EUROPEAN DRUG POLICIES AND ENFORCEMENT

European Drug Policies and Enforcement

Edited by

Nicholas Dorn
Director of Information Development
Institute for the Study of Drug Dependence, London, Great Britain

Jørgen Jepsen
Associate Professor of Criminology
Director of the Centre for Alcohol and Drug Research, Århus, Denmark

and

Ernesto Savona
Professor of Criminology
Director of Research Group on Transnational Crime
Trento University, Italy

First published in Great Britain 1996 by
MACMILLAN PRESS LTD
Houndmills, Basingstoke, Hampshire RG21 6XS
and London
Companies and representatives
throughout the world

A catalogue record for this book is available
from the British Library.

ISBN 0-333-63334-2 hardcover
ISBN 0-333-65221-5 paperback

First published in the United States of America 1996 by
ST. MARTIN'S PRESS, INC.,
Scholarly and Reference Division,
175 Fifth Avenue,
New York, N.Y. 10010

ISBN 0-312-12926-2

Library of Congress Cataloging-in-Publication Data
European drug policies and enforcement / edited by Nicholas Dorn,
Jørgen Jepsen, and Ernesto Savona.
p.   cm.
Includes bibliographical references and index.
ISBN 0-312-12926-2 (cloth)
1. Narcotics, control of—Europe.   I. Dorn, Nicholas.
II. Jepsen, Jørgen.   III. Savona, Ernesto Ugo, 1943–
HV5840.E8E94   1996
363.4'5'094—dc20   95-33035
                                                               CIP

10   9   8   7   6   5   4   3   2   1
05   04   03   02   01   00   99   98   97   96

Printed and bound in Great Britain by
Antony Rowe Ltd, Chippenham, Wiltshire

Contents

List of Figures

List of Tables

Preface and Acknowledgements

Throughout Europe, the 1990s have seen increasing polarisation between drug trafficking-control measures and drug user-control measures. On the one hand, exceptional legal powers, more intrusive policing methods and high-level police cooperation between countries. On the other hand, a range of local and national policies on drug users favour social integration rather than punishment. Policies towards traffickers and users collide at the sites of local drug markets and 'open drug scenes', invoking very disparate and often volatile responses. What can be learnt?

The development of the European Union has implications for drug control through internal Justice and Home Affairs, and through the EU's external policies. Europol is intended to facilitate police cooperation on drugs intelligence throughout Europe, though an inter-governmental basis for its operation has proved problematic. The prospect of deepening of the EU opens up questions about policing and drug control in a confederal context. EU enlargement to include eastern European countries provides fresh challenges for drug enforcement, democracy and legality. Trade and development policies of the EU offer opportunities to encourage alternatives to coca cultivation in Latin America. What are the options for the future? These are the questions raised and explored by contributors to *European Drug Policies and Enforcement*.

The modest project leading to this book has been a model of European cooperation: an initial idea which both broadened and deepened as it became reality. The editors and contributors thank all those who assisted in cities, countries and European agencies. Here the editors would like to acknowledge a small number of agencies, groups and individuals who, although of course they have no responsibility for the collection as published, nevertheless made it possible.

We are especially grateful to our host institutions: the Institute for the Study of Drug Dependence (ISDD), London, which hosted the project and its coordinating editor; the Centre for Alcohol and Drug Research, Århus, which organised a nordic seminar on methodological aspects of research on drug markets and enforcement, feeding into the book; the Research Group on Transnational Crime (TRANSCRIME), Trento and the National Institute of Justice, Washington. Additionally, the European Monitoring Centre for Drugs and Drug Addiction, Lisbon, and DGI of the European Commission, Brussels, are thanked for their encouragement of pan-European drug policy research and for some practical networking opportunities.

Amongst individuals who made the work possible, Rachuel Yrigoyen Fajardo, Andean Commission of Jurists, drew our attention to Humberto Campodónico's work, while Simone White, of the London School of Economics and Political Science, translated the Spanish. Andy Atkins at the Catholic Institute for International Relations, London and Elizabeth Joyce, Oxford University, also helped on Latin American aspects. Research staff at ISDD read the manuscript, Oswin Baker helped with the subediting, Keith Povey copy-edited, and Annabelle Buckley has been a decisive and effective commissioning editor.

NICHOLAS DORN
JØRGEN JEPSEN
ERNESTO SAVONA

Notes on the Contributors

Hannes Alpheis
Sociologist, formerly at the Department of the Interior, now with the Finance Department, Hamburg, Germany

Ada Becchi
Professor of Economic Policy in the Planning School of the Institute of Architecture of Venice, Italy; Member of the Parliament in the 10th legislature (1987–92), Italy

Humberto Campodónico
Economist; specialist in development, international economics and drug issues; member of DESCO (Centre for Studies on and Promotion of Development), Lima, Peru

Nicholas Dorn
Director of Information Development, Institute for the Study of Drug Dependence (ISDD), London, Britain

Hermann Fahrenkrug
Sociologist, Senior Researcher at the Swiss Institute for the Prevention of Alcohol and Drug Problems, Lausanne, Switzerland

Cyrille Fijnaut
Professor of Criminology and Criminal Law, Catholic University of Leuven, Belgium and also Erasmus University, Rotterdam, The Netherlands

Andrew Fraser
Director of DAIS (Drug Advice and Information Service), Substance Misuse Directorate, South Downs Health NHS Trust, Brighton, Britain.

Michael George
Director, Chartered Clinical Psychologist and Manager of Drug and Alcohol Services, Worthing Priority Care NHS Trust, Worthing, Britain

xi

Liesbeth Horstink-Von Meyenfeldt
Public Prosecutor, Ministry of Justice, The Hague, The Netherlands

Jørgen Jepsen
Associate Professor of Criminology, Århus University, Director of the Centre for Alcohol and Drug Research, Denmark

Lau Laursen
Research Associate, Centre for Alcohol and Drug Research, Århus University, Denmark

Maggy Lee
Researcher, criminologist, Institute for the Study of Drug Dependence, (ISDD) London, Britain

Leif Lenke
Associate Professor of Criminology, Department of Criminology, University of Stockholm, Sweden

Börje Olsson
Sociologist, Senior Researcher at CAN (Swedish Council for Information on Alcohol and other Drugs), Stockholm, Sweden

Ernesto Savona
Professor of Criminology and Director of TRANSCRIME, the Research Group on Transnational Crime, University of Trento, Italy

Introduction: Local, National, Pan-European, International

Nicholas Dorn, Jørgen Jepsen and
Ernesto Savona

In most member states of the European Union, a sharp escalation
of the war on drug traffickers coexists with a reluctance to
criminalise people simply for possessing or using illegal drugs.

Sitting very awkwardly between the anti-trafficking and the
user-integration measures is the unresolved question of how to
respond when trafficker meets user – when tidy distinctions
between two worlds may often be hard to maintain. This is the
focus for Part I of this book, which presents perspectives on the
experiences of cities and countries in policing the middle ground,
'retail' drug markets. From the viewpoint of control systems, user–
dealers (drug users who may occasionally or often sell drugs) have
a foot in two contrasting moral camps, the dangerous and the
pathetic, and so provide a conundrum for control policy.

The challenge is greatest when drug sellers meet buyers in large
numbers, in public, as in the now-defunct Needle Park of Zürich,
or in Hamburg or Copenhagen (see Chapters 1 and 3). Then a
host of dramatic issues arise – of public outrage, public order,
public health and public safety. What have been the experiences
of European towns and cities in respect to the 'retail' end of drug
markets, the publicly visible street markets, the 'open drug
scenes'? Because this is such a public issue, involving so many
people not just rhetorically and emotionally (as fascinated
spectators at a distance) but also often face-to-face and in their
everyday lives (witnessing disruption in their immediate communities), it has been and remains the most problematic aspect of
drug control policy. European cities, their political authorities,

1

policing agencies and welfare networks have been learning as they go along, in a series of trial-and-error social experiments, responding to open drug scenes. If there is a way of summarising these histories then we could say that the first response is repressive in the tradition of anti-trafficking policy; the second represents a degree of accommodation to the resilient nature of local drug scenes, coupled with attempts to address the health and welfare issues of users and to reconcile their rights with the rights of non-users; and the third demonstrates the emergence of a new and creative control 'mix' (which remains problematic in its implementation and consequences).

Part II of the book moves on to policing and policy-making at national levels, with attention to domestic policy-making on drugs and to pressures from neighbouring countries and sub-regional organisations (for example, the Nordic Union). With exceptions, which will be later described, European drug policies since the Second World War have been relatively liberal when it comes to drug users (as distinct from traffickers) and during the first half of the 1990s they became more so. An example of this trend occurred in April 1994, when the German Constitutional Court ruled that the police and prosecution authorities do not have an absolute duty to bring charges against cannabis users – thus bringing this major European country closer to the policy of some other EU countries, such as Britain. There, cannabis possession remains technically criminalised but people are rarely targeted for possession alone; when arrests do take place, they are normally followed by formal warnings (police cautions), not only as regards cannabis possession but also sometimes for possession of small amounts of 'harder' drugs. Some other countries go further, pursuing a consistent decriminalisation policy for possession of all drugs, either *de facto* – for example, the Netherlands, which issued guidelines restraining prosecution for drug possession – or *de jure*, for example Italy, which decriminalised possession of all drugs by referendum in April 1993, and Spain, which decriminalised possession of all drugs as part of the reaction against the Franco years. Contributors focus on the tightening of the Dutch drug policy on cannabis cafés, the party politics of drug control in Sweden, the nature of Italian drug control, and the development of drug control discourses in the Scandinavian context.

In Part III the question of European cooperation against drug trafficking is discussed in the context of the broader development of the EU's internal policies on Justice and Home Affairs. As, the Treaty of Union signed at Maastricht confirms in its third 'pillar', the member states are committed to work together against drug trafficking and money laundering, amongst other matters. The background to this is a convergence of member states' policies in which police powers have been enhanced, penalties have soared, drugs intelligence systems developed, and the joys and pitfalls of pan-European police cooperation explored. A much debated matter is the relationship between (i) the intergovernmental system of arms-length police cooperation between EU member states and, (ii) more integrated approaches based on movement in a federal or confederal direction. The latter might involve transfer of powers from the member states and national agencies, in two directions: 'upwards' to pan-European policing against drug traffickers and other criminals (cf. German preferences for the development of Europol), and also 'downwards' to provincial or local agencies, according to the principle of subsidiarity.

This is a hotly contested area, also one in which much is at stake in terms of effective drug control, the future of European law, indeed the future shape of the European Union. Three chapters survey the ground, one of which is a 'framework' chapter and two offer 'case studies'. The setting up of Europol (whose first responsibility is cooperation on intelligence on drug trafficking) provides a case study of intergovernmental cooperation. As for drug policy-making in a federal or confederal system, the events around the Platzspitz in Zürich provide a dramatic case study of the interaction of top-down, national drug policy (in this case, favouring health and welfare) and a 'bottom-up' response by local authorities (bearing in mind public safety and order). Although Switzerland did not join the EU, nevertheless many of its internal political structures and processes are interesting from a broader European point of view, in drug control as in other matters. One possibility is that Switzerland (and other federal or confederal countries) may offer a model for the balance-of-power in future between drug policy-making by administrations at different levels (pan-European, national and city levels). On the other hand, the events of 1996 and later may lead to a more centralised form of policy-making, privileging only one of these levels, perhaps the national, governmental level. At the time of writing, the Platzspitz, and Europol (ironically, perhaps, situated in the Netherlands) stand as icons of these two futures.

Finally, there are of course external, foreign policy aspects to the EU's involvements in drug control. Money laundering, where the developed countries have relatively recently introduced what are intended to be globally applicable controls, may not be the sure-fire solution to drug trafficking that some imagined, not least because developing countries may find them difficult to implement. Nevertheless, recent advances in anti-laundering cooperation may have some potential internationally. Two contributors debate this: in Chapter 12 there is a detailed exposition and call for cooperation to make the newly introduced control work. This is followed by a short but powerful critique (Chapter 13), suggesting that liberalisation of the economy undermines any possibility of controlling money laundering, at least in the Latin American context. The book rounds off (Chapter 14) with an ambitious attempt to survey external drug policies of the EU – embedded in the Union's broader polices on enlargement, security, trade, aid and development. Where possible, throughout the book, implications are drawn out for future policy and linkages are made between the various sectors and level of local, national, pan-EU and external policies on drugs.

Editorial perspectives

As editors, we have much in common while also holding distinctly different perspectives. Jørgen Jepsen, a Danish associate professor of criminology, holds a human rights, anti-'war on drugs' perspective, characteristic of much of southern Scandinavian criminology. Readers will recall that Denmark was profoundly split over ratification of the EU Treaty of Union – Jepsen was amongst those opposing it, for a number of reasons, including the perception that a stronger EU might mean a less tolerant Danish society and more 'war on drugs'. He has done work on civil rights in several contexts including that of southern Africa.

By contrast, Ernesto Savona, as an Italian who has lived though the Tangentopoli corruption scandals (the crossover of crime, business and public administration), sees the strengthening of domestic and international law as necessary for the democratisation of society. Also a professor of criminology, Savona has carried out work for UN bodies and at the US National Institute of Justice, and his work is characteristic of the modernising, pro-international tendency in Italian society and criminology.

Nicholas Dorn is a British criminologist and is particularly interested in the post-Maastricht development of European Union policies on Justice and Home Affairs – where policies on policing and on drugs function as a highly visible marker – and on EU external policies. Where Jepsen defends civil rights by opposing any further tightening of drug polices in his country, Savona champions international drug-related legislation as the leading edge in a more general clean-up, Dorn calls for the strengthening of our abilities to 'think European' in analysing internal and external policies of the EU.

Part I

Policing Local Drug Scenes

1 Copenhagen: A War on Socially Marginal People

Jørgen Jepsen

The following account of recent developments in low-level drug policing in Denmark – 'the war on drug users' – refers to a major three- to four-year police operation aimed at tackling the drug problem with saturation policing, particularly in two areas of Copenhagen – Vesterbro and Christiania. While these actions were seen by the police as central elements of its drug strategy ('Narko-strategi 90'), they gave rise to much public criticism, involved huge financial costs and – as several critics have claimed – considerably increased the misery of street addicts.

This issue is not unique to Denmark. But against the background of Denmark's traditional self-image as a welfare society, it seems reasonable to ask: where are the models for these dramatic actions? Have they been effective? What have been the costs? What is the justification for this massive investment? What are the long-term effects?

Behind the 'effectiveness' question lies the problem of explicit versus implicit goals: is the main aim of the investment to improve the drug situation – or is it to give the police a new, badly-needed legitimacy in the face of criticism of their inability to slow the importation of illicit drugs?

DRUG USE, MISUSE AND LAW ENFORCEMENT IN DENMARK: AN OVERVIEW

The actual level of drug use in Denmark is not known. The country has no systematic registration of drug users or clients at treatment institutions and no 'clearing house' for such information, although measures are under way to improve monitoring

9

drug use, motivated by the emerging European Monitoring Centre for Drugs and Drug Addiction (EMCDDA). Nor is it known to what extent police action is effective in keeping drug trafficking and drug use down. In contrast to the increasing belief in the benefits of police repression in Sweden (see Strindlund, 1991), Danes are a lot more sceptical.

At present, therefore, most of the assumptions forming the basis for policy decisions are based mainly upon guesstimates from those working in the field, be it within the police or social services. The Copenhagen police estimate (Københarns Politi, 1991) that there are some 2–3,000 heavy drug users in greater Copenhagen. Most of them were assumed to be intravenous users, but in recent years the AIDS threat may have persuaded many to use other methods of administration.[1] It was also estimated some years ago that there are around 8–10,000 heavy drug users in Denmark as a whole. There are indications that this figure has fallen, as those users who present themselves to treatment institutions and social services tend to be getting older, while the recruitment of new clients has seemed to be slowing down. This may mean that the actual number of users in Denmark has decreased in the last five to ten years, leaving a 'hard core' in contact with the institutions.

But it may also mean that new users have not come to the attention of the authorities. Users of cocaine in 'yuppie' circles may not be recognised, nor may the users of ecstasy, if they do not develop serious symptoms. Police seizures of cocaine and dance drugs are not very frequent or substantial, prompting the question: are the drugs simply not used, or are their users simply not known?

Given this background, it is questionable whether the present level of drug use is a problem – and whether it is a social problem meriting the allocation of large police resources. Since nobody knows the exact magnitude of the phenomenon, its status as 'a problem' is a subjective and political matter. Police maintain that it is a serious social problem. Sociologists maintain that it is not, and would certainly be less so if law enforcement did not exacerbate it (Winsløw, 1984, 1989; Balvig, 1985).

The police, after all, have a traditional professional and institutional interest in defining phenomena as law enforcement matters. The drug problem is only one major example. Drugs, social unrest, demonstrations, squatters and 'autonomous groups' with hints of terrorist connections, have all proved effective as levers for obtaining more public funding for the police.

For many years Danish police have maintained that their aim is to eradicate drug trafficking. If they pursue street-level dealers, it is only as the means to an end of reaching the 'Mr Bigs' (in Danish: *'bagmändene* ('the men behind', a term also used in connection with economic crime). For a long time, the image was one of a hierarchical mafia-type organisation, with a few financiers behind several layers of lower-level dealers, and the use of *agents provocateurs* was the preferred investigation technique. After several years of case law development for regulating this type of investigation, there were attempts to legalise it in 1985, along with phone-tapping. However, both legalisation of *agents* and of the use of anonymous witnesses ran into hard opposition in Parliament. While phone-tapping was legalised to the satisfaction of the police, anonymous witnesses were totally prohibited in 1985. The use of *agents* was heavily circumscribed in 1986, so this technique became considerably less useful for the police. Today, tapping and tip-offs seem to be the major tools in drug trafficking investigation (see Jepsen, 1989b and 1993).

Despite these obstacles to policing, Danish newspapers have regularly contained dramatic reports on seizures of large consignments of illegal drugs, while the Danish police have harvested hemp fields in several parts of the country where old-time hippies have discreetly been cultivating high quality cannabis (see Table 1.1).[2] Nevertheless, it had become increasingly clear by the end of the 1980s that seizures and harvests did not stop drugs pouring into the country. In occasional dry periods, addicts might turn to diverted legal drugs – particularly dextropropoxiphene obtained from arthritis-ridden pensioners, which caused several deaths among Danish users (Winsløw, 1987). They also learned to mix cannabis with strong beer and various medicines (e.g. benzodiazepines), which introduced a pattern of poly-drug use in contrast to the previous pattern of drug-specific subgroups and subcultures.

Since the late 1980s, therefore, law enforcement officials have unofficially conceded that they cannot 'do the job' of fighting drugs alone. On the official level, some of the most ardent police advocates of increasing repression have called for more prevention and treatment efforts from the social and health sectors. Some of them have loudly complained, for example, that the Copenhagen

Table 1.1   Illicit drugs seizures, Denmark, 1984–93

	1984	1985	1986	1987	1988	1989	1990	1991	1992	1993
Opium (g)	3	42	6	0.7	500	1324	248	3897	303	287
Heroin (kg)	23.8	5.4	17.3	13.4	29.2	36.7	26.7	30.8	38.5	28.3
Methadon (ml)	2095	1333	2944	7542	5024	9175	11893	17161	17416	18461
Methadon tablets	2653	574	2102	1404	1235	4000	2687	4516	4527	3089
Kokain (kg)	6.5	0.5	7.1	25.6	9.7	54.9	28.1	39.6	21.4	11.2
Amfetamin (kg)	2.0	4.0	10.2	56.2	29.8	23.9	26	23.6	73.6	11.8
LSD (doser)	265	35	76	110	11	25	258	26	86	140
Hash (kg)	658	510	472	1235	1369	729	1250	1703	2152	1227
Marihuana (kg)	74.0	78.6	43.2	32.4	26.8	19.7	228.5	73.0	109.6	106.5
Cannabinol (kg)	0.1	0.5	1.1	0.8	0.5	0.9	0.7	0.2	6.2	0.2
Hamp plants (kg)	3387	1149	1665	1007	8636	2372	3050	2222	9209	4336

Source: Politiets Årsberetning (Annual Report of the National Chief of Police), 1993 (Rigspolitichefen, Copenhagen, 1994).

social services are inefficient and irresponsible in their provision of treatment and services for addicts. The Copenhagen police have often maintained that the arrested addicts they have delivered to treatment centres,[3] have been turned away or have quickly left, frustrated with the unsatisfactory treatment on offer.

Thus, for the last few years in Copenhagen, the relationship between the police and the treatment sectors has been strained, the police complaining of inefficiency and unwillingness on the part of the treatment sector, which in turn complains that the police harass addicts and add to their misery instead of concentrating on traffickers. These developments form the basis for some of the events that have occurred during the Copenhagen police's major operations against the open street-level drug scene between 1989 and 1993, epitomised in two major wars on drugs and their users – 'Politiaktion Vesterbro' (1990–91(93)) and 'Politiaktion Christiania' (1992–93).

THE COPENHAGEN WAR ON DRUGS IN THE STREET

The beginning: Politiaktion Vesterbro

Vesterbro – a working-class section of Copenhagen to the north of the central railway station with some 40,000 inhabitants – has been a 'problem area' of the city for many years. In the early 1960s, the local street life of down-and-outs, drunks and prostitutes (hitherto accorded local tolerance, sympathy and charity), underwent considerable change with the legalisation of pornography. The 'good old prostitutes' now had competition from porno mags, films and live sex shows. Tourists began to invade the area and gradually the hotels near the railway station grew bigger and better. Today, they are one of the travel companies' favourite dumping grounds for tourists, some of whom enjoy the short walk to sin and vice, others of whom deplore it.

Throughout the 1970s and into the 1980s, local residents complained to the city government about the deterioration of their neighbourhood. When the drug addicts and dealers followed on the heels of the pornographers, they had had enough, but no one seemed to pay attention to their repeated protests. Vesterbro almost seemed out of bounds to public intervention; every town has its vice section, and the tradition for tolerance became a neat excuse for doing nothing. Gradually the decline became worse, with drug prostitutes patrolling for curb-crawlers in the Halmtorvet (Haymarket), pimps and down-and-outs loitering more drunk than ever. Moreover, drug dealers were conspicuously visible at the so-called 'sharp corner' of Istedgade (at the very heart of the area). Some of their equally visible customers were from the neighbourhood, though many (as much as 40 to 50 per cent) came from other parts of Copenhagen – or from outside the city altogether.[4] And so Vesterbro became an open drug scene, with needles and syringes discarded under the trees of the Sønder Boulevard and in children's playgrounds, while dilapidated council buildings became places for the lowest grade addicts to fix, sleep and die in the rags and debris.

In 1989 the police began clearing the Istedgade 'sharp corner' of dealers, users and fixers. As a 'payoff' the addicts were given a 'fixing shelter' at Halmtorvet, but they never used it and stayed on the streets. Once again, the local citizens protested to no avail.

For two weeks in the summer of 1990, in its prime-time Sunday evening slot, Danish TV featured lengthy reports on the situation in Vesterbro, where locals felt threatened by the influx of new Gambian drug dealers in particular (allegations were made that the Danish drug dealers did not like the competition from black foreigners). When they interviewed officials, reporters were told by the police that it was a matter for the social services, by the social services that the housing department had to clear and renovate the buildings, and by the housing department that it was a matter for the police.

Now, four years later, something is being done about the housing situation at Vesterbro, but at the time the only measure taken was to install better locks in the few remaining doors. The Copenhagen drug services have been in a state of limbo since then, with no capacity to motivate the addicts to leave the area for treatment; the only recourse has been to call in the police.

In August 1990 the Copenhagen police announced its 'Narkostrategi 90', which was originally envisaged to last from three to four months. The official elements of the strategy included:

reinforcement of the preventive efforts;
increased investigation of the *bagmänd* ('men behind') and the flow of money in the drug environment;

increased uniformed police presence in the drug scenes;
increased drug education and training of police officers;
increased cooperation with social authorities and other agencies
(Københavns politi, *Årsberetning*, 1990, p. 2).

Within this general framework, the police highlighted the following aims of its specific actions in Vesterbro:

to make the area safer for residents, shop owners, tourists and others;
to attempt to 'clear up' crime;
to limit the supply of narcotic drugs;
to limit the number of people living outside Vesterbro, who go there to commit crime (including the buying or selling of drugs);
to provide a cleaner environment;
to refer drug addicts to social services for treatment (*ibid.*, p. 8).

Politiaktion Vesterbro started on Monday, 20 August 1990, and a preliminary report was circulated in September 1991, covering the year to 18 August 1991. The idea of a time limit of three to four months of intensive action followed by a period of stabilisation was revised – the intensive presence continued at least for the first year, but even in late 1992 the police presence was huge. It involved several uniformed patrols, on average 30 persons on a 24-hour basis. They operated from a van stationed a block away from the 'sharp corner', to which those arrested were taken for questioning, cautioning and – later – fining.

The technique was to ask people about their reasons for being in the area. If their reasons appeared unsatisfactory, they would receive an oral warning, then two more oral warnings, then a written warning and finally, on the fifth occasion, they would be fined. They would also be ordered to leave the area immediately after a warning.

The action not only involved suspected drug dealers but also users (who represented by far the largest proportion of those stopped), potential buyers, drunks, vagabonds, pimps and prostitutes. This solution to the problem of an invading drug scene led to the dispersal, harassment and punishment of a traditional clientele in the name of cleanliness and order (and to an inability to distinguish between the victimisers and the victims).

The action – which was highly visible and attracted considerable attention, both locally and nationally – initially met with the approval of local residents and hotel and shop owners. The police summed up the results of the first year as follows:

Vesterbro has acquired a nicer look and a cleaner environment; the usual hangouts for addicts and others in the streets are gone; it has become safer for residents, shopkeepers, tourists and others;
the supply of drugs has been limited;
it has been made more difficult for new drug users and persons living outside Copenhagen to contact dealers on Vesterbro;
addicts have been referred for treatment to social services;
a public debate has been initiated on the adequacy of the current drug treatment policy.

As for the results in relation to crime, the police reported:

the number of penal code offences registered in the area fell by 17 per cent compared to the previous year;
the number of addicts arrested and charged with property crimes has fallen during the campaign;
the number of persons contacted, arrested and charged with drug-related offences has fallen considerably in the area during the campaign;
in the central parts of Vesterbro, the decline in crime has been as follows: robbery −37 per cent, breaking and entering −6 per cent, theft from cars −47 per cent, violence −37 per cent;
in the rest of the area covered by the local police station (no. 1) the development shows: robbery +9 per cent, breaking and entering −17 per cent, theft from cars −31 per cent and violence −12 per cent. It is specifically stated that 'Eriksgade [a street] which was previously plagued by drug dealing, addicts in the stairways etc. and other criminal persons – including certain ethnic groups (Gambians, etc.) has been cleansed.'

Seen through these rose-tinted police spectacles, the action was an unconditional success. Initially, local residents, shopkeepers and hoteliers – and most tourists – felt the same. But as the net tightened and the measures became tougher, the locals began to regret the results of their demands for peace – they had been plunged into a war instead.

The most ardent criticism came from the staff of the Maria Church Social Services, who felt their clients were being chased away and their services violated by the police action. The police asked for permission to enter the church premises so as to catch drug dealers, but – much to their dismay – the priest's protests secured the asylum function of the church. Instead they would have to catch dealers and users as they left the church premises.

During the first period (20 August 1990 to 3 February 1991) 16,853 man hours were spent on patrol activities in the area. In the second period (4 February to 18 August 1991) 9,992 hours were invested. Throughout the two periods, the police bus and the foot patrol issued a total of 6,259 oral warnings, 528 written warnings and 1614 charges for violations. Furthermore, 3442 arrests were made, 519 of which were of people already wanted by the police. 91 people were turned over to social authorities.

When the official treatment institutions proved to have insufficient resources, the police contacted a private institution, built on a modified Minnesota-model but with very tough treatment practices.

However, others – the local social service institutions, the church (including the priests of the Mariakirken) and the old alcoholics and prostitutes – felt differently. They saw the whole action as a brutal harassment, which resulted in a harmful increase in the misery of addicts (which is, for instance in Sweden, an explicit aim of such low-level policing: Strindlund, 1991).

There were indications that in 1992/3 many of the addicts and dealers were scared or pushed away from Vesterbro. In other parts of town – some not very far from the boundaries of the police action area – both addicts and dealers were reported to have taken up new stands and hangouts, most prominently at Nørrebro, another old working-class section of town which for some years had managed to play down its former image as a 'reserve' for addicts.

By 1994, however, it appears that the whole action had been in vain and that users and dealers were gradually returning to their old haunts in Vesterbro, now with a distinct 'colouring' of the picture through the growing number of Gambian dealers, easily identifiable in the street scene. Once more, bona fide residents and local groups complained that the police did not do the work and demanded stronger action.[5] The situation seems to reflect the old maxim of nature abhorring a vacuum – as soon as police pressure diminishes, the void is filled again by the drug street scene.

To some extent this may be seen as an indication of a lack of other places for users and dealers to go. The treatment sector in Denmark had for many years been shrinking rather than expanding, and the police repeatedly complained that they had no treatment alternative to prison when dealing with addicts.

These problems came to the fore of political attention in 1994 after the publication of a Government White Paper in which the Ministries of Justice, Health and Social Affairs hinted at a slight shift in drug policy from law enforcement and police action towards treatment and welfare measures.

Since the publication of the White Paper, a lively debate has taken place in the mass media. Based on several TV programmes critical of police action and pointing to the need for a more welfare-oriented policy, a debate is still running (as at Spring 1995) on strengthening the treatment system and playing down the role of law enforcement. Models from Holland and Switzerland, and lately from Germany, are being discussed as more relevant to the Danish situation than the repressive Swedish model.

The police carried on as usual for some time, but following statements from the Minister of Justice and the Attorney General in the summer of 1994 that prosecutors and police should stop the 'stressing policy' against street users, police action at street level has been toned down.

Meanwhile, the streets of Vesterbro are left in a state of limbo. The maintenance of public order is lagging, while treatment institutions and low-threshold assistance schemes are patently unable to accommodate even the serious drug users. Plans to rebuild a treatment system are underway, but will take a long time to implement. In the meantime drug addicts and police officers are equally bewildered about the future. In such a situation, drug dealing in streets of Copenhagen may increasingly come to resemble the situation in Zürich or Frankfurt.

DRUG POLICING AND 'THE FREE CITY OF CHRISTIANIA'

The Danish interplay between police and the open drug scene has nowhere displayed such a peculiar and politically conflictual development as around the drug market in the so-called 'Free City of Christiania'.

The course of events merits both a brief overview of the history of Christiania and its interaction with the Danish authorities (the police in particular).

In September 1971 – at the height of the squatter movement in Denmark when 'the spirit of 1968' was still alive – a group of hippies and political activists crawled through the broken fence of an old barracks in Copenhagen and declared the area 'liberated'.

The area – some 35 hectares situated only a couple of kilometres from the city centre – contained several former military buildings of very differing quality. Many artists, students, intellectuals and even university professors took up some of the better buildings and renovated them beautifully (one of them, with a large wall painting, still draws artistic attention). At the other end of the scale, drug users, psychiatric patients and common criminals holed themselves up in the more squalid quarters where they did nothing to improve the conditions.

Over the following years the population of the place – announced as a Free City and christened Christiania as an allusion to the royally-inspired name of the locality, Christianshavn – grew to some 1000 residents (with some 300–400 more in summer). The community was awarded status as a 'social experiment' by the Social Democratic government in June 1973, with a promise that the occupants would be allowed to stay for at least three years. Somewhat surprisingly, this decision was supported and carried out by the Minister of Defence, Keld Olesen, who represented the formal ownership of the land.[6] The Free City of Christiania has been the focus of controversy between the political left and right ever since.

The new conservative government elected in December 1973 agreed with the Lord Mayor of Copenhagen that the place should be closed before 1 April 1976. Supporters of Christiania took their case to the Supreme Court, claiming that the promises of the previous government had given them the right to remain on the land. The case was lost, but by the time of the decision the political majority had changed. In February 1978 parliament allowed Christiania to continue – albeit upon several conditions, including demands for 'legalisation' of buildings, pubs and jobs and a regulation of land utilisation.

For some years, the Christiania experiment was largely supported by the majority of politicians and the general public. Gallup polls have shown varying proportions of supporters and detractors. Prior to the 1978 parliamentary decision, public (and political) opinion was very positively influenced by a TV documentary of an ordinary family which moved into Christiania for one week and converted from scepticism to warm support. Later on, however, the proportion of the population wanting to close down Christiania changed from 47 per cent in 1981 to 62 per cent in 1982 (when Sweden heavily criticised the open cannabis market, see Chapter 8), although it fell again to a minority in 1984 (AKF Report, see Jaeger *et al.*, 1993, p.65).

Christiania – as a true grass-roots movement – has a flat, anti-authoritarian decision-making structure. It has always been difficult for the surrounding society to make agreements and 'deals' with the Free City: a 'parallel' society such as Christiania will inevitably be a thorn in the side of more conservative elements in general and to law enforcers in particular. As pointed out in the 1993 AKF Report, this led to a learning process on the part of government and to the development of new, responsive modes of government as opposed to traditional constitutional or 'sovereign' forms. In particular the history of Christiania during the period 1986–93 represented a development of new modes of government, based upon negotiation, with respect to Christiania's status as an 'alternative society'.

Over the years Christiania has carried the burden of living with deviants, violent gangs, drug users and other social problems foisted upon it by the surrounding city. In the late 1970s, many of the stronger initiators and culture-carriers left, both as a reaction to the growing problems and to the political pressures put upon the experiment.

The frustration of the first wave of Christiania was partly a reaction to the increasing 'slummification' and incapacity of the community to make and live up to agreements, but it also reflected disappointment at the external demands for normal-isation/legalisation.

In the AKF Report of 1993, the following items are presented as foci for negotiations – but also as instances of conflict:

(1)   the issue of the pubs – in particular the problems of licensing, auditing, taxation and public order;
(2)   the plans for utilisation of the Northern Area (the most attractive part);
(3)   which community expenses could be charged as rent contribution to the social security system for the roughly 50 per cent of inhabitants on welfare;
(4)   the status of a 'framework agreement' between Christiania and the Ministry of Defence.

The biggest step towards 'normalisation' in the drug field was taken by the 'Christianites' themselves in November 1979, when the 'People's Movement Against Hard Drugs' launched the 'Junk Blockade' and evicted all junkies and hard drug dealers.[7] Since then, the drug scene in Christiania has almost entirely revolved around cannabis, a drug symbolising the area's demand to be free from the norms governing Danish society.

It is precisely this symbolic status that has been the focus of conflict between Christiania and the surrounding political environment. Moreover, behind the image of Christiania as an experiment in alternative and self-sufficient lifestyles lay the reality of a community increasingly dependent upon the Copenhagen social services.[8] Hence the 'Lex Christiania', passed in 1989 under the name of 'Act on the Use of the Land of Christiania' (no. 232), which demanded several adjustments and concessions to legalisation and 'normalisation'.

Christiania, the police and the authorities

In the 1970s the Copenhagen police developed a confrontational relationship with Christiania, not only because of the drug scene, but also because they found stolen goods in many of the buildings when they made large-scale searches in the area. The inhabitants of the more dilapidated buildings in Christiania also represented a more marginal and at times highly criminal group than the 'cultured' inhabitants. They were tolerated – and in some instances even protected – by other Christianites. But the internal relationships were rather ambiguous: the more professional criminals – including the 'Bullshit Gang' which took over the cannabis trade for a few months – were a distinct foreign element in Christiania, while criminality among the 'deprivation-type' inhabitants was treated as a social problem through support and inclusion (see Balvig, 1987 as quoted in Jepsen, 1989a). To the police, however, they were all criminals.

The conflicts between Christiania and the Copenhagen police worsened when in the 1980s police conducted night searches in a rather rash fashion. An increasing number of complaints were lodged with the police complaint board, and when that turned out to be ineffectual, court cases were brought for unwarranted searches and arrests, resulting in ever-increasing awards of damages to Christianites.

The main conflicts, however, occurred around the open drug scene, where hash dealers increasingly applied marketing techniques which drew unfavourable attention from the police, the general public and interested local, national and international politicians. The situation became so tense that in the early 1980s, the open scene (located near the entrance of Christiania and hence vulnerable to police action) was moved back into the interior of the Free City, where one of the central thoroughfares now became known as 'Pusher Street'.

By the late 1980s police raids into the interior of Christiania became common affairs and the confrontations became more violent as time went by. Christianites would throw stones at the unpopular *uropatruljen* – 'unrest patrols' – when they entered Christiania in plainclothes (or rather, in various attempted disguises). Alternatively, they would be 'shouted out', pursued by a host of barking dogs, who would emphasize the message with bites if they got the chance.

Consequently, the patrolmen stationed a group of uniformed riot police outside Christiania, to come to their assistance when things got out of hand. Several policemen were wounded, some rather seriously, during the battles that raged into the early 1990s. Between September 1992 and May 1993, for example, ninety policemen were injured in Christiania.[9]

The decision to normalise Christiania initiated a long period of negotiation between Christiania and the authorities. A special Christiania Secretariat was established within the Ministry of

Defence in December 1989 and a steering committee was set up, with representatives from the Ministry of Defence (responsible for the 'civil aspect' of the normalisation programme), a respected social worker with extensive experience of addicts, and a county official, formerly head of the government's Alcohol and Drug Council.

This steering committee had to fight a hard battle to obtain compromises between the political field, Christianites and the police. On the one hand, they had to carry through the process of 'normalisation', including securing taxes and legal conformity from the many unlicensed restaurants and pubs which had sprung up over the years. On the other hand, they had to obtain the cooperation of Christiania's inhabitants, which required many concessions respecting the uniqueness of the social experiment.

The cannabis market, however, was the real sticking point, vividly highlighting the ideological and political conflict between the alternative society and its surroundings. While the Christianites often drew more sympathy to their cause than the police (possibly due to unwise and excessive force on the part of the unrest patrol and its successors)[10], the surrounding society could still not accept the open cannabis market in Pusher Street.

By 1993 the conflict reached the point where even the steering committee was threatening the closure of Christiania. The process of normalisation had slowed and the cannabis market was blossoming, to the outrage of politicians in Copenhagen and abroad. On the other hand, court cases and private videos which were broadcast on national TV, demonstrated the aggressiveness and violence of the police to such an extent that other politicians and lawyers demanded the delineation of police activity in the Free City.

Faced with police harassment, the citizens of Christiania made their own register of police actions, illustrated by the following account of police control of Nemoland, one of the pubs at the centre of controversy. During the period 1 January to 8 June 1993, Nemoland was visited by 491 police patrols, involving a total of 2457 police officers. From this, only ten warnings resulted – mainly for lack of orderliness/cleanliness. On only three occasions was the place closed down for the rest of the day – because of the presence of cannabis on some customers.

16 March 1993 was an illustrative day, as described by the locals:

At 10.25 four uniformed policemen arrived. Nothing found.
10.50: Four uniformed policemen sit at the tables, doing
nothing.
12.10: Four uniformed officers just sit.
12.30: Five UPs [unrest patrol officers] arrive. They check
people and tear up flowers from the flower stalls. Found
nothing.
15.15: Four uniformed policemen arrived. Found nothing.
16.08: 20 UPs arrive. Nothing found.
21.35: Seven uniformed policemen arrive. Nothing found. . .
and so the days go on. . .

But behind the arguments such as a demand for law and order
and a demand for 'normalisation' of police activity, other interests
and motives were at play.

Freedom and profit – Christiania and the drug discourse

On the legalistic side were police and politicians who wanted
Christiania closed down – almost at any price, people who had
been working intensely toward that goal for years.

The other side was more complex. It included the Christianites
who saw the prohibition against the use of cannabis as
unreasonable and against the spirit of the Free City. Most of
these were active users themselves, but others were liberal-minded
Christianites and sympathisers who more or less wanted to use
Christiania as a working example of the possibility of living un-
dramatically with endemic use of cannabis.

But behind these well-meaning or simply naive anti-prohibitionists stood the actual dealers in cannabis, profiting well from
the market. The police clamp-downs in 1989 and again in 1992
had seriously dented their income and they had an unmistakeable
economic interest in upholding the trade and protecting it as far
as possible from legal restrictions. Some of them could be seen as
'cultural' Christianites with a special attachment to cannabis, but
most of them were simple racketeers, simultaneously alien
elements and parasites on the all too tolerant body of the Free
City. They not only exploited the weaknesses of the community,
they also used the liberal political discourse as a defence against
both the demands from outside for moderation and the demands
from inside for solidarity.

In the turbulent period from mid-1993 to the spring of 1994, this covert battle between the repressive and the exploitative environments of Christiania over the body of the idealistic experiment played a major role not only in local politics but in the national and international discourse on drugs. The course of this argument highlighted the difficulties of establishing an accommodating climate between the all-out advocators of legalisation and the primitive law-and-order proponents. This appears to be a general feature of the Danish drug discourse – that each party maintains its claims on supremacy, with complete disregard as to the consequences of their actions.

Christiania Patrol and the 'normalisation move'

In the autumn of 1993 the 'normalisation move' was at its height. Police invaded restaurants in Christiania, removing furniture and closing down unlicensed shops, while also harassing cannabis users and dealers. The police had previously appeared in uniform for a while, but due to the distance to the market at Pusher Street, the dealers – thanks to an effective warning system of salaried watchboys on mountain bikes – always managed to move their goods before the patrols hit them. The police therefore changed their tactics and began stopping and searching people leaving Christiania. In this way, they intercepted a large number of relatively minor, recreational buyers, finding cannabis or other forms of illegal possessions (weapons, stolen goods, etc.) on up to 70 per cent of 'suspects'. But the Christianites soon found a counter-tactic – they tricked and provoked the police into searching them and then demanded damages (which they invariably won) for wrongful arrest. The police success rate plummeted to around 30 per cent.[11] To cover their embarrassment, the police decided to try once more with a new plainclothes patrol.

In 1993 a special 'Christiania Patrol' was established, staffed by local circuit police officers, but this plainclothes squad soon ran into trouble again. They succeeded in moving in on dealers through inventive disguises – one, for example, impersonated a wheelchair user, and suddenly jumped out of his chair to arrest a man selling cannabis. But these operational successes led to other problems – with the National Association for the Handicapped (the wheelchair episode) and with politicians worried at the

violent encounters between Christianites and the police. Indis-
criminate use was made of tear gas (in one case a tear gas grenade,
thrown over the Christiania fence by an angry policeman, landed
in a children's playground, sending kids coughing and screaming
into the school).

At the same time it was becoming apparent that perhaps the
police 'stress tactics' were having little impact on the actual drug
market in Copenhagen. The number of recorded cases of
professional drug crime and trafficking was falling steadily while
the number of users and small-time dealers detained rose: this
went on while cannabis prices remained constant or even fell.

The questioning of the street-level operations found a surprising
proponent in the Minister of Justice, Erling Olsen.

Christmas 1993 – and thereafter: whose common sense?

On 13 December 1993, Olsen hinted that the police should be
more flexible in cannabis law enforcement and the handling of
minor offences in Christiania, although later that month he had to
retract much of his pragmatic instruction (*Politiken*, 22 December
1993) as his right-wing government co-allies required a clear
denunciation of cannabis.

The question of whether it would be in accordance with legal
principles to have different rules for Christiania than for the rest of
the country became the formal framing of the conflict. After all,
'inequality of law', in the form of adjustment to local situations, is
common practice in Danish law enforcement. This allows for
different levels of sentencing and different police priorities in
different parts of the country, even though this is rarely
acknowledged officially.

Despite retreating to the position of formal equality of law
throughout Denmark, only the next day – on the 23 December –
Erling Olsen released a press statement confirming a deal between
the Christiania steering committee and the residents of Christiania. In return for a reduction in police activity the Christianites
would 'keep down the cannabis market' through self-policing.
Olsen also issued an order to the local police to appear in
Christiania only in uniform.

The police union responded by calling in the Labour
Inspectorate Office to document the dangers of police work in
Christiania. However, the Inspector merely stated that police

work was no more dangerous in Christiania than elsewhere. The next move on the police's part was simply to stay away from Christiania. The official justification was that there would be no point in patrolling in uniform and that the special Christiania squad was being dismantled. Everyone else, though (including Christianites wanting police protection from violence), saw this move as a covert strike action, as a demonstration against the Minister of Justice.

Despite an order from the Minister of Justice to resume ordinary police work in Christiania (such an order being demanded by the police union, *Morgenavisen Jyllandsposten*, 18 January 1994), the police remain away, this time due to 'other work'.[12] As a consequence, the market in cannabis is said to be flourishing again.

But in the meantime, the conservative parliamentary majority dictated an ultimatum to Christiania in January 1994: either everything would be 'normalised' (or rather legalised – *lovliggjort*) before mid-April, or Christiania would be closed by 1 February 1995. This legalisation would not only require restaurants and buildings to be torn down – together with the fence surrounding the Free City (to allow easier escape for police patrols in trouble) – but also involve a complete cessation of the cannabis trade.

The ultimatum did result in some 'normalisation' activity, which satisfied parliament. But in reality, the fence had not been torn down and the cannabis trade only tapered off temporarily.

Until the end of April, when Folketinget (parliament) was scheduled to discuss the situation, the media focused on Christiania and the legality issue. The Christianites found the government's demands too restrictive and even the cannabis dealers in Pusher Street threatened a 'strike' if the measures were forced through (*Politiken*, 27 March 1994). The Minister of Justice hailed this threat – which was actually carried out in a media circus as of 6 April – and asked that it be made permanent. But after parliament granted a stay of execution – acknowledging the action undertaken to normalise conditions while demanding further progress on all fronts – the public eye again left Christiania and the cannabis pushers to themselves.

Both the Deputy Police Inspector of Copenhagen (in a report quoted by *Politiken*, 23 January 1994) and representatives of the Christiania contact group (*Politiken*, same day) have declared that the intensive police activity in Christiania in 1993 had the effect of hardening and professionalising cannabis dealing. Only the tough dealers – 'rockers' and 'the autonomous' – are believed to have held out while the remaining 'old timer' hippies have disappeared.

A year on (November 1994) there seemed to be a return to the *status quo ante*, in the sense that the cannabis market is still there and the police patrol only sporadically or not at all. Restaurants have been normalised, some buildings torn down, and both Christianites and the police are licking their wounds. As for the latter, the wounds include court decisions indicating that many of the searches carried out by the police had insufficient legal grounds (see, for example, *Politiken*, 19 October 1993 and 27 January 1994) and therefore merit the award of damages.[13] Furthermore, a disciplinary fine (but no penal sanction) was imposed upon the police officer who had thrown the tear gas grenade into Christiana (*Politiken*, 21 September 1993).

Summing up – the attempts to crush the open cannabis market in Christiania have been unsuccessful, the main result being a loss of prestige for the police.

A NEW DANISH DRUGS POLICY ON STREET LEVEL?

In the spring of 1994 the Attorney General reminded local police chiefs (who are also local prosecutors) of his instruction of 1969 to respond to first-time cannabis possession offences only with a warning and to concentrate efforts on professional dealers. Denmark has no prohibition or penalisation of drug use, and possession of cannabis for own use should be dealt with leniently.

Both Nordic politicians and Danish police reacted negatively to this order, which in reality did not do much more than confirm an earlier Danish decision to differentiate between hard and soft drugs and to be 'soft' on users and small-time user–dealers.

Officially then, Denmark at present is in line with the emerging pragmatic approaches of places like Amsterdam, Hamburg (see Chapter 3), Frankfurt and Zürich.

In the long run, this implies a reduction of law enforcement efforts and the decriminalisation of cannabis. Such prospects do not satisfy Denmark's Nordic sister countries, and in the spring of 1994 Erling Olsen was pressed by his government colleagues (in particular the Christian People's Party and the Centre Democrats) to confirm that the latest developments did not imply any acceptance of even a minor trade in cannabis. Any more pragmatic policy would once again have to be implicitly, rather than explicitly, carried out.

Danish police officials still maintain that any relaxation of street harassment of drug users and minor dealers will require a clear mandate from Parliament, preferably in the form of a change in the law,[14] and it is quite clear that the present parliament – more right wing after the 1994 election – will not allow such a decision. In legal terms, such a change in the law is not necessary for police to behave differently. Both the instruction from the Attorney General and the traditional freedom of action for the police would be a sufficient basis for police discretion in relation to minor cases of cannabis possession. The problem is of course that beat officers, with their traditional views on cannabis and their hostility to Christiania, hide behind this formalistic argument and the politicians accept it.

Now that Sweden has decided to enter the EU, the Union may become the platform where the intra-Scandinavian drug discourse is played out. It remains to be seen whether this will result in further efforts to fight the illegal cannabis market in the streets of Denmark, be it in Vesterbro, Christiania or elsewhere in the country. But the low-level law enforcement developments of 1990–94 have shown that the limits of the law and of the police have been reached.

Whether local inhabitants fight alongside the police, as in Vesterbro, or against the police, as in Christiania, repressive actions will hardly be allowed to reach their desired levels of 'efficiency'. Important groups maintaining demands for sensible police behaviour and for the rule of law still seem able to prevent an all-out war on drug users and on Christiania – at least for the present.

NOTES

1. The Pompidou Group Multi-City Study reports: 'HIV seroprevalence amongst IV drug misusers in Copenhagen is estimated to be stable at between 8 and 15 per cent . . . The relatively low rate is attributed to adopting a preventive rather than repressive approach to drug

misusers' (Council of Europe, 1994, p.16). The last sentence indicates a
rather rosy view of actual practice in Denmark.

2. For some years Danish farmers were allowed to grow poppy seeds for
    export to be used on German buns. Several addicts harvested the
    poppies prematurely and got reasonably potent but impure opium.
3. See Københavns Politi, Narkotikasekretariatet, 1991, p. 38.
4. See *Københavns Politi, Årsberetning*, 1991, p. 34.
5. See, for instance, *Politiken*, 21 November 1993, in which a local group
    of residents complain both about insufficient police action and about
    the market dispersal which has pushed the dealings just a few blocks
    down the street.
6. A more extensive summary in English of the history of Christiania may
    be found at the end (pp. 345–62) of a report published in 1993 by the
    County and Municipal Research Institute (AKF): *De offentlige
    myndigheder og Christiania* (The Public Authorities and Christiania), by
    B. Jæger, L. Olsen and O. Rieper (the AKF Report). The following
    section of the present paper draws considerably on this report.
7. Representatives of the 'People's Movement' also tried to cooperate
    with the police by targeting professional junk dealers for arrest, but
    conflict arose when the police indiscriminately arrested junk dealers
    and hash pushers. This was the last time Christiania attempted any
    serious negotiations with the Copenhagen police.
8. In 1980 the local welfare office estimated that about a third of the 850–
    900 winter inhabitants were on welfare payments. In summer the
    number of residents increased by some 300–400 persons, of which
    around half were estimated to be on welfare (AKF Report, p. 55).
9. Parliamentary reply by the Minister of Justice to the Conservative MP
    Viggo Fischer.
10. Documented extensively by 'The Christiania Legal Group' on the basis
    of statements from victims of police violence, court cases, witnesses and
    videos. The material collected over the years has been made available
    both to the present author and to succeeding Ministers of Justice as
    well as to responsible police officials.
11. Personal communication from Police Inspector Poul Lind, head of the
    local precinct.
12. *Ibid.*
13. In 1992 490 persons were awarded damages for unwarranted arrests
    and searches, double the number of the preceding year (*Politiken*, 19
    October 1993).
14. Personal statement of police inspector Poul Lind to the author, 25
    October 1994.

REFERENCES

Alkohol og Narkotikarådet (1989) *Narkotika: Forhindrer forbud forbrug?*
    (Drugs: Does Prohibition Prevent Use?), Report on a conference at the
    Falkonercentret, 13 October 1989.

Bach, N. (1992) *Stofmisbrugerbehandling i Danmark: en evaluering af behandlingsindsatsen på dette område* (The Treatment of Drug Abusers in Denmark: An Evaluation of the Treatment Efforts in This Field) (Randers: mimeo).

Balvig, F. (1985) 'Narkotikaens betydning for kriminalitetsniveauet' (The Influence of Drugs on the Level of Crime), *Narkotika og kontrolpolitik* (report on a seminar at Rønne, Bornholm, Nordiska Rådet, Stockholm).

Balvig, F. (1987) *Den tyvagtige Dansker* (The Thieving Dane) (Copenhagen: Borgen).

Council of Europe (1994) *Multi-city study: Drug Misuse Trends in Thirteen European Cities*, written of behalf of the experts from the thirteen cities by Richard Hartnoll.

Folketingstidende (1993/4) *Forespørgsel no. F15 til justitsministeren og forsvarsministeren (om forholdene på Christiania)*. Besvarelse og debat 20 January 1994, pp. 5248–339 (Parliamentary interpellation on Christiania).

Jepsen, J. (1989a) 'Privatization of Social Control – Four Examples from Scandinavia', in R. Hood (ed.), *Crime and Criminal Policy in Europe*. *Proceedings of a European Colloquium*, Centre for Criminological Research, University of Oxford.

Jepsen, J. (1989b) 'Drug Policy in Denmark', in H.J. Albrecht and A. van Kalmthout (eds), *Drug Policies in Western Europe*, Kriminologische Forschungsberichte aus dem Max-Planck-Institut für ausländisches und internationales strafrecut, Freiburg i.Br. vol. 41.

Jepsen, J. (1993) 'Criminal policy, drug trafficking and consumption', in J. L. Diez-Ripollès and P. Copello (eds), *La actual politica criminal sobre drogas: Una perspective comparada*, Instituto Andaluz Interuniversitario de Criminologie, Tirant lo Blanch Derecero (Valencia).

Justitsministeriet (1993) *Pressemeddelelse – om politiets indsats på Christiania.* (press release from the Minister of Justice on police activity in Christiania), 22 December.

Justitsministeriet, Socialministeriet, Sundhedsministeriet (1994) *Bekæmpelse af Narkotikamisbruget. Elementer og Hovedproblemer* (Multi-departmental policy statement on drug problems and drug policy).

Jyllandsposten (Morning Daily, various issues).

Jæger, B., L. Olsen and O. Rieper (1993) *De offentlige myndigheder og Christiania* (The AKF Report) (Copenhagen: Amternes og Kommunernes Forskningsinstitut).

Krarup, O. (1977) *Christiania-dommen. Udskrift af Ostre Landsrets dombog. Med indledning af Ole Krarup* (transcript of the Superior Court decision in the Christiania case, with comment by Krarup, Professor of Administrative Law and one of the barristers for Christiania) (Copenhagen: Informations Forlag).

Kruse, S., J. Winsløw and A. Storgaard (1989) *Narkotikakontrol i Danmark* (Drug Control in Denmark) (Copenhagen: Alkohol og Narkotikarådets Skriftserie 14).

Københavns Politi Årsberetning (Annual Report of the Copenhagen Police), various years.

Københarns Politi, Narkosekretariatet (1991) *Narkotika-Strategi 90. Beretning om Københavns Politis Indsats på Vesterbro i Tiden 20 August 1990 – 19 August 1991* (Report on the Activities of the Copenhagen Drug Police at

Vesterbro), ed. J. Sperling and J. Pedersen (Copenhagen: Københavns Politi, Narkosekretariatet).

Lund, T. (1993) 'Vor narko-politik er helt absurd' (Our Drug Policy is Totally Absurd), *Det Fri Aktuelt*, 28 October 1993.

Madsen, B. (1981) *Sumpen, liberalisterne og de hellige: Christiania -et barn af kapitalismen* (Copenhagen: Social og sundhedspolitisk gruppe).

Politiken various issues.

Rigspolitichefen (1993) *Notat om uropatruljer* (Copenhagen, 8 July 1993) (material on *uropatruljer* from the Office of the National Chief of Police).

Rigspolitichefen (1994) *Politiets Årsberetning 1993* (Annual Report of the National Chief of Police).

Storgaard, A. (1992) *Straf for Narkotikahandel* (Penalties for Drug Trafficking) (Aarhus: CANFAU, University of Aarhus).

Strindlund, H. (1991) 'Det *ska* vara svårt att vara missbrukare', in *Vi ger oss aldrig, Rapport från Regeringens Aktionsgrupp mot Narkotika, Stockholm* (It should be hard to be a drug abuser, in We Never Give In, *Report from the Governmental Action Group against Narcotics*).

Sundhedsstyrelsen (1991) *Alkohol og stofmisbrug blandt unge (udarbejdet af Dorrit Schmidt)* (Alcohol and Drug Abuse among Adolescents) (Copenhagen: National Directorate of Health).

Sundhedsstyrelsen (1993) *Alkohol og narkotikamisbruget 1992* (Abuse of Alcohol and Drugs, 1992) (Copenhagen: National Directorate of Health).

Winsløw, J. (1984) *Narreskibet* (Ship of Fools) (Copenhagen: Socpol).

Winsløw, J. (1987) 'Drug Abuse Treatment as a Cause of Excess Mortality among Danish Drug Abusers', *Scandinavian Studies in Criminology*, vol. 8, pp. 81–100.

Winsløw, J. and Ege, P. (1984) *Stofmisbrug, kriminalitet og metadon* (Drug Abuse, Crime and Methadone) (Copenhagen: Alkohol- og Narkotikarådet).

2 London: 'Community Damage Limitation' through Policing?

Maggy Lee

Open drug dealing at city or street level has been well documented in the United States and in Europe (see Zimmer, 1987, 1990; Uchida and Forst, 1994; Worden *et al.*, 1994; Beschner and Bower, 1985). In Britain, claims such as 'London is now the centre of a £3 billion addiction industry'[1] and 'Crack "turf wars" sweep Britain'[2] have made banner headlines in the national and local press. Drug trade in Manchester was reportedly 'enforced by teenage hitmen with Uzi sub-machine-guns and sawn-off shotguns'.[3] Amidst the resultant public demands for safer streets, various police forces have set up 'drug-free zones', installing closed-circuit television cameras and mounting high-profile anti-drug operations to tackle the open, visible drug trade.

These activities broadly fit the trend that many researchers have identified as 'low-level drug enforcement' within Britain (Dorn and Murji, 1992). 'Low-level' in theory, is taken to mean the suppliers and users at the retail level of the drug market, with police reorganisation and intelligence development broadly mirroring the perceived hierarchy of the market (see Dorn *et al.*, 1991; Miles, 1993; Wright *et al.*, 1993). But what low-level drug enforcement entails in practice, and how it relates to wider developments in policing in Britain, remains largely unexplored. This chapter discusses some of the preliminary findings of an on-going two-year research study on low-level drug enforcement and policing.[4] In particular, this chapter describes and analyses the efforts of the Metropolitan Police Force to reduce the level of drug

33

activity and improve community safety in one part of London through a high profile operation known as Operation Welwyn.

Operation Welwyn, which brought together a special squad of police officers from four neighbouring police divisions, started in 1991 and is still running at the time of writing. The Operation went through at least three different phases: phases 1 and 2, both of which were described by senior and frontline officers as 'straightforward' anti-drug operations with limited impact on the open, visible drug market, were rarely referred to in public. It was phase 3 of the Operation – involving 'partnership' between key individuals within the police, local councils and other local agencies – that was publicly hailed as a success by local residents groups, council leaders, the Metropolitan Police Commissioner, Labour Party politicians (*King's Cross News*, no. 3, Spring 1994) and the Prime Minister alike (HM Government, 1994). So what were the main elements of the policing strategy in King's Cross?

A CASE STUDY

The highly publicised police operation in King's Cross coincided with the publication of a report from the Advisory Council on the Misuse of Drugs (ACMD), *Police, Drug Misusers and the Community* (1994). This report argued that in developing their local policing strategies, the police along with other 'partners' must develop ways 'to limit the harm to individuals and damage to the community from drug misuse' (p. 25). In the context of street-level drug enforcement, a 'community damage limitation' approach would aim at 'reducing the fear of drug-related crime to finance drug misuse, crime associated with drug dealing and the threat to public health' (pp. 26–7). How this orientation towards community interests actually works in practice is best understood as an evolving phenomenon at the local level. In their conclusion, Dorn and Murji (1992, p. 169) argued that:

> This suggests a negotiated, emergent character to low-level drug enforcement producing a multiplicity of approaches, rationales, compromises and evaluations of outcome . . . If things turn out well, then the decade may see forms of LLDE that reduce the extent of drug distribution *and* reduce social harm associated with low-level drug markets. But the practice

of LLDE at a local level could also entail a raft of other possibilities which may be viewed as much less desirable.

(emphasis as in original)

This chapter draws upon the case study of Operation Welwyn to illustrate the 'negotiated' and 'emergent' character of low-level drug enforcement against a background of wider developments in policing in Britain.

Methodology

The fieldwork on which this chapter is based was carried out between April and October 1994, and was threefold. First, the qualitative methods included an examination of police statistics and relevant public documents. Second, fieldwork involved observations of multi-agency meetings and 'shadowing' the Operation's uniformed and plain clothes officers over a two-week period. A research diary was kept to provide a snapshot of encounters between the police and others in various settings (including 'known' or 'suspected' drug dealers/users), patrolling activities, surveillance and other forms of intelligence gathering. Up to eighty contact hours were spent in informal discussion and semi-structured interviews with senior and rank-and-file police officers, drawing on their experience, understanding and expectations of policing and other 'partnership' activities in the King's Cross area. Third, semi-structured interviews were conducted with ten local council administrators, housing managers, community safety practitioners and drug agency practitioners with knowledge and experience of working on issues of community safety and/or drugs in the locality.

The local setting

King's Cross is an inner-city area in London with a resident population of some 16,000. It is a racially mixed locality with a high proportion of white residents. The area is dominated by the railway terminal, which handles over 100,000 passengers each weekday and links London to the north-east of England and to Scotland. Apart from the blocks of cheap hotels, local businesses are largely made up of small shops such as fast-food restaurants, convenience stores, bookmakers, offices and a few larger organisations. In their joint bid for central government funding, the local Boroughs and Training and Enterprise Councils described King's Cross in the following way:

> Heavy traffic, congestion, pollution and parking problems are the daily experience of residents and visitors. Road accident statistics are higher than the regional average. The area has a cluttered street-scene, and the ad hoc transport interchange contributes to the lack of coherence, the absence of civic pride and identity. It is essentially a borderland, crisscrossed by administrative boundaries.
>
> (Camden Council *et al.*, 1994, p. 2)

Inter-racial tension in the area was known to be long-standing, and racial attacks were seen by the police as on the increase:[5]

> In racial incidents reported from January to August 13, 28 of the victims were white, 54 were Asian, and 13 were black.
>
> (*Guardian*, 17 August 1994)

Historically well-known for its street prostitution problem, King's Cross in the early 1990s also acquired the reputation of being 'a drugs market place' (*Hampstead and Highgate Express*, 26 February 1994). Partly because of the accessibility and anonymity the location provided, the area in and around King's Cross station was described by some police as 'a common market for drug dealing' – no need for an established connection and offering high turnover of crack and heroin. Police videotapes of the area showed groups of suspected drug dealers congregating outside the bookmakers, burger bars and post office. Local press articles also recalled the bleak picture of people dying after taking high-purity heroin and 'parents forbidding their children to visit the local playground because of the used needles and condoms lying around' (*Hampstead and Highgate Express*, 25 February 1994).

Central to this commonplace construct of the local drugs scene was a perceived problem of dealers coming from outside the 'community'. Whilst acknowledging that a few of the drug pushers and buyers lived in the local hotels, senior and frontline police officers believed that the majority of dealers routinely travelled into King's Cross from other parts of London. Because of the demographic characteristics of the local drugs scene, police actions effectively resulted in large-scale arrests of black dealers.

Despite this, officers had no qualms about the high proportion of black arrestees – over 60 per cent according to police statistics (see below). Both senior and frontline officers stressed that dealers were not singled out because they were black: 'it so happened that the local drug market is dominated by Afro-Caribbean and to a lesser extent Italian dealers.' Police videotapes of dealers in action were routinely produced in court to substantiate the case for prosecution. As one local council community safety practitioner admitted, although there was 'some initial unease', as 'a very high proportion of the people that were being arrested [on the police videotapes] were black people, the evidence seemed to be there.'

This racial dimension to a local drugs problem is arguably of crucial consideration to the way a locality is policed. The ACMD Report (1994, pp. 22–3) pointed out that in some areas, street-level police activities which appear to bear particularly on certain groups (for instance, young, unemployed Afro-Caribbean male cannabis street dealers) may remain 'a rubbing point between the police and some people within ethnic communities'. In King's Cross, however, the working assumption of an external, transient problem population reinforced the notion of an homogeneity of 'community' interests. For instance, one local council administrator described this apparent consensus in the following way:

> 'Here in King's Cross, if the police operation was seen to be successful, if the number of dealers out on the streets seemed to be declining, if there's less overt drug dealing, then that was the goal or end product that local people were concerned about. There's evidence to suggest that the drug dealers and drug users were from without King's Cross. So there's a general willingness within the local area to regard these people as outsiders and as bad outsiders . . . I certainly think we've got policing by consent in King's Cross.'
>
> (Interview with local council administrator)

Similarly, from the police point of view, the use of vigorous policing tactics against crack cocaine and heroin dealers which might have created public order problems in other black 'communities' (see Keith, 1993; Graef, 1990; Dorn *et al.*, 1992) was regarded as largely unproblematic in King's Cross:

> 'King's Cross station is a potentially explosive public order area. It's a transit point and lots of people hang out there or

congregate there. But I don't see robust enforcement as a problem. People don't mind being stopped and searched as long as it's being done professionally or if they have nothing to hide. It's not the number of officers being deployed, it's not even the number of stop and searches being made that matters. It's the style of policing, their professionalism, that matters . . . It's not like we've flooded the area with our officers. We've never done that, and we haven't got the resources.'

(Interview with Chief Inspector in charge
of Operation Welwyn)

But as we shall see, the notion that the police simply delivered what the 'community' wanted is far too simplistic. Rather, drug enforcement in King's Cross stood at the intersection of a variety of interests, tensions and competing demands. As a police operation aiming to deliver what some sections of the population wanted (i.e. robust enforcement against others), Operation Welwyn generated new sites of negotiation and alliance as well as social conflict.

Communities as customers for policing: the national setting

The anxieties directed towards the local drugs scene went beyond disapproval of the buying and selling of drugs *per se*. In its reference to King's Cross, a local council community safety document spoke of 'the large and law abiding population [living] in increasing fear as every corner and doorway became a haven for dealers and prostitutes and the streets and open spaces were littered with syringes, condoms and the general detritus of the criminal activity' (Camden Council *et al.*, 1994, p. 21). This construction of drugs as a multi-faceted problem is nothing new. Implicitly, what was needed was safer streets or the so-called 'defensible space', typified by 'The Five Towns Initiative' and 'Safer Cities Projects'.[6] Crime Concern – a charity set up with initial Home Office funding – was launched in 1988 to promote crime prevention partnerships, encourage the involvement of the commercial sector and to manage locally based partnerships in designated Safer City areas. In addition, the 1991 Report of the Standing Conference on Crime Prevention (the Morgan Report) firmly placed the notion of local delivery of 'community safety' in the forefront of political and police discourse. Multi-agency crime prevention forums and community safety partnerships which had been in their infancy in the mid-1980s, were rapidly becoming standard practice by the early 1990s.

This orientation towards the concerns and priorities of 'the community' has been mirrored in the restructuring of police roles and responsibilities. A principal element of the Metropolitan Police reorganisation in the 1980s, and now pressed ahead nationally in the Government's White Paper, *Police Reform* (1993), is to devolve routine policing to self-contained local command units, focus managerial power on the division, and, theoretically, make it responsive to local communities' needs. Using the 1990s language of new managerialism, local 'communities' are seen as 'customers' for policing. The attempts both within and outside the police force to draw in a wider social context in discussing policework are laudable (for instance, Alderson, 1984; Scarman, 1981; Wells, 1987). But this vision of policing is also potentially powerful as a political tool to redefine successful policework at a time when, as in other public services, the activities, costs, resource use and performance of different forces have been under intense official scrutiny (Audit Commission, 1990; Sheehy Report, 1993). The apparent rising crime rates and falling detection rates,[7] when combined with evidence of 'poor performance and failures that range from incivility and aggressiveness to corruption' (ACPO, 1990), raise fundamental questions about the cost-effectiveness of the police. Chief police officers have since tried to reorientate the culture of policing around an explicit mission of service and ethos of consumerism, partly as self-engineered change to preserve the organisation but also in response to central government's reform agenda. As Reiner (1994) has pointed out, this emphasis on 'quality of service' and service delivery is arguably 'policing designed for the age of the Citizen's Charter'.[8]

In the context of drug enforcement, such developments have found their expression in the ACMD Report (1994), *Police, Drug Misusers and the Community*. First, the police are urged to accept that what their local customers want may not simply be the unattainable 'elimination' of the drugs trade. In pursuing a policy of 'containment', the police along with other 'partners' must develop ways to minimise the 'level of harm done to the local community'. This broadening of policing objectives fits with the police's own argument that – as in other areas of police activity – performance cannot be measured solely in the quantifiable terms of detection rates and drug seizures.

Secondly, divisional-based enforcement strategies should be developed in conjunction with the most appropriate local agencies. For example, the police could support local authorities in their efforts to carry out environmental improvements 'such as better street lighting, public buildings and amenities', which in turn would be linked to police efforts 'in returning areas to normality'. At the same time, 'the community', through its Neighbourhood Watch and 'active citizens' (e.g. informants) would share frontline responsibilities in 'street level enforcement'. In this way, a new division of labour between the police and 'the community' can be conceptualised.

Transforming King's Cross

Operation Welwyn phase 3 (whose senior officers submitted evidence to the ACMD Working Party) illustrates in a concrete and localised form some broader developments in policing generally and drug enforcement specifically.

In 1991 and 1992, under phases 1 and 2 of the Operation, a total of 174 suspected drug dealers and buyers had been arrested. Officers, however, believed the impact they had on the drug market was short-lived: 'We would arrest someone. The problem would only go away for two days, and then that dealer or punter would be replaced by someone else' (Operation Welwyn plainclothes police officer).

Local resentment against the drugs problem had culminated in a public protest march in October 1992 involving over a hundred families, children and local residents' groups. Residents' representatives appealed to the local Labour Member of Parliament and the Deputy Commissioner of the Metropolitan Police and demanded that 'something must be done'.

On taking charge of the Operation in November 1992, the Area Commander in Number 1 Area of the Metropolitan Police set the following policing objectives:

To improve the quality of life for the residents, commuters and people who work in or pass through the Kings Cross area by reducing crime (drugs, prostitution and associated criminality) and reducing the fear of crime.

(London Drug Policy Forum, 1993, p. 13)

This broadening of policing objectives linked in with the Area Commander's attempt to recondition the minds of the police 'so that they don't just focus on results like arrests but actually work towards improving the well-being of the local community' (Interview with Area Commander). A squad of forty plainclothes and uniformed officers was used to police an area of roughly one square mile. There was no single purpose to the Operation – success was to be judged by a complex set of criteria:

'It's about results, yes, but it's not just about arresting people. Operation Welwyn is the policing side of the partnership. It's anything at all that impacts on crime and brings the area back to normality. It's about social and economic regeneration.'

(Interview with Area Commander)

There were three main elements to the policing strategy under this new phase 3 of the Operation – namely, partnership, targeting and surveillance, and intensive patrolling.

Partnership

First, there was an attempt to build an alliance with 'the community' and other non-police agencies. This partnership approach involved collaboration between three divisions of the Metropolitan Police, British Transport Police, the two local councils (Islington and Camden), Islington Safer Cities Project, Camden and Islington Family Health Services Authority, Camden and Islington Health Authority, local 'community' and business representatives, Neighbourhood and Tenants Associations and voluntary organisations. A King's Cross Joint Working Party was set up in November 1992 and, following that, a King's Cross Community Safety Initiative with a Partnership Coordinator funded by the local councils. A free King's Cross newspaper was circulated to homes and businesses to inform them what was happening in the area. A referral scheme was proposed so that drug users, the homeless and others who arguably made up the area's 'transient' population could be referred back to their own 'home' authorities for support. There were also plans to set up a primary care centre to provide medical and counselling services for people with needs 'related to alcoholism, homelessness, drug abuse, prostitution and mental illness' (King's Cross Community Safety Initiative, 1994). Attracting central government funds and investment from big business was seen by all parties as the long-term solution to crime and urban decay in the area. Indeed, the police stressed that they had a legitimate role to play in the fight against the causes of crime and had rallied behind the local councils' applications for the government's new Single Regeneration Bid. It was this partnership approach which arguably transformed the 'feel' of King's Cross and turned Operation Welwyn into one of the Metropolitan Police's two most publicised showpieces (the other being the London-wide burglary-focused Operation Bumblebee).

The partnership approach also shaded off into 'multi-agency policing' (Wright, 1986), which involved the mobilisation of non-police resources towards policy-defined goals. The interpenetration of police and non-police goals and activities was facilitated by the vague and open-ended concept of improving the well-being of or limiting the damage to 'the community'. On the one hand, partnership in King's Cross encompassed any form of 'good work' perceived to have some beneficial impact on the locality – for instance, improving public health and the area's physical appearance by better refuse collection, better street lighting and through a scheme to clear discarded syringes. On the other hand, the policy-defined goals were oriented towards drugs and crime control. The local councils and central government's Urban Partnership Funds set out to improve security on King's Cross housing estates by installing entry-phones and closed-circuit television, limiting the number of entrances to the estate and building new perimeter fencing. Plans were also made 'to install closed-circuit TV in major public areas to make the streets safer' (King's Cross Community Safety Initiative, 1994). Police crime prevention officers worked with the local councils, housing associations, London Transport and private businesses to 'design out' places where drug dealing and prostitution seemed to take place. Joint actions were taken to secure doorways and alleys, seal off railway arches and board up derelict buildings. By driving the drug dealers, buyers and users from the less visible locations onto the streets, such multi-agency efforts facilitated police surveillance and targeting work ('they have nowhere to hide; the police can take them out one by one').

Where the policy-defined goals were framed in terms of drugs and crime control, the mobilisation of non-police resources towards policy-defined goals also meant that police enforcement tactics became increasingly enmeshed with what Cockburn (1977) described as the management of cities and people. As one local council administrator explained,

'You've heard about the raid on the Carlisle Hotel, which in itself was a very significant operation in that it involved a small number of Council officers being made aware of the details of an armed police operation. First of all, the police indicated that this is what they're going to do. But they also wanted to know what the Council could do because their concern was that they could go into this hotel and probably make a few arrests. But it's likely that the hotel would then be used for dealing again in a short period of time. What could the Council do or the Fire Brigade do to provide a more permanent solution to this? . . . We could take out a Control Order, which is basically the Council taking environmental health action and bringing the hotel under council management . . . The police operation took place fairly late at night. Then the very next morning the Environmental Health people served the Control Order and closed the place down. So that's an example where we try to think what we can do with our powers and resources to back up a police operation which is therefore a more coordinated, corporate approach to the problem.'

(Interview with local council administrator)

Indeed, the Metropolitan Police Commissioner in a public conference cited the closing of the Carlisle Hotel by the local council under the Housing Act as a 'vivid example of multi-agency partnership in action' (*King's Cross News*, Conference Special, no. 3, Spring 1994). On another occasion, the police raided a flat allegedly used for drug dealing. Following that, the Islington Council served an eviction order on the tenant.[9] The *Police Review* (22 July 1994) cited another example of partnership where the Operation Welwyn team 'raided a crack house at 2 p.m. one afternoon and made five arrests. At 2.20 p.m. the local council arrived to cut off the electricity and at 2.30 p.m. the place was demolished.' One side effect of multi-agency policing was that 'good' results in drug enforcement in the conventional sense of drug seizures or court-based punishment were not always necessary to justify police activities. As one police officer pointed out,

> 'It doesn't matter whether we find large amounts of drugs or not . . . In the end we didn't charge anyone with drug-related offences. That didn't matter because we already had an agreement with the local authorities. They used their planning powers to evict those people immediately after the raid. From a policing point of view, we've managed to close down a crack house. It's a good result in that sense!'
>
> (Operation Welwyn plainclothes police officer)

In this process, alliances were formed to facilitate the local delivery of what the ACMD's Report has termed 'vigorous, focused, street level enforcement'. Raids, street clearance operations, targeting and surveillance (see below) all became publicly legitimised as a necessary part of the total package of 'returning the area to normality'.

Targeting and surveillance

Targeting and surveillance was a central aspect of the Operation throughout its three phases. Operation Welwyn officers worked with about twenty undercover police officers, who posed as buyers purchasing crack cocaine or heroin from the dealers. In Operation Welwyn as in many other drug enforcement operations[10], the case built up relied heavily on video evidence of deals taking place and detailed observation logs filled out by officers on surveillance. Three observation points were set up (for instance, above the rail station) to monitor all activity in the area with the aid of high magnification camera equipment. The logs included details about exchanges and the clothes that alleged dealers were wearing. Once the test purchasing phase was completed by the undercover officers, plainclothes officers armed with the dealer log book would go out with four to five arrest teams (each with four to five uniformed officers) in a 'swoop' operation to identify and arrest the dealers caught on video.

Surveillance was also facilitated by the local authorities. As one officer stated,

'Local authorities allowed us to use vacant council flats where we could film the drug deals. When the cherry tree blossomed and blocked our view, they came to trim the tree for us. That's total cooperation!'

(Operation Welwyn plainclothes officer)

Another aspect of the targeting strategy involved gathering intelligence on the local drugs scene, crime patterns and active drug dealers.[11] The need to cultivate useful informants, to establish 'a rapport with the low life in the area', as one plainclothes officer put it, meant the relationship between the police and the policed was highly negotiatory in nature. As one officer explained,

'Plainclothes police work doesn't necessarily mean anonymity. I know what most of the dealers are up to and they know me . . . They know I'm not here to cause any grief and they'll tell me things. But these people know the score. They know that they can still get arrested anytime.'

(Operation Welwyn plainclothes officer)

The police claimed that through targeting, intelligence gathering and surveillance, over 200 suspected drug dealers were identified and most of them arrested under Operation Welwyn 3. In terms of the punishment meted out by the court, the Operation had a conviction rate of 96 per cent with an average prison sentence of two and a half years.

Intensive patrolling

A special squad of Operation Welwyn officers was deployed to guarantee a highly visible police presence on the streets. Intensive patrolling (including an extra 25 officers from the Territorial Support Group at one point) was seen as important in reassuring 'the community' that something was being done about the drugs problem. With such a concentration of intensive patrolling activities in an area of roughly one square mile, Phase 3 of the Operation also substantially increased the risk of arrest in King's Cross – but not just for drug dealers and buyers. According to Operation Welwyn's statistics, the police arrested or cautioned a total of 2,000 people between 1993 and 1994 for various types of illegal activities (possession of drugs, obstruction through swallowing of drugs, soliciting, kerb-crawling, placing prostitute adverts in public phone boxes, etc.).

Even when unable to make arrests, Operation Welwyn officers set out 'to keep the pressure on the low life' by acting as what Sagarin and McNamara (1972) called a 'judicial punitive body'. In effect this meant harassing suspicious people in known drug areas by stopping them, questioning them, perhaps searching them, and telling them to move on. Between 1993 and 1994, a total of 4,000 stop and searches were recorded by Operation Welwyn officers:

> 'The general tactic is to keep the pressure on the low life, keep hassling them, and try to re-establish some control over the area. Some of them would stay away at least while we're around.'
>
> (Operation Welwyn uniformed police constable)

Of course, such techniques represent nothing new to most specialist officers in police basic commands; they are not unique to drug enforcement but have been generally referred to as 'inconvenience policing' (Reiner, 1991). But there is a down-side to the use of such techniques. As the following example from my research diary shows, intensive patrolling when paired with a policy that upheld a spatial realisation of criminality, had the potential to generate new sites of tension between the police and the policed:

> 3p.m. Wednesday afternoon. Went out with one uniformed officer on patrol. Officer said 'everything seemed normal' outside King's Cross station. Two men walked towards us; both white in their late 30s; dressed in dirty jeans and jackets, one carrying a plastic bag and the other carrying an old travelling rug. The officer said to me that one was a 'known drug user'. Officer stopped him; asked him where he was going. The 'known drug user' said he was just 'passing through' and was 'not causing any grief'. The other man looked annoyed for being stopped. Officer told both to 'go the other direction' and said, 'This is my territory, I don't want any trouble from you'. The other man started swearing. Said the officer has 'no right to stop them'; that he is 'infringing on [their] liberties'; that they are just 'crossing the road like everybody else'. Both ignored officer's instruction to turn back. The other man started

swearing again. Officer told him to stop swearing or else would 'book him'. The 'known drug user' looked on, not quite knowing what to do. The other man tried again to cross the road. Officer moved to try and block his way. 'Known drug user' said again 'we're not causing any grief'. Officer eventually let them both pass through.

(Extract from research diary)

Competing demands and the problem of displacement

Whilst senior officers stressed the success of the Operation (both in terms of achieving 'hard' results and in forming alliances with 'the community'), there was a sense of frustration amongst some frontline officers that they were making a limited impact on the drug trade even in the third phase:

'The streets are a lot quieter partly because the dealing is now more covert. We've managed to take out many dealers; a lot of them went inside [prison]. But some of the dealers we arrested under Welwyn 1 have come out and are back on the streets again.'

(Operation Welwyn plainclothes officer)

The ACMD's report and the work of many researchers (Dorn *et al.*, 1992; Keith, 1993; Zimmer, 1987; Uchida and Forst, 1994; Worden *et al.*, 1994) have pointed to the ways in which drug sellers adapt to police presence. In King's Cross some dealers allegedly adapted by varying the location and time of sales. 'Runners' were also increasingly used by some dealers to seek out and notify known buyers of the time and location of the deal. The apparent success of the police at reducing overt dealing and generating alliances in one part of the area seemed to have produced tensions with key players and resident groups in other parts of the area. One senior officer in the neighbouring division was publicly critical of Operation Welwyn because it had displaced the drug problem to his division and had since launched a smaller-scale operation just one mile from King's Cross (interview with Detective Chief Inspector). A local drug agency also claimed its outreach workers had extended their activities to the nearby Euston station because the Operation had dispersed some of their clients to other sites:

'No doubt the level of overt activities of drug selling has been reduced as a result of such intensive police activities. I mean, they put lots of resources into such a small area and they're determined to produce results. But the impact of the police activities seemed very sporadic. What the operation has done is to push the drug dealing off the commercial area into a wider area for instance the housing estates. I think their activities have pushed what is initially a problem within a radius of one quarter of a mile from King's Cross off to a radius of one half of a mile.'

> (Interview with local drugs agency manager)

Despite the working assumption of an homogeneity of 'community' interests, multi-agency policing in King's Cross occupied a place at the intersection of multiple interests and sometimes competing demands within 'the community'. For instance, after representations from the police, the local council restricted the licences of local fast-food outlets. Late-night cafés were asked to close earlier so that prostitutes and 'dealers had nowhere to duck into' (*Guardian*, 15 November 1993). This did not go down well with some local businesses and they looked set to challenge the council's curfew through the courts.

Similarly, some local residents complained that they were the 'unwilling victims' of an Operation which only succeeded in displacing the problem to their housing estates.[12] As one local newspaper described on its front page:

Somers Town is becoming London's new drugs and sex Mecca with pimps, hookers, and crack-pushers seeking refuge there as Operation Welwyn flushes them out of King's Cross . . . 'It's shameful. This area has always had its fair share of crime, but it has never been known as a red light area like King's Cross – until Welwyn,' she said.

(*Camden and St Pancras Chronicle*, 11 August 1994)

Although there is no hard evidence to suggest that drug activities in nearby estates were directly caused by Operation Welwyn, some local residents clearly believed that was the case. As one local council housing manager argued,

'What the police have done is that they have broken up the drugs problem in and around King's Cross station into pockets of smaller problems all over the area. That's what the local residents think, and that's why some of them want the Operation extended, some demand the use of private security guards on some council estates, video cameras and entry-phones, and others want to build an eight-foot wall around their estate to keep the drug users away.'

(Interview with local council housing manager)

For the police, the dilemma was that the language of 'community safety', with its stress on responsiveness to customer needs, meant a variety of constituencies could now identify themselves as having a legitimate voice in the creation of policing policies. Since Welwyn was such a highly publicised Operation, it became inextricably linked with *any* fluctuation in levels of drug activity in the King's Cross and surrounding area.

DISCUSSION

The achievements of Operation Welwyn were more apparent in stimulating social and environmental improvements in a deprived area rather than in containing the drug trade in King's Cross. The real extent of covert dealing and displacement of the drug problem was difficult to ascertain and therefore remained a contested issue. Indeed, research evidence elsewhere suggests that sustained impact of drug enforcement activities on the community can only be achieved as a result of much wider gentrification of the area (c.f. Zimmer, 1990; Keith, 1993). In the short run at least, the official acknowledgement of King's Cross as a high-profile drug problem area had in effect prompted the local councils, health authorities and other social agencies to tackle some of the most obvious signs of *urban deprivation*. To the extent that local liaison processes facilitated environmental and social improvements which made a difference to the everyday lives of some local residents and commuters, alliances between the police and the 'community' (albeit fragile and shifting) could be regarded as a success.

But any attempt to understand and assess drug enforcement activities must also take into account the harsher realities of contemporary policing. Activities such as raids, intensive patrol-ling, targeting, stop and search and the involvement of social agencies in some police operations, are inherently grounded in social conflict: they involve the policing *of*, and interventions *against*, certain individuals and groups of people. As we have seen, Operation Welwyn also involved an intensification of conventional policing tactics in urban 'trouble-spots'. The ACMD Report (1994, p. 21) recommended that policing tactics such as stop and search should be adopted 'as an essential element of street-level policing providing there is quality control and that outcomes are properly monitored'. So far, key partners of the police did not regard it as part of their role to discuss or raise questions about frontline policing activities in King's Cross. To some extent, more information and better monitoring may be useful in ensuring that intensive policing tactics formerly reserved for public order situations (as in the controversial 'saturation' tactics of the 1980s) do not become normalised as just another form of vigorous, focused street-level policing. Ultimately, the challenge for the police and those social agencies involved in multi-agency policing must be to deliver a drug enforcement strategy that can limit not only the 'damage to communities' but also the potential excesses of policing in British cities.

NOTES

1. *Evening Standard*, 6 September 1993.
2. *Today*, 22 October 1993.
3. *Observer*, 12 July 1992.
4. Acknowledgements: Building upon past research activities on drug referral and policing, Dr Nicholas Dorn and I developed this project and the Smiths Charity Trusts funded it at the Institute for the Study of Drug Dependence. The research work would have been impossible without the help of Commander John Townsend and Chief Inspector Paul Hoare and the cooperation of all those who agreed to be interviewed and/or observed in ethnographic work. I am most grateful to my colleagues who commented on drafts of this chapter, especially Nicholas Dorn, Jane Mountency, Toby Seddon and Oswin Baker at ISDD. None of these people has any responsibility for the presentation, analysis or conclusion arrived at here.
5. In August 1994 the stabbing of a 15-year-old white male in King's Cross, allegedly by a group of Asian youths, sparked off speculations of a 'race attack' and an apparent backlash against the Asian (mainly Bengali) community (*Guardian*, 15 August 1994).

6. As part of the Home Office crime prevention initiative, the Safer Cities Programme extended the earlier Five Towns Initiative in 1988. For further comments see Crawford (1984), pp. 497–520; King, (1989), pp. 291–312; Tilley (1993), pp. 40–57.
7. Although the limitations of official crime figures are well known, the apparent falling clear-up rate – from nearly 50 per cent in 1950 to 29 per cent in 1991 (Home Office, 1992) – has been politically damaging for the police.
8. For a discussion of the Charter initiative, see Doern (1993), pp. 17–29; Cooper, (1993), pp. 149–71.
9. Joint action taken by the police and housing authorities in the United States has often taken a more extreme form. In Alexandria, Virginia, for example, whole families were evicted from public and private housing and then blacklisted (Moran, 1990). Similarly, in Charleston, South Carolina, under a police anti-crime programme called 'Take Back the Streets', criminals were systematically thrown out of housing projects and 'flying squad officers monitored ex-convicts who lived in the community' (Meese and Carrico, 1990).
10. See Dorn *et al.* (1992), pp. 106–11.
11. This strategy of targeting criminals (such as prolific burglars) rather than crime was also echoed in the Audit Commission's Report (1993) that 'every BCU officer should, for example, know who are the top ten local target offenders'.
12. Whilst the ACMD's Report acknowledged the potential problem of geographical displacement in drug enforcement, it also accepted the displacement of open drug trade from a public place to a private house, as something positive in terms of 'community damage limitation', i.e. restoring 'a public amenity for the benefit of the wider community' (ACMD, 1994, p. 27).

REFERENCES

Advisory Council on the Misuse of Drugs (ACMD) (1994) *Drug Misusers and the Criminal Justice System, Part II: Police, Drug Misusers and the Community* (London: HMSO).
Alderson, J. (1984) *Law and Disorder* (London: Hamish Hamilton).
Association of Chief Police Officers (ACPO) (1990) *Setting the Standards: Meeting Community Expectation* (London: ACPO).
Audit Commission (1990) *Effective Policing: Performance Review in Police Forces* (London: HMSO).
Audit Commission (1993) *Helping with Enquiries: Tackling Crime Effectively* (London: HMSO).
Breschner, G. and W. Bower (1985) 'The Scene', in B. Hanson *et al.* (eds), *Life with Heroin* (Lexington MA: Lexington Books).
Camden Council, Islington Council, CENTEC and CILNTEC (1994) *Destination Kings Cross – Single Regeneration Budget Proposal.*

Clarke, J., A. Cochrane and E. McLaughlin (1994) *Managing Social Policy* (London: Sage).

Cockburn, C. (1977) *The Local State: The Management of Cities and People* (London: Pluto).

Cooper, D. (1993) 'The Citizen's Charter and Radical Democracy: Empowerment and Exclusion within Citizenship Discourse', *Social and Legal Studies*, vol. 2 (2), pp. 149–71.

Crawford, A. (1994) 'The Partnership Approach to Community Crime Prevention: Corporatism at the Local Level?', *Social and Legal Studies*, vol. 3 (4), pp. 497–520.

Crime Concern (1994) *Annual Review 1994: Towards a Safer Britain* (Swindon: Crime Concern).

Doern, G. (1993) 'The UK Citizen's Charter: Origins and Implementation in Three Agencies', *Policy and Politics*, vol. 21 (1), pp. 17–29.

Dorn, N., K. Murji and N. South (1991) 'Mirroring the market?', in R. Reiner and M. Cross (eds), *Beyond Law and Order* (London: Macmillan).

Dorn, N. and K. Murji (1992) 'Low Level Drug Enforcement', *International Journal of the Sociology of Law*, vol. 20, pp. 159–71.

Dorn, N., K. Murji and N. South (1992) *Traffickers: Drug Markets and Law Enforcement* (London: Routledge).

Dixon, D., A. K. Bottomley, C. Coleman, M. Gill and D. Wall (1989) 'Reality and Rules in the Construction and Regulation of Police Suspicion', *International Journal of the Sociology of Law*, vol. 17, pp. 185–206.

Graef, R. (1990) *Talking Blues: The Police in Their Own Words* (London: Fontana).

Hayeslip, D. (1989) 'Local-level Drug Enforcement: New strategies', *National Institute of Justice Report*, no. 213, March/April 1989 (Washington, DC: NIJ).

HM Government (1994) *Tackling Drugs Together – A Consultation Document Strategy for England 1995–1998* (London: HMSO).

Home Office (1992) *Criminal Statistics: England and Wales 1991*, Cmnd 2134 (London: HMSO).

Home Office (1993) *Police Reform*, White Paper, Cmnd 2281 (London: HMSO).

Horton, C. and D. Smith (1988) *Evaluating Police Work* (London: Policy Studies Institute).

Keith, M. (1993) *Race, Riots and Policing: Lore and Disorder in a Multi-racist Society* (London: University College London Press).

King, M. (1989) 'Social Crime Prevention à la Thatcher', *Howard Journal of Criminal Justice*, vol. 28 (4), pp. 291–312.

King's Cross Community Safety Initiative (1994) *Partners Against Crime* (London: King's Cross Community Safety Initiative).

London Borough of Camden (1994) *Community Safety in Camden: Working Together for a Safer Borough* (London: Borough of Camden).

London Drug Policy Forum (1994) *Drugs and Community Safety: Promoting a Partnership Approach* (London: Metropolitan Police).

Maguire, M. (1994) 'Crime Statistics, Patterns, and Trends: Changing Perceptions and their Implications', in M. Maguire, R. Morgan and

R. Reiner (eds), *Oxford Handbook of Criminology* (London: Clarendon Press).

McLaughlin, E. and J. Munci.e. (1994) 'Managing the Criminal Justice System', in J. Clarke *et al.* (eds), *Managing Social Policy* (London: Sage).

Meese, E. and B. Carrico (1990) 'Taking Back the Streets', *Policy Review*, Fall, pp. 22–30.

Metropolitan Police (1993) *Metropolitan Police Service Charter* (Metropolitan Police: London).

Metropolitan Police (1994) *Review of the Year 1993–94* (London: Metropolitan Police).

Miles, R. (1993) *Ruffling Feathers: Is Drug Enforcement for the Birds?* (MA dissertation, Essex University).

Moran, J. (1990) 'High Noon in Alexandria: How we Ran the Crack Dealers out of Public Housing', *Policy Review*, Summer, pp. 78–81.

Policing (1991) 'The Way Ahead', special issue, vol. 7 (3).

Reiner, R. (1991) *Chief Constables* (Oxford: Oxford University Press).

Reiner, R. (1992) 'Policing a Postmodern Society', *The Modern Law Review*, vol. 55 (6), pp. 761–81.

Reiner, R. (1994) 'Policing and the Police', in M. Maguire, R. Morgan and R. Reiner (eds), *Oxford Handbook of Criminology* (London: Clarendon Press).

Sagarin, E. and MacNamera, D. (1972) 'The Problem of Entrapment', in R. Dahl and G. Dix (eds), *Crime Law and Justice Annual 1972* (Buffalo: William S. Hein).

Sampson, A., P. Stubbs, D. Smith, G. Pearson and H. Blagg (1988) 'Crime, Localities and the Multi-Agency Approach', *British Journal of Criminology*, vol. 28 (4), pp. 478–93.

Scarman, Lord (1981) *The Brixton Disorders* (London: HMSO).

Sheehy Report (1993) *Report of the Inquiry into Police Responsibilities and Rewards*, Cmnd 2280 I, II (London: HMSO).

Standing Conference on Crime Prevention (1991) *Safer Communities: The Local Delivery of Crime Prevention through the Partnership Approach* (London: HMSO).

Smith, D. and Gray, J. (1983) *The Police in Action* (London: Policy Studies Institute).

Stubbs, P. (1987) 'Crime, community and the multi-agency approach: a critical reading of the Broadwater Farm Inquiry Report', *Critical Social Policy*, vol. 20, pp. 30–45.

Tilley, N. (1993) 'Crime Prevention and the Safer Cities Story', *Howard Journal of Criminal Justice*, vol. 32 (1), pp. 40–57.

Uchida, C. and Forst, B. (1994) 'Controlling street-level drug trafficking: professional and community policing approaches', in D. Mackenzie and C. Uchida (eds), *Drugs and Crime: Evaluating Public Policy Initiatives* (Thousand Oaks: Sage).

Wells, R. (1987) 'The will and the way to move forward in policing', in J. Benyon and J. Solomos (eds), *The Roots of Urban Unrest* (Oxford: Pergamon).

Worden, R., T. Bynum and J. Frank (1994) 'Police Crackdowns on Drug Abuse and Trafficking', in D. Mackenzie and C. Uchida (eds), *Drugs and Crime: Evaluating Public Policy Initiatives* (Thousand Oaks: Sage).

Wright, N. (1986) 'The new Metropolitan Police Strategy and its Implications for the Campaign for Police Accountability', *Critical Social Policy*, vol. 17, pp. 75–8.

Wright, A., A. Waymont and F. Gregory (1993) *Drugs Squads: Law Enforcement Strategies and Intelligence in England and Wales* (London: Police Foundation).

Zimmer, L. (1987) *Operation Pressure Point*, Occasional Paper of the Centre for Crime and Justice (New York: University School of Law).

Zimmer, L. (1990) 'Proactive Policing against Street-level Drug Trafficking', *American Journal of Police*, vol. 11 (1), pp. 43–74.

Zimmer, L. (1993) *Policing Inner-City Drug Scenes: Lessons from New York*, paper presented at 4th Conference of European Cities on Drug Policy, Hamburg, December 1993.

3 Hamburg: Handling an Open Drug Scene

Hannes Alpheis[1]

With 1.7 million citizens, Hamburg accounts for roughly a tenth of the German drug problem (Germany having 60 million inhabitants in the west and 20 million in the east). This over-proportionate share of drug users is also accompanied by an unusually liberal (for Germany) drugs policy. Mayor Voscherau has a nationwide reputation for being the first German politician to promote a policy of decriminalisation. Hamburg is, therefore, rather unique in the German drug scene.

Situated in the northern part of Germany, Hamburg is the second largest city in the country. With its large harbour, it plays a pivotal role in east–west and Scandinavian trade – drug trade included. Many of the drugs seized in Hamburg are not for the local market but for other parts of the world. Nevertheless, the Hamburg market is easy to access, resulting in a relatively low price for drugs (especially heroin). This factor is partly responsible for a high number of hard drug users (estimated at 8,500 in 1994), which is only comparable nationally to Berlin and Frankfurt. This high number undoubtedly influences the city's drug policy, for – as it is a city state – not only does Hamburg have some legislative leverage on the federal system, but it is also free to shape its own handling of the drug problem.

This chapter reports on developments in the last six years. Outlining the Hamburg situation should shed some light on the features peculiar to Germany, while also focusing on a problem encountered in almost every European city with a large drug using population: public safety.

BACKGROUND

Hamburg drug policy: steps towards 'Hollandisation'

Every available indicator shows that, after years of stagnation, illicit drug use has increased since 1987 (see, for example, the first register of hard drug users by the police as well as the number of drug-related deaths,[2] Figures 3.1 and 3.2). Figures in Hamburg at the end of the 1980s were as high as in Amsterdam at the beginning of the 1980s, but seem to have reached a saturation point by 1992, when they stabilised.[3] Hamburg tried to learn from the Amsterdam experience, and sought to 'Hollandise' its drug policy by taking a public health approach rather than a criminal justice approach. This is widely applauded, even by the police force. In 1989 Mayor Voscherau announced the shift in drug policy, which included expanded methadone treatment, detox facilities, low threshold assistance (harm reduction) and a depenalisation of drug users. At the same time, the fight against smuggling and trafficking was intensified.

Due to the different German legal system, the Amsterdam approach could not be transferred lock, stock and barrel to Hamburg. For instance, the principle of strict legality (mandatory prosecution) meant the German police force had to prosecute every offence which came to its attention. Since generally only a judge could abandon a prosecution, it was difficult to adopt more pragmatic approaches (as in the Netherlands, where a principle of expediency prevails).

To promote the public health approach, Hamburg tried to change national drug law. In September 1992, the federal Drug Enforcement Act was finally reformed. Under the revised law, the prosecutor's office is free to drop a case where further trial is obviously counterproductive. This initiative paralleled German juvenile law with its discretionary powers of prosecution and its aim to help and educate offenders. This does not, however, alter the fact that the officer on the beat still has to follow up a possession case. Although this will not usually result in a sentence,[4] German drug users still face the possibility of their small amounts of illicit drugs being seized by the police. It is possible though that police officers, anticipating the juridical results of their activities, may modify their reaction (turning a blind eye) to possession offences.

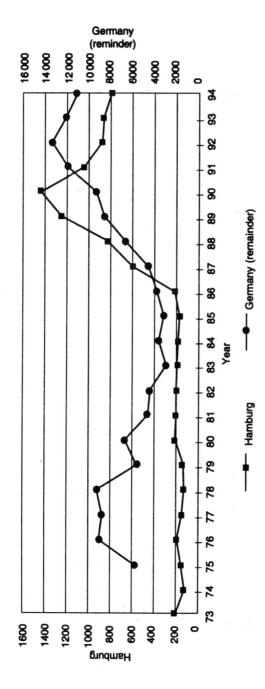

Figure 3.1   Epidemiological indicators: first time registered drug users, 1973–94

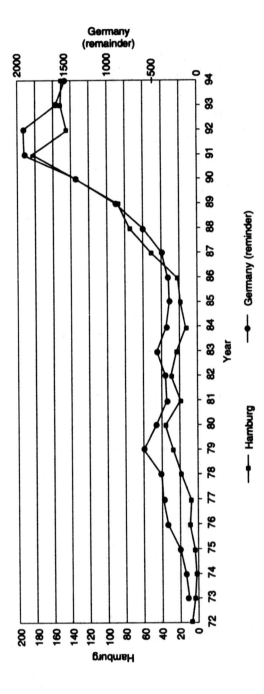

Figure 3.2   Epidemiological indicators: drug-related deaths, 1972–94

The 'Hollandisation' of drug policy – penal reform and expanded methadone treatment – is the first step towards liberalisation. It brings to public attention the idea that drug using behaviour cannot be cured by criminalisation, although it also accepts that drug policy needs public approval. If this step is widely accepted, one can think of further legalisation moves. In March 1992 the city state of Hamburg launched another initiative to change national drug law – allowing the medical prescription of substances such as heroin within certain settings (i.e. scientific research). In order to prescribe heroin experimentally to some 200 addicts, Hamburg needs to alter federal law, and although its amendments passed the chamber of the Länder (Bundesrat) it is not very likely to pass the conservative federal parliament (Bundestag).

The social ecology of an open drug scene

Bearing in mind the late 1980s goals of Hamburg's drug policy (harm reduction and depenalisation), it came as a shock when in 1990 the local government announced a crackdown on an emerging open drug scene in a downtown quarter of the city. Drug policy needs to be accepted by the public, but the consequences of an open drug scene can find no public acceptance, neither from the local inhabitants who are affected directly nor from those affected indirectly via the media. Hence the reorientation of Hamburg's drug policy, including the option to fight open drug scenes, even by prosecuting drug users.

An open drug scene is defined as stationary gatherings of drug users in public where trafficking and drug use is visible, even to an outsider. An open drug scene is tied to the following consequences:

drug injection in public (parks, doorways, shops, playgrounds, schoolyards, public toilets);
littering (used syringes, condoms, human excrement);
drug trafficking in public (by individuals and gangs);
drug-related crime (shoplifting, burglary, robbery);
violence within the drug scene (including use of weapons);
declining shop revenue (danger of bankruptcy and a succession of unlet properties).

An open drug scene focuses public attention on the negative effects of a liberal/harm reduction approach. An open drug scene also tends to reinforce itself, recruiting new dealers, users and support facilities. Other citizens, especially those living nearby, will not tolerate such developments for long. And there are examples in other cities (like Arnhem in the Netherlands) of citizens not only demonstrating but taking the law into their own hands.

Certain factors favoured the emergence of an open drug scene in the Hamburg quarter of St Georg, situated at the central railway station and east of the central business (and shopping) district:

> Since the opening of the railway station in 1906, St Georg[5] has been one of Hamburg's traditional red light districts (the other being St Pauli with its famous 'Reeperbahn' situated at the harbour west of the central business district). That means that higher levels of tolerance towards deviant behaviour exist side by side with *low visibility* of the individual deviant.
> A high ethnic 'minority' in the resident population (around 40 per cent, up to 60 per cent in some areas) also contributes towards *low visibility*, especially for Turkish/Kurdish dealers, as Turks are the biggest ethnic group in St Georg (with almost their own infrastructure).
> The proximity of the central railway and underground station allows for *easy accessibility*.
> Cheap hotels and 'bed and breakfast' houses also make for *easy accessibility*. As well as regular customers there are addicts on public welfare, ex-offenders and refugees who are placed here by the welfare department because it is not possible to find accommodation elsewhere for them. (Recently, the city has begun reducing the proportion of 'problematic groups' in St Georg's hotels.)
> St Georg offers good *economic opportunities* for junkies. The big department stores (for shoplifting) are nearby on the other side of the railway station, and St Georg has its own structure in the red light business, with less organised prostitution than in St Pauli. Prostitutes are usually working freelance, which opens up opportunities for juvenile prostitutes as well. These conditions meet the needs of female (and male) drug addicts trying to make some money.

The deviant subculture around the central station has become a 'home' for some drug users, long before they started taking heroin. This is connected with the *convenience* of knowing the people and the place.

The above factors attract a drug scene which by itself opens up the typical *economic opportunities* for drug users through dealing and running. This reinforcing effect of an open drug scene is fostered by Hamburg's function as a national and international market for heroin.[6]

Last but not least, there are the *conveniences* of drug users' everyday life: Hamburg's largest assistance provider (the Drob Inn,[7] with needle exchanges and low threshold services) is located in St Georg.

During the 1980s Hamburg undertook intense measures in St Georg to regenerate the quarter and secure residential opportunities. The programme had the goal of attracting young families with children into the quarter and was quite successful. This success, however, is now endangered with the emergence of the drug scene which might trigger what is known in urban sociology as the process of succession (see Park, 1936, Cressey 1938, Duncan and Duncan 1957, Hoffmeyer-Zlotnik, 1982). There is a danger that the young families will move out of the quarter to be succeeded by people already associated with the drug scene. The influx of these people reinforces the tendency of the remaining young families to move out, which would in turn open up the door for the next step in succession. Schelling (1972) describes how this process of 'neighbourhood tipping' can finally drive an existing majority out of the quarter.

THE STRUGGLE AGAINST THE OPEN DRUG SCENE

The fight against the open drug scene started in September 1990. Massive police forces were mobilised towards the Hansaplatz, a square already known throughout Germany for its open drug scene. Up to 100 uniformed police officers searched junkies and dealers, in an unexpected swoop which was not declared to be a solution to the drug problem. The action was only aimed at the fostering of public security – the interests of drug users being no longer compatible with those of the rest of the locals. In a way this action was something of a natural experiment: nobody knew how the scene would react. Below, I will describe what happened based on observations and then discuss the implications of such developments.

The dissolving of the Hansaplatz scene in Autumn 1990 was partly due to the change of season. In winter there are usually less 'outdoor activities' to observe in St Georg. When spring comes, prostitution as well as drug using generally becomes more visible again. Whilst the Hansaplatz remained 'clean' for the next twelve months, the junkies started to gather again in Spring 1991 in a shopping street nearby that was used by far more citizens than the relatively remote Hansaplatz. Shop owners and their customers quickly began to complain, and the owners soon engaged private security.[8]

At the same time all groups in the area took action to shut the last bolt-holes for addicts: landlords and residents locked stairwells, schoolyards and parking lots were ringed with steel, public institutions put security guards on their doors. The City of Hamburg developed a security programme for the central railway station that included closing part of the tunnel system. Due to the shut-down of 'retreat zones', open drug consumption became more frequent in the street (or in the trains). The junkies were forced to relocate, in groups of up to 100 people, directly in front of the central station. As approximately 250,000 people change trains each day at the station, the drug users ironically became *more* visible.

The public also demanded intensified action from the enforcement authorities. In September 1991 the police set up a drug coordination group, its task being to organise the various police units which operated in the St Georg area. The drug coordination group's strategy was tied to the goals of Hamburg's drug policy – in other words, the group was not using the opportunities opened by the federal drug law which would have meant writing lots of crime reports and criminalising junkies. Instead, the police used the 'Hamburg Law on Security and Order', which allows for banning people from certain areas in case of danger. This was used to send away junkies from critical zones. From September 1991 to May 1992 the forces controlled (in more than 9,000 additional shifts, an average of about 40 a day) almost 25,000 people in the streets of St Georg, banned more than 15,000 people yet only wrote about 550 crime reports (an average of 2.3 a day).

This tiny number of crime reports indicates that even within the principle of legality (mandatory prosecution) there is room for different policing strategies. In this case keeping the situation under control (by staying on the street, moving addicts on) was considered more important than writing crime reports against junkies.

But the situation did not clear up in the winter of 1991. Junkies continued to hang around St Georg. There were no more large concentrations at the railway station, no open consumption or trafficking. Nevertheless, they were still there and they gathered at the Drob Inn. There were several reasons for this: the Drob Inn offered shelter during winter, there were more junkies around than in previous years, and the police were very cautious about taking action there, so as not to interfere with the harm reduction aims of the institution.

The social workers at the Drob Inn went on strike in January 1992 to mobilise the public against the overcrowding and police tactics. But the city government continued its strategy of not allowing an open drug scene to emerge. At the same time, a pressure group started to promote shooting galleries and needle parks to give the junkies shelter and to remove them from the eyes of the public. These ideas became popular in the Green Party and sections of the Social Democrats. After all, the idea is an appealing one: open up some special areas where drug users do not disturb anybody and where they can be reached by drug agencies. The same ideas guided the setting up of the open drug scene at the Platzspitz in Zurich, Switzerland (see below). The city government, however, rejected the idea partly because the setting up of shooting galleries violates German law and also because it was afraid of an influx of hard drug users from other cities and countries.

Due to the exceptional summer of 1992 – the best weather in 45 years – the number of visible drug users in St Georg increased dramatically. As the police continued moving people on, the scene trickled into the whole quarter. Drug users were almost everywhere – in the parks, in squares, churchyards, playgrounds, schoolyards, in garages, backyards, entrances and doorways – more or less openly injecting drugs.[9] There was almost no displacement[10] towards other quarters. Local police units in other areas of town would intervene at the first sign of gatherings of drug users in their district. But perhaps more importantly, the environment and familiarity of the area meant that street junkies liked and stayed in St Georg.

The omnipresence of hard drug users once again stimulated action by the local residents. They joined a weekly demonstration under the slogan *Macht endlich Drogenpolitik* (Drug Policy Now). Young left-wing residents (social workers, teachers, and students) led the protest. The anger and distress arose not so much out of a specific deterioration of *public safety* during that summer. St Georg is a typical inner city area, and although these areas usually face higher crime rates than others, statistics of the most common crimes (those which concern local residents most) showed no dramatic increase in the summer of 1992. Obviously, therefore, public safety was not the primary concern: other threats to public health, such as littering or the presence of dirty people living in unhealthy conditions, were of greater urgency. This indicates that local residents preferred to address the *public health and social care* implications, reflected in the slogan Drug Policy Now. There were no slogans such as Junkies Out or calls for imprisonment and compulsory treatment.

In Autumn 1992, joint action was undertaken by the city's departments of health, of youth and education, and of urban development to bring relief to the quarter. One intention was to decentralise the drug scene by providing low-threshold facilities in other parts of town. This is not an easy task since the respective local populations usually protest strongly when they learn that such a venture is to be instigated in their neighbourhood. Nevertheless, resources for four additional low-threshold facilities were provided in winter 1992. The first agency (an old bus) opened in March 1994 in the east of Hamburg, and the second in summer 1994 in the south. These will add to the existing six agencies (one in every district) outside the inner city.

A couple of measures were also designed to help local residents of St Georg regain their quarter: additional kindergarten workers, longer opening hours for the local youth club, guards and additional cleaners for playgrounds, a local drug prevention programme, school janitors, additional social workers in schools, expanded opportunities for school lunches[11] and a community centre for the elderly. Last but not least, St Georg was put on the disadvantaged areas programme (*Soziale Brennpunkte*), set up to address low turnouts in certain areas in the 1991 local elections. This means that the area is targeted for further development measures. The first step was to cultivate a developmental expertise, for which a series of roundtable meetings were conducted. This part of the process is double-edged, as it hones and articulates local resident opinion while also having the potential to create expectations which cannot be fulfilled. At the very least, this procedure should enhance communication between citizens and strengthen the social ties within the community.

After launching the package of instant measures in November 1992, public interest ebbed. One reason was the decline in the number of addicts on the streets (it was winter). Another reason was an overall decline in drug users (see the figures on epidemiological indicators above). Nevertheless throughout this period, the police kept up the pressure with additional units available because of a relative calm in other areas (few violent demonstrations, no football riots, no organised attacks on refugees/asylum seekers). To attune police action to the views of the local low threshold Drob Inn, regular meetings between both sides were set up. This resulted in better relationships, allowing, for example, the police to ban people from hanging around outside the Drob Inn without arousing protests from the social workers. Such regular meetings were slowly opened to other interest groups so that they now serve as a police/community liaison committee.

In 1994 there was still a visible drug scene near the central station, numbering 70 to 100 people who gathered to meet friends, swop information and exchange drugs. These people are in very bad health and arouse the sympathy of passers-by. The former distinctions of 'junkies' and 'alcoholics/homeless' have now dissolved. Nevertheless, it is assumed that junkies would exhibit very different behaviour if they had the chance to establish an open drug scene. The police will therefore continue to keep moving them on and ensure a certain degree of decent (or at least discreet) behaviour.

OPEN DRUG SCENES IN A COMPARATIVE EUROPEAN PERSPECTIVE

It is difficult to compare the drug scenes and policies of different cities in different countries. If one relies on the definition of an open drug scene given above (open drug dealing and consumption) one has to say that very few scenes in Europe fulfil the 'requirements'. There are also variations in size: whereas Frankfurt or Zürich have sometimes had over 1000 drug users at any one time in one spot, 70–100 users in Hamburg's central station in the summer of 1994 pose different questions for local authorities. A comparison of local measures must not only take into account the qualitative and quantitative aspects of the phenomenon but must also look at local, regional and national attitudes towards minorities in general and drug users in particular. If one studies such attitudes, one finds for example, that there are more similarities between Hamburg and Amsterdam (or the Netherlands) than between Hamburg and southern parts of Germany. These different local mentalities open up yet another range of opportunities for local authorities.

A comparison of European drug scenes identifies a certain type of city – for instance, Amsterdam, Zürich, Frankfurt and Hamburg (Bless *et al.*, 1993; also Renn and Lange, 1995) – containing an estimated population of thousands of hard drug users. These cities have all tried to implement liberal drug policies based on harm reduction. At the same time, they experienced more or less 'open' drug scenes. They also share broader similarities, being business and trading centres with religious roots in Protestantism. And together, these cities, as the 'Frankfurt Group', took the initiative to challenge national and European drug policies and to promote a 'new way'.

A common feature of the drug scenes in these cities is that they established themselves in or near residential quarters. These quarters are usually inner-city areas with old housing and are therefore also at risk of 'neighbourhood tipping' through the processes of invasion and succession. Measures to counteract such processes of deterioration and ghettoisation lead to an opposing tendency – urban renewal programmes may lead to population movements going under the rubric 'gentrification'. (On gentrification in Hamburg, see Dangschat, 1991; for a discussion of the link between gentrification and police action in inner city areas see, Zimmer, 1990; also Zimmer, 1994, for a critical discussion of the New York experience.)

A high proportion of young urban professionals in the residential areas which are also locations for local drug scenes will help the articulation of protest and participation (formal or informal) in the political debate, since the well-educated are well-informed about the 'rules of the game' and are more able to use mass media effectively. This leads to greater public awareness in these areas than in those areas with the same degree of nuisance but a different local population. The specific social structure of the gentrified residential quarters offers local administrations the chance to interact with local residents, tailoring specific measures to the needs of the quarter and stimulating mechanisms of informal social control which are the *sine qua non* for the prevention of neighbourhood tipping. So it is the neighbourhoods which attract wider interest that display the most progressive perspectives; the neighbourhoods which remain almost silent, however, face a bleak future.

For these reasons, the location of a drug scene is critical. When it settles in places where local residents are not affected (like the Zürich Platzspitz – see Chapter 10) then there is little coordinated public pressure against such a situation. But when Zürich's closing of the Platzspitz led to an influx of drug users into residential quarters nearby, it triggered mass protests by the residents and forced the government to tolerate the scene at an abandoned railway station, Lettenstieg.[12] Frankfurt tried to shift part of the scene from an inner city area (Taunusanlage) to an abandoned industrial quarter (Schielestrasse), where the environmental conditions for the emergence of an open drug scene do not prevail. Similarly, Amsterdam's attempts to push drug users out of inner-city areas have led to drug scenes in the suburbs which are not so overt and yet make the delivery of user services more difficult.

The measures taken by the respective towns against inner-city drug scenes contain both 'pull' and 'push' effects. On the 'pull' side, they provide alternatives to living on the scene: methadone treatment programmes and municipal shooting galleries (*Gassenzimmer* in Zürich). Similar institutions (*Fixerräume*) are not yet allowed under German federal law, but Hamburg and Frankfurt have expressed their interest in establishing such institutions.[13] The two cities are also interested in conducting scientific research to test the effects of prescription of heroin and other opiates to hard-core drug users (research which is already under way in Switzerland and planned in Amsterdam).

Experience of methadone treatment shows that even a very broad low-threshold supply of methadone would not completely eliminate unwanted and drug-seeking behaviour. Therefore, all the cities use some additional deterrence policies. Zürich and Amsterdam admit that they have been too lenient during a phase of 'unbounded tolerance towards addicts'.[14] The first element of this 'push' strategy is to make a distinction between 'citizens' and 'outsiders' (e.g. drug users). Under this policy (in Dutch, *oentmoedigings beleid* – discouragement policy), services are only open to citizens, while outsiders are to be sent home or persuaded to return to their cities or countries of origin. This results in a number of paradoxes, such as low-threshold institutions for which a special entry permit is needed. *Oentmoedigings beleid* strategies can be found in Zürich, Amsterdam and Frankfurt.

Another element of the push strategy is to prevent drug users' antisocial behaviour through policing. These interventions are seen as 'in the interest of people in the vicinity, for whom drug use often causes a considerable nuisance, as well as of addicts themselves' (City of Amsterdam, 1992, p. 24). The tactic which is used in Amsterdam, Frankfurt and Hamburg is 'the ban', by which individuals are banned from one spot or part of the town. These measures – which include searching people for small quantities of drugs – are aimed at both the maintenance of public order and the prevention of the establishment of open drug scenes which will seriously affect public security. Last but not least, the open police presence is intended to increase feelings of security.

As mentioned before, local residents are not only disturbed by threats to public security but also by threats to public health and by scenes that arouse sympathy. People feel that help is needed but that they themselves are not able to provide the adequate services (out of lack of professional knowledge and because of the number of such instances). So they would like to see other agencies intervene. This is yet another reason for the provision of outreach/street work for drug users. Amsterdam and Zürich provide services that are continually seen out on the streets and serve as a bridge between drug user and the 'social services'. In Amsterdam there is also a helpline at the public health department which people can call when they see homeless people needing help, which sends out a team to assess the situation. Another service in Amsterdam is *vroege hulp* (early help) which provides medical and social care for arrestees at police stations.

All these services have two purposes: they provide help for as many drug users as possible and they assist local residents (at least psychologically) to cope with the observable human misery.

According to local customs and standards of social work they may also contact those individuals who do not ask for help on their own account. Whereas such an approach is not common in Hamburg, the 'street junkie project' in Amsterdam offers a choice to drug users who are repeatedly in conflict with the police to either serve their entire sentence with no time off for probation or enter a rehabilitation clinic. They have to complete the entire drug rehabilitation treatment, otherwise they still go to prison (City of Amsterdam, 1992, p. 27). This programme, although some social workers have been very critical about it, seems to have had some success.

CONCLUSION

After four years of action in Hamburg, the drug scene has been driven from the relative remoteness of Hansaplatz Square into public view. With every move the scene became more visible. This was possibly also due to rising numbers of addicts in the streets: people who developed a drug habit in 1987/88 (when the current wave started) may after five to six years be in such a condition that street life becomes inevitable.

Assuming that drug-related behaviour is not totally inelastic, i.e. it is in a way opportunistic,[15] there is reason to believe that police action to some extent changed the structure of the street scene. Those who have access to alternatives (buying and consuming drugs in private dwellings, abstinence, treatment, etc.) will leave the scene when the going gets tough. This typically means those addicts with best resources (both social and financial). Those who stay on the scene are those who are the most problematic users (polyuse). The closure of zones of retreat combined with this negative selection of junkies will lead to a rising recklessness in every respect: violence and visible misery may increase. Therefore the remaining part of the scene will deteriorate and challenge the aesthetic sentiments of local residents even more than before.

Indeed, it has to be pointed out that local authorities of some cities may sometimes use the label of an 'open drug scene' to include a range of activities that disturb aesthetic feelings. As a result, measures against homeless people, alcoholics, cannabis users, runaways, and the like are justified on the ground of tackling the 'open drug scene'. There is therefore a danger that the 'open drug scene' argument can be used for other purposes (for instance, maximising profits or presenting a clean city), especially in areas with direct economic interests, such as shopping centres, or areas that attract specific public attention.

The dynamics of the street scene are not only influenced by the intensity of police work but also by the existence of alternatives to street life that have to be provided by other agencies (e.g. welfare and youth departments). In 1992, when there were roughly 300 people on methadone maintenance programmes out of Hamburg's estimated 9,500 addicts and the waiting list for 'low threshold' detoxification was six months long, the only thing that could be achieved by police action was to divide up the problem and distribute it around the city so that every quarter had to bear a burden.

It would not be enough to justify the ongoing police action that was also observed in Zürich, Copenhagen and Frankfurt by its aim of gaining public approval for a certain drug policy. One should bear in mind that there is a close connection between drug-related 'problem' behaviour and prohibition.[16] It is prohibition which is responsible for the circumstances under which drug users live as street junkies. High drug prices combined with criminalisation for trafficking are responsible for a high level of problematic behaviour in the streets. Police action is always directed against the symptoms and not at the causes of that behaviour. Politics should make clear that intensified street control is not aimed at solving the drug problem (not even regionally) but that it is directed against the side effects of prohibition, and that there are a number of reasons to believe that problems with open drug scenes would diminish with free availability – regulated or not – of drugs.

POSTSCRIPT: FURTHER DEVELOPMENTS

The head of the Hamburg Department of the Interior, Senator Hackmann, resigned in 1994 in the context of indications of police misbehaviour in connection with the policing of Hamburg's open drug scene. It seems that inappropriate force may have been used against suspected drug dealers; some incidents, particularly concerning the treatment of black persons inside the police station, appeared to be infused with racism.

The Department of Justice set up a Commission to check allegations of excessive force or racially motivated behaviour in three inner city 'red light' areas. The Commission found that, out of 118 police cases in which the prosecutor's office had not proceeded to court, the police's Internal Affairs Division had not acted properly in 53 cases. Furthermore the prosecutor's office itself had failed to adhere to standard procedures in 55 cases. As a result of the Commission's work legal proceedings were taken against the police in seven cases.

At the time of writing, these cases are under review and there will be further hearings, so any remarks made here must be preliminary. On the one hand, one should bear in mind the thousands of cases in which searches and arrests took place, during the period described in this chapter. In this perspective, the relatively small number of cases of police misconduct coming to light supports the familiar idea of the occasional 'rotten apple' in the police. On the other hand, police subculture and its 'them or us' mentality does seem compatible with misconduct of the types alleged (see Rudovsky, 1992). In most industrialised counties, there are structural factors – for example, minority group involvement in drug dealing, and a strongly loaded public opinion – that make police misconduct in this area rather predictable. If so, then perhaps it is not just the few apples which are rotten, but something is wrong with the apple industry.

NOTES

1. The views expressed here are those of the author and not necessarily those of the Hamburg Department of Interior.
2. This includes not only deaths by overdose but also other deaths related to the misuse of illegal drugs: suicide, traffic accidents, etc. Overdoses accounted for roughly 96 per cent of drug-related deaths in Hamburg in the last four years.
3. One common objection against these statistics is that they only reflect police activity in a field where crime is usually unreported.

Interestingly enough, the correlation between the number of drug deaths (which is not dependent on police activity and therefore can be taken as an independent variable) and the number of first time registered drug users is $r = 0.90$ for Hamburg and $r = 0.87$ for the rest of Germany. The correlations between the number of drug deaths and all other indicators that are usually presented in police statistics regarding drug-related crime are extremely high (Pearson r ranges from 0.75 to 0.94). So as the drug problem gets more and more serious (indicated by the number of deaths), the police respond and reproduce almost exactly the same changes in the statistics of registered addicts.

4.   At least in relatively liberal states as the City State of Hamburg, Hessen or Schleswig-Holstein.

5.   The place has a long-standing tradition of unpopular utilisation: a leper hospital was founded at the end of the 12th century, and a gallows and knacker's yard were located here by the mid–16th as well as plague graves. Later on social institutions such as the charity school (1694) and the alms house (1788) were sited in St Georg. See Möller, 1985, p. 59.

6.   This nationwide attraction is supported by the fact that in 1990 only 71 per cent of newly registered opiate users in Hamburg were citizens of the city. In 1991 (1992) the share was even lower: 67 per cent (66 per cent) although it climbed to 81 per cent in 1993.

7.   Spelt with a 'b' for Drogen*b*eratung (drug counselling) and run by a non-governmental organisation.

8.   According to German law, private security forces are only allowed to operate on private property. But they were seen on the street and did hassle drug users.

9.   In the words of the residents the whole quarter became a 'single big shooting gallery'.

10. For displacement effects, see also Lowman, 1992, pp. 1–17.

11. In Germany, school usually lasts from 8.00 to 13.00 so that pupils have lunch at home.

12. This paragraph is based on personal communication with officials from the respective cities.

13. Since 1995 Frankfurt offers two 'Gesundheitsräume' (health rooms) for similar purposes.

14. 'Up to the early eighties, the Amsterdam policy was characterised by virtually unbounded tolerance towards addicts. This is what made Amsterdam so attractive for addicts from abroad, which in turn resulted in mushrooming problems' (City of Amsterdam, 1992, p. 14).

15. A notion that is reflected in the frequent mentioning of the weather or the season as a precondition for the emergence of open drug scenes. The question of commitment and motivation is also crucial in other public order discussions (for instance, see the Lowman/Matthews 1992 controversy on policing street prostitution).

16. This view does not focus on the negative effects of prohibition regarding organised crime and law enforcement agencies, which are addressed in other sections of this volume.

REFERENCES

Bless, R., M. Freeman, D. Korf and T. Nabben (1993) *Urban Strategies to Open Drug Scenes*. *Report prepared for the 4th Conference of the European Cities on Drug Policy, Hamburg, December 1993* (The Amsterdam Bureau of Social Research and Statistics).

City of Amsterdam (1992) *The Amsterdam Drug Policy* (Amsterdam: Information and Public Relations Department).

Cressey, P. (1938) 'Population Succession in Chicago: 1898–1930', *American Journal of Sociology*, vol. 44, pp. 59–69.

Dangschat, J. (1991) 'Gentrification in Hamburg', in J. van Weesep and S. Musterd (eds), *Urban Housing for the Better-off – Gentrification in Europe* (Utrecht: Stedelijke Netwerken).

Duncan, O. and B. Duncan (1957) *The Negro Population of Chicago: A Study of Residential Succession* (Chicago: University Press).

Hoffmeyer-Zlotnik, J. (1982) 'Community Change and Invasion: The Case of Turkish Guest Workers', in J. Friedrichs (ed.), *Spatial Disparities and Social Behaviour. A Reader in Urban Research* (Hamburg: Christians).

Lowman, J. (1992) 'Street Prostitution Control. Some Canadian Reflections on the Finsbury Park Experience', and 'Against Street Prostituion', *British Journal of Criminology*, vol. 32, pp. 1–17; p. 400.

Matthews, R. (1992) 'Regulating Street Prostitution and Kerb-Crawling. A Reply to John Lowman', *British Journal of Criminology*, vol. 32, pp. 18–22.

Möller, I. (1985) *Hamburg* (Stuttgart: Klett).

Park, R. E. (1936) 'Human Ecology', *American Journal of Sociology*, vol. 42, pp. 1–15.

Renn, H. and K. J. Lange (1995) *Stadtviertel und Drogenszene. Eine vergleichende Untersuchung zur Belästigung durch 'offene' Drogenszenen in europäischen Großstädten* ('Urban Quarters and Drug Scene', Studie im Auftrag der Europäischen Kommission, Hamburg).

Rudovsky, D. (1992) 'Police Abuse: Can the Violence Be Copntained?', *Harvard Civil Rights and Civil Liberties Law Review*, vol. 27 (2), pp. 465–501.

Schelling, T. C. (1972) 'The Process of Residential Segregation. Neighbour-hood Tipping', in A. H. Pascal (ed.), *Racial Discrimination in Economic Life* (Lexington, Mass.: Heath).

Zimmer, L. (1990) 'Proactive Policing Against Street-Level Drug Trafficking', *American Journal of Police*, vol. 9, pp. 43–74.

Zimmer, L. (1994) 'American Inner Cities and Drug Policing: Strategies that Maximize Harm to Individuals and Communities', in L. Böllinger (ed.), *De-Americanizing Drug Policy: The Search for Alternatives for Failed Repression* (New York and Frankfurt: Lang).

4 Southern England, Drugs and Music: Policing the Impossible?

Andrew Fraser and Michael George

'I'm surprised that it took them so long . . . It was the worst kept secret in the world that it [the dance club] was a monster drug party!'

(Arrested raver)

Drugs are a consumer product for which there is a simple relationship between demand and supply. Without consumer demand there is no economic or practical sense in establishing or maintaining supply networks, and it is against these distribution networks that enforcement agencies almost exclusively direct their operations. However any disruption of drug supply networks as a result of police operations can only be transient – consumer-driven supply networks rapidly reform or mutate to meet unchanged or displaced consumer demand.

The 'drug problem' of a particular area is therefore a result of consumer demand and not the supply network of a particular drug. Consequently police action (targeted as it is against supply) can have little effect on the overall 'drug problem'. At best, police action causes suppliers similar delivery problems to those any supplier of fast-moving consumer goods has to overcome; police action may temporarily affect supply but will rarely touch demand. Police operations do not generally reach the hearts and minds (though they often reach the pockets) of the end user. This hypothesis is based on eight years' observation of the interactions between police operations, supply networks and drug use in Worthing, a coastal town in the South of England. The hypothesis advanced seems independent of the particular class of drugs in the demand–supply relationship, at least as far as opiate and 'dance culture' drugs in this study are concerned.

A LOCAL STORY

The town of Worthing

The development of Worthing town has followed a familiar pattern – from a small fishing village to a holiday resort, from a relatively prosperous light industrial centre through to the commercial, economic and social problems of the 1990s.

The Victorian expansion of the rail network and some well publicised royal visits to the area helped transform Worthing into a popular Edwardian seaside holiday resort. However, unlike its brasher neighbours, Brighton and Littlehampton, Worthing had a less commercialised and more sophisticated ambience, which attracted older, white-collar holiday-makers. This image and the comparatively mild weather was also responsible for the town's expansion between the two world wars as a haven for pensioners ('Costa Geriatrica') and London commuters.

From the late 1950s, the town succeeded in attracting industry to compensate for a declining tourist trade. Pharmaceutical production, light engineering and the head offices of large insurance and banking companies all relocated to the area. However, in the 1980s Worthing was badly affected by recession and unemployment, with their associated social ills. Today, the rare day tripper will see empty shops, industrial units for rent and a faded, rundown sea front, pier and promenade.

In comparison with neighbouring towns the population distribution is heavily skewed towards older residents. The 1981 Census shows 31.7 per cent of the population under 30 years old, compared with 38 per cent for Brighton, the nearest neighbouring town of comparable size. For those in their twenties (the group most likely to present to drug treatment services) the difference is even more striking – 10.6 per cent compared to 14.7 per cent. An active College of Technology and the county-wide College of Art, both located in Worthing, slightly redress this age imbalance by bringing into the town young commuters both for daytime study and night time leisure/entertainment. With a population of

99,970, Worthing is however the largest town in West Sussex. With a similar number living around the town in overspills, satellite developments and rural communities the catchment of the Health District is just over 200,000.

There are advantages over national studies in focusing on long-term drug using sub-cultures within a relatively closed system such as Worthing. Despite its disproportionate number of elderly residents, the town has had significant local drug use and related problems since the 1960s. Drug use is not a static phenomenon and Worthing has replicated the drug use trends and changes reported nationally over the past thirty years. It is almost as if someone had shut all the doors and allowed the natural course of evolution to take place with relatively few individuals either leaving the system or entering the system from outside. Furthermore, if as we believe, Worthing is representative of national trends, then local policing strategies and outcomes have implications for national policies.

Parameters of the research

The Worthing study focuses on police actions and their outcomes, both planned and unplanned, against two widely different drug distribution 'scenes' and their customers:

1986–90: Endemic heroin use in a tightly bonded cohort of Worthing residents;
1990–93: Epidemic use of ecstasy and other 'dance culture' drugs by a very loosely bonded group of attenders at a large local night club where a promoter was running regular 'all-night' raves.

The interest in comparing and contrasting these two drug scenes (heroin and 'dance drugs') is that the police viewed them as presenting uniquely different problems, both on the issues of responsibility:

'Clearly the problem was recognised . . . but getting something done about it was a different problem entirely . . . The rave/ ecstasy scene, if it was recognised was ignored. It was made clear to me when I came on the Unit that we don't touch clubs or pubs – that is down to the local station . . . it's out of our remit.'

(Detective Sergeant Force Drug Unit)

Also on policing:

'Because of the narrow low-age band of both customers and traders, undercover work by plainclothes officers was impractical and intelligence from the market was of poor quality.'

(Detective Chief Inspector Special Units)

'It's not like kicking in doors . . . That's pretty standard and both we and the druggies know how to behave . . . There's a protocol to that . . . But hundreds of kids on ecstasy . . . If you kicked down a rave door you'd have a riot . . . They don't know the rules!'

(Detective Constable Divisional Drug Unit)

In short, the rave scene was, from the police viewpoint, a new and 'unpredictable' public order problem with unclear and unresolved unit responsibilities.

Local agencies cooperating in the study

In theory, Sussex Police organise their response to drug use around the recommendations of the Broome Report. A Force Drug Unit of about thirty officers concentrate their activities against medium-level dealers as well as coordinating drug intelligence. At Divisional level, uniformed and Divisional detective officers are involved in drug investigations. In the main their activities are centred on simple possession offences, small scale (retail) supply and drug related crime – usually acquisitive crime. In practice, as for most other police forces, reality intrudes. Problems with staffing and pressures on Divisional Commanders to redirect priorities into other areas has meant that the Broome Report and its recommendations has been honoured in theory rather than in practice. There is only one Divisional (street) Drug Unit in the whole county and even that is under regular threat of disbandment. Specific Divisional activity against drug dealing and use is rare, depending on the whims of the local Commander and/or applied pressure from the local residents or media. This leaves the Force Drug Unit starved of its local intelligence reports gleaned from low-level offenders via unofficial plea bargaining. The Force Drug Unit attempts to adhere to its designated role as perceived in the Broome Report (targeting medium-level dealers). However, it is continually being pressurised by Divisional Commanders to move 'down-market' and deal with 'local trouble spots'.

Worthing is served by two community drug agencies from separate Health Regions. The town's drug users obviously do not conform to officially designated catchment areas and present to either or both agencies as their fancy takes them. Consequently, pooling and triangulation of data between the two agencies has facilitated the plotting of comprehensive and accurate local dealer/user networks. Longitudinal observation has allowed monitoring of changes and trends in both drug distribution and use.

Unusually, over the eight years of this study both agencies had built up similarly strong relationships with Sussex Police. Most agencies, due to the sensitive and confidential nature of their client work, are rightly cautious of any association with enforcement agencies. However, the unique multi-agency forums of the East Sussex Drug Advisory Council (ESDAC) and the equivalent council in West Sussex (WESDAAC), allowed both agencies to build up joint initiatives with the Sussex Police in areas such as training, court diversion schemes and alternatives to custodial sentencing. This led to the enthusiastic cooperation of Sussex Police when it was proposed to begin a longitudinal study of the effects of police activity on drug distribution and use within Worthing. Funding from South East Thames Regional Health Authority and a Pompidou Group Fellowship made this proposal a reality.

Similarly, drug distributors and users were also forthcoming on their experiences and activities both with drugs and the police. Field workers are rarely in the position of having access to entire drug distribution–user networks. Likewise it is unusual to be able to observe the effects of police operations on both drug distribution networks and their end-user 'customers'.

Whilst police and policed willingly gave their time to be interviewed and talked frankly as to their roles in, and perspectives on, police operations, it was unfortunate that in spite of repeated approaches, one key actor, Interdance, the local rave promoter, declined to cooperate with, or be interviewed by the researchers. In some respects this was quite understandable. They always had the most to lose: the late night licence essential to their company's commercial success.

ACTION AGAINST HEROIN DISTRIBUTION/USE

Historical background

Worthing's original nucleus of heroin users was seeded and supplied in the 1960s through the unusually liberal prescribing practices of a local general practitioner (GP). On his death the established local demand for opiates was met by English Language students from Iran, who smuggled heroin into the UK. These young entrepreneurs used heroin exportation/importation as a means to circumnavigate hard currency controls brought in by the Iranian government.

This source of heroin dried up when the Islamic revolution brought a degree of stability and control back to that country. Worthing users responded with cooperative and entrepreneurial initiatives, obtaining heroin either from London wholesalers or importing directly from the Netherlands through links with Worthing expatriates living in Amsterdam.

In the early 1980s, the increased professionalisation of illicit heroin distribution networks reached Worthing, and by the summer of 1985, three independent though occasionally cooperating large heroin wholesaler–dealer networks were quickly establishing a virtual monopoly for local supply.

Concurrent with the development of the heroin distribution network, and equally important for the local drug scene, was the emergence of a large group of socialising heroin users. Their social and focal point was a pub in the town centre which had for a number of years served both as a meeting and market place for dealers and their drug using customers. Although most drugs were available, the pub was primarily a heroin marketplace.

A stable distribution network based on pyramid selling and socialisation led to an increase in endemic heroin use, whilst competitive retail outlets in the same marketplace brought constant supply and a more or less stable price and purity. At any one time, the distribution pyramid was made up of the three large heroin wholesalers, three or four smaller wholesalers and six to ten retail dealers servicing and supplying around 130 heroin dependent 'customers'.

Police operations

Until the spring of 1986, Worthing's Divisional Drug Unit (Street Unit) followed a pattern of 'stop and search' of known users which often resulted in prosecution for possession or other drug-related offences such as acquisitive crime. Whilst this strategy led to increased and better intelligence through 'plea bargaining' and minor inconvenience to end users, its effects on the drug dealing networks were minimal. However, in a change of strategy in the summer of 1986, after extensive and expensive surveillance, the Force Drug Unit arrested all the large wholesalers in three related strikes (Operation Mauritius). Worthing's heroin distribution network was completely destroyed.

It could be naively assumed that the removal of the large suppliers would restrict the availability of heroin. However with unmet demand, as in the past, resourceful users quickly organised replacement supplies from neighbouring towns whose distribution networks had been left untouched by Operation Mauritius. The distribution pyramid rapidly reformed with a new pecking order, as new entrepreneurs and wholesalers moved in to fill the vacuum created by the police activity. In a very short time, in spite of police statements to the contrary, heroin supply was once more able to meet Worthing's demand.

Despite the apparent 'success' of Operation Mauritius, public (and parental) concern was mounting over 'the heroin pub'. In response to this pressure, the Divisional Drug Unit raided these premises (Operation Anthill) a few weeks after the Force Drug Unit's operation against the dealing network. As a public relations exercise, the Divisional Force invited the media to view the operation. The resulting heavy national coverage did not hide the fact that very few of those detained in the raid were caught in actual possession of drugs: the bar floor was littered with drug deals discarded by their owners to avoid prosecution.

The police used this operation to commence proceedings against the licensee and staff of the public house for allowing their premises to be used for the distribution and consumption of drugs, although the charges were mysteriously dropped after two days in the Crown Court. More 'usefully', the police action was used as an explicit threat to the managers of other local public houses not to allow their premises to become the new social centre for the heroin users.

Immediate impact

Without its vital social/trading centre the Worthing heroin network fell apart: Operation Anthill had not touched the dealing network or its staff, but the Divisional action against the social centre was much more effective in the long term than the Force action against the traders. As a National Drug Intelligence Unit (NDIU) report (Fraser and George, 1988) pointed out, it was 'particularly interesting to see how these two quite unrelated police actions caused total and long-term disruption of the heroin supply and use scene'.

In a mood of high confidence the Worthing Divisional Commander announced that the drug problems of Worthing were over and as a result he was disbanding the local Divisional Drug Unit and redeploying its staff elsewhere.

The next few months were a time of great instability for the heroin using cohort. Of course in the past there had been minor hiccups in heroin supply but these had never lasted more than a few days and were no more than an inconvenience. Yet without the 'market', scoring heroin became almost impossible. Some moved onto other drugs including GP-prescribed pharmaceuticals, others moved to a different town whilst still more switched their dependency across to alcohol, causing the police further problems through high profile street drinking and an increase in alcohol-related offences. Treatment was an option for others, and some simply gave up using and began employment in a more or less honest fashion within the irregular economy.

The loss of the social centre and the dispersal of the user group was a real blow to the unity and cohesion which was a feature of the heroin using cohort. This change was particularly striking to cohort members returning to Worthing after spells in prison or living elsewhere.

Some eight months later, after a few false starts, a new social and trading centre developed in another town pub. The heroin supply network had declined with the decreasing demand; now with the new marketplace it grew rapidly back to shape – almost everything and everyone returned to the original status quo. In the long run, the combined police operations had absolutely no effect whatsoever.

Longer-term consequences: from the police view

Few police officers, either from specialist or general units, feel that either of the operations against heroin was successful in eradicating or even suppressing heroin use in Worthing. In fact, they believe that drug use has become more visible since the operations. This may be a direct result of the closure of the social/ market centre, which led to the dispersal of drug use and users throughout the town, giving the impression of an increase in prevalence. Likewise, user displacement on to benzodiazepines and/or alcohol led to a greater likelihood of arrest for public order offences – reinforcing the police's impression that there were more of them about.

However, a number of conclusions (some positive, some negative) can be drawn:

> Operations aimed at closing social and dealing centres are more effective than those directed at individuals in a drug distribution network.
> Successful operations may stop heroin availability in an area in the short term, but without a continuing police presence and pressure, distribution networks re-emerge.
> Police actions against a dealing network for a particular type of drug generally leave those for other drugs untouched. Some (e.g. amphetamine) may even flourish, since displacement leads to an increased demand for the 'new' drug while police attention is focused elsewhere.
> Drug distribution methods used by networks readily mutate to accommodate particular police activity, e.g. from a social centre to a house-based dealer operation.

From the heroin user view

Lack of availability leads heroin users to a range of displacement activities:

> alcohol misuse, leading to an increase in offending, for example more public order and alcohol-related crime;

increased pressure on General Practitioners to prescribe benzodiazepines and synthetic opioids;
increase in trade and use of street amphetamine powder (speed);
alternative activities within the irregular (black) economy such as moonlight minicab driving, 'lump' labouring, antique 'knocking', etc.

There is a strong link between the actions of the law enforcement agencies and initial therapeutic contact of heroin users. When street heroin is not easily and reliably available, treatment (oral methadone) becomes an acceptable alternative.

Prior socialisation, commonly held values and a sense of community against a common foe (society with its rules and regulations) was a binding factor which held many of the heroin 'career' members of the cohort together during the long period of heroin drought. Members 'lost' during the drought were less committed to the concept of a full-time heroin using career.

There was a noticeable increase in overdoses and deaths during the drought as users began injecting opiates designed for oral consumption (e.g. Diconal or Palfium). The incidence of overdoses and deaths dropped to their pre-drought levels when the heroin dealing networks re-established themselves.

When heroin returned to the area with a regular and reliable dealer network, most users dropped their displacement drugs/activities and switched back to heroin. The exceptions were those who had displaced onto the drugs of inactivity – alcohol and benzodiazepines – who were unable to make the change back.

ACTION AGAINST DANCE-DRUG DISTRIBUTION AND USE

Historical background

In the summer of 1991 national tabloid, broadsheet and broadcast media focused on ecstasy as the new drug of concern. This media attention highlighted the alleged popularity and prevalence of ecstasy and to some extent amphetamine and LSD, as part of the entertainment package of raves and pay parties. This increased public awareness and anxiety both of the drugs themselves and of large groups of young people assembling in unsupervised (or difficult to supervise) locations.

Worthing's own association with the rave dance culture was initiated by the activities of a promoter (Interdance) at a local venue (Sterns Night-Club). Sterns is a purpose-built night-club located 3 miles outside Worthing on the edge of the South Downs, reached by a sole access slip road off the main Worthing–Littlehampton coastal road. The recession had heavily hit Sterns's traditional business – middle-class over-25 couples wanting a weekend dance location with a late night licence – a sort of steak and Status Quo set.

The arrival of the 'rave' scene was a commercial lifeline for the management. Through the skills and aggressive marketing efforts of the rave promoters, Interdance, Sterns rapidly became the 'scene' for young people from a wide catchment area. Many of the customers lived far beyond the county's boundaries, and the promoters chartered private coaches to ferry the less mobile ravers to the club. The club's accessibility to the car-owning young was also a key to its success – people were prepared to travel from Portsmouth in the west, Hastings in the east, or even from as far inland as South London to sample its delights.

The club was isolated, with no residential properties within 800 metres, and was built underground to achieve planning permission in an area of outstanding natural beauty. As a consequence there were few complaints about the noise or problems with parking for the 2000-plus ravers that might arrive in 700 to 800 cars every Saturday night.

Although these raves caused few specific problems for Worthing residents, there were media-inspired fears that drugs were routinely available and being consumed at the club. However, unlike the heroin use reported earlier, this general public anxiety did not initially manifest itself as pressure on the Divisional Police to react. The operations against drug dealing at Sterns were part of a planned and coordinated response rather than a knee-jerk reaction to public opinion.

Apart from general media-generated hype, or non-specific parental anxiety, police had specific intelligence concerns about the club and its raves:

'From the intelligence I was given I accept that there was a drug problem up there. . ... I could tell from my walking around

the club . . . that there was a lot of people high on drugs in that
club . . . We were getting a lot of information from other forces
that drugs were readily available and dealers were coming in
from South London and the Portsmouth area.'

(Division Superintendent)

The intelligence referred to by the uniformed Superintendent
would appear to have come from out of the area, via the Force
Drug Unit. This was later confirmed by one of their officers:

'A year prior to the operation we started, that is to say the Drug
Unit started, to be passed information of a general nature about
the volume of drugs being sold and used in the night-club when
it started being used as a rave venue. . .. It went on from there,
as the information started to filter in, not just from Sussex but
from other forces such as Hampshire and London . . . The club
was starting to become the main venue for sale and use in
particular of ecstasy and amphetamine sulphate. . .. A large
amount of information was coming in which was not specific,
but that information started to become more specific and it
became clear that people were attending there from South
London and Hampshire for the purpose solely of knocking out
quite large quantities of gear.'

(Detective Sergeant, Force Drug Unit)

One of the spurs to police action was professional pressure as a
result of intelligence gathered from neighbouring forces. Another
was the uncomfortable feeling that Sussex Police were being made
to look impotent in the eyes of club management, dealers, users
and professional colleagues:

'I'd never seen anything like it, never saw the police there when
I was dealing.'

(Wholesale dealer)

'You never saw the police there, either inside or outside the club
. . . sometimes you saw them waiting at the exit to the road in a
patrol car or in the top car park in the morning when everyone
was leaving . . . but they were just watching and did nothing.'

(Rave customer)

'. . . what I won't have is dealers taking the piss and that's what
they've been doing.'

(Division Superintendent)

'It was a law unto itself!'

(Detective Constable, Force Drug Unit)

'On a personal note it was almost as if it had a reputation for being untouchable – and once I heard that, it really crowned it for me. It became clear to me that a lot of people thought that we were impotent and were not prepared to do anything . . . worse still in the pay of someone – and that was even mooted as well.'

(Detective Sergeant, Force Drug Unit)

And so, professional pride in combination with intelligence from other forces stimulated Sussex Police to plan an operation against the 'un-policeable' rave scene at Sterns.

Unique constraints of the rave operations

There could be well over 2000 attenders at a Sterns/Interdance rave. Although only some would be under the influence of mood-altering chemicals, all had the potential to be hostile to police intervention.

Such a situation causes unique public order/safety problems. There had been no public order constraints mentioned by officers involved in Operation Anthill (discussed earlier), which had been directed against no more than 150 heroin users in a group social setting. In the words of a Divisional Drug Unit officer, 'They know how to behave'; the same could not be said of the younger rave attenders.

The police fully appreciated that they were in a delicate area – a clumsily mounted operation could so easily degenerate into a fully fledged riot:

'It was completely beyond our means to consider doing a raid there – for public safety.'

(Detective Sergeant, Force Drug Unit)

'I decided that it wasn't in the interests of public safety to carry out a police raid.'

(Division Superintendent)

A second constraint on the club-based operation was the police mistrust of the rave promoter Interdance. The relationship between the police and Interdance had always been difficult. Part of the total 'entertainment package' for an unknown number of Interdance rave customers was the recreational use of 'dance drugs'. Heavy-handed club security would lessen the appeal of Sterns – driving customers towards other promotions with laxer rules or more tolerant security. However, Interdance was also aware that continuing commercial success was dependent on retaining a late night licence.

With all these conflicting pressures Interdance blew hot and cold over the drugs issue, reacting with a mixture of moral surprise, rhetoric and titular action. Their attempt to walk the three-stranded tightrope of politics, public relations and profit led to intense police suspicion:

> 'They want to keep their licence . . . so they put on this squeaky clean act.'
>
> (Detective Constable, Force Drug Unit)

> 'It wasn't just a punter problem . . . I wouldn't trust the management.'
>
> (Detective Sergeant, Force Drug Unit)

As a result of their strong suspicions of the Interdance management, the police decided that any operation would be mounted without either the knowledge or the solicited cooperation of Interdance.

As indicated above, the Worthing Divisional Drug Unit was disbanded following the short-term success of operations Mauritius and Anthill. This was helpful as it removed a competitive layer in police management and put an end to the rivalry between Force and Divisional Drug Units which had led to a reluctance to share information. As a result of the disbandment, a new and 'excellent cooperation' between the Force Drug Unit and the uniformed Division developed, and there was now a free and mutual exchange of intelligence:

> 'They [the Force Drug Unit] offered their assistance and cooperation.'
>
> (Division Superintendent)

'It was a pleasure working with him [Uniformed Super-intendent] and the blokes under him . . . An excellent cooperation.'

(Detective Sergeant, Force Drug Unit)

While there were no competitive constraints between the specialist and generalist units, there were however intra-unit problems:

'The biggest single problem was the internal politics in my unit.'

(Detective Sergeant, Force Drug Unit)

This was caused by disagreements within the Force Drug Unit as to its role – traditionalists believed that it should be directed against middle-level heroin dealers, while the 'young Turks' claimed that large scale distribution of 'dance drugs' should be the primary target. This still remains an on-going debate within the unit.

Finally, finance and manpower were constraints which continually reduced the size and scope of the original operational plan:

'We were promised a number of things from Headquarters that didn't materialise . . . It was obvious that the powers that be started to pull in the purse strings and say "No, it's down to you matey and you'll run it basically from your own resources" . . . it got watered down – mainly due to . . . the cost of the whole operation.'

(Detective Sergeant, Force Drug Unit)

As indicated earlier the club was out of town so it was not a source of nuisance complaints such as the police regularly received about clubs in Worthing. Policy-makers and planners therefore believed that a large operation would be a waste of resources. Further-more, if it resulted in the closure of the club, the problem could be displaced into the town centre:

'Let sleeping dogs lie . . . If it were stirred up too much, all those disgruntled punters would end up in town and could cause serious problems.'

(Detective Sergeant, Force Drug Unit)

Despite these constraints and factors, a joint operation between the Force Drug Unit and uniformed Divisional officers was planned and executed.

A series of police operations

Financial, manpower and public order considerations led to a scaling-down of the original plan to a series of smaller operations based on the diversion of selected cars arriving at the club to a separate car park for searching.

The police used informant intelligence as one criterion to select cars to stop and search. This suggests that the target group for the first of their series of operations (Operation Rosemary) was wholesale dealers rather than retailers or end users.

'We were looking for known drug dealers . . . A great deal of research had gone into the operation . . . I knew the vehicles we were looking for and the people . . . 75 per cent of the cars that we pulled in had drugs on them . . . That shows the success of our intelligence.'

(Division Superintendent)

'Firstly, we did have a spotter some miles up the road but in the event this was not particularly effective . . . Secondly, we had an officer at the entrance to the lower car park in the drive . . . where any car would have to stop for the club's security check . . . which gave the officers a chance to select any vehicle they felt was necessary. There was some basic information about vehicles and punters . . . and there was an informant there . . . I'll say no more.'

(Detective Sergeant, Force Drug Unit)

'Three main factors . . . Intelligence, an informant and Drug Unit officer's experience.'

(Detective Constable, Force Drug Unit)

All participants (including those arrested) agreed that Operation Rosemary was conducted with speed, efficiency, good humour and a high degree of professionalism. Customers arriving at the club, unless they were selected for stop and search, were unaware of what was happening. The police also took pains to conceal from the club management both the timing and pre-operation activities. However, the operation's success was also paradoxically its problem:

'We filled up the vans much quicker than we had anticipated, certainly within an hour of the first stop . . . We had to stop when we could physically detain no more.'

(Detective Sergeant, Force Drug Unit)

'A lot of people we were looking for didn't show because we left early . . . It was much more successful than we had anticipated . . . The dealers were impressed with the operation . . . In fact they passed comment that it was good!'

(Division Superintendent)

Operation Rosemary resulted in nineteen arrests with seizures of between 250 and 300 ecstasy tablets/capsules, plus quantities of amphetamine sulphate, LSD and cannabis resin. Initial triumph was somewhat dented when forensic analysis reported that many of these so-called ecstasy tablets were non-controlled anti-histamines, but as one officer put it:

'They went there to flog them as Es . . . Con people if you like . . . Although I think that some of the dealers were surprised to find out that their gear was duff! [no good].'

(Detective Sergeant, Force Drug Unit)

But with the system clogging up with processing procedures (documentation, interviewing and the thousand and one post-arrest bureaucratic tasks), Operation Rosemary missed its main aim – arresting high-level wholesale market dealers. With many ravers buying their drugs on their home patch and carrying them into Sterns (thus avoiding being ripped-off by unknown dealers at the venue), it was inevitable that when searched they would be easily arrested and clog up the system, diverting police effort away from the large wholesalers:

'What the police should have done is to have stopped cars leaving which had just a few minutes before driven up to the car park . . . It's important to realise that the big boys buying and selling never went to the raves at Sterns . . . just the car park . . . But then that's a public car park and some of the people arriving and leaving are just up there to walk their dogs – there was an old woman who used to take a pet parrot up there and let it fly around.'

(Wholesale dealer)

Operation Rosemary and the lessons learnt from it became a pilot for a second and larger operation. Six months later, a similar police operation took place on a much larger scale. Its code name was Operation Suffolk and it resulted in another fifty-four arrests. The operation showed signs of both sophistication and a change in police tactics. One in three of all the cars stopped contained drugs, predominately ecstasy. One in four people stopped were in possession of illegal drugs. At this point the police introduced the informal 'Three Es Rule', which resulted in 28 of those arrested being released without charge, even though they had been found in possession of up to three doses of a Class A drug. It was deemed that these were for personal use and that the time, effort and paperwork involved in prosecution would not be 'cost-effective'. Individuals with more than three ecstasy tablets were deemed to be in possession with intent to supply and formal steps to prosecute were made. Initial forensic analysis once again indicated that much of the so-called ecstasy seized was non-controlled anti-histamines.

Operation Suffolk undoubtedly benefited from the lessons learnt from Operation Rosemary. The informal 'Three E's Rule' prevented the system becoming clogged up and allowed the police to concentrate their efforts on 'real' dealers. Although much of the forensic bureaucracy was done on site (searches, statements and finger-printing) once again the police ran out of transport to ferry arrested ravers to the police station. However, this time they hired commercial vehicles, allowing the operation to continue.

After Operation Suffolk, Sussex Police conducted similar but smaller operations against Sterns/Interdance customers on a more or less regular basis. Each operation has trawled in a predictable number of customers 'in possession' and generated the predictable media coverage. Police, Interdance and Worthing Borough Council Licensing Committee became locked in a complex battle over Sterns's late night licence; continuing police operations can be viewed as a tool to apply pressure on the Licensing Committee. It would seem that local media coverage was stage managed by the police to disproportionate levels, with senior officers available for media comment at even the most minor of Sterns-related court cases. Operations had changed from being a physical 'War on Drugs' to a media 'War of Words' directed against Sterns/Interdance.

Outcomes: from the police view

Operations directed at closing or restricting socialisation/drug dealing areas are more effective than those directed at individuals in dealing networks. Policing of 'un-policeable no-go areas' is possible without provoking public order offences.

Publicity resulting from arrests made during Operations Rosemary and Suffolk was effective in convincing the licensing committee to withdraw Sterns's late night licence and raising local awareness of the link between raves and drug use. There was an increase in cooperation between Force Drug Unit and uniformed Division. The Force Drug Unit now sees 'dance drugs' as a legitimate operational objective. There was, however, little or no decrease in drug use within the club. There was also an increase in public order offences as a direct result of 'displace-ments' due to the police operations, namely unofficial raves on public land after the introduction of 'early closure' at Sterns and growth in the number of pay parties in private and unoccupied town centre properties.

There is now, though, a degree of retrograde security cooperation between Interdance and the police, with Interdance regularly handing over 'sacrificial lambs' caught by Club security staff in possession of small quantities of drugs.

From the ravers' view

Public pressure led to Interdance losing its late night licence. This resulted in 50 per cent drop in attendance as mobile ravers chose other late-licensed clubs and growth in the number of 'high risk' unofficial raves without security or paramedical cover.

There is little or no change in drug use at Sterns. Although dealers are now reluctant to run the gauntlet of potential roadblocks, users continue to pre-purchase drugs on their home ground. This results in drugs being found in more police-stopped cars – giving the impression that the problem is getting worse. Once ravers make it to the club they are safe, since police have never conducted operations within Sterns. The deterrent effect of arrest was further undermined by the re-arrest of some of the same people in both Operations Rosemary and Suffolk.

Interdance have adopted a siege mentality as the police have used the success of their operations as evidence to oppose

Interdance's applications to run raves throughout southern England.

CONCLUSIONS

This study looks at police operations against two very different drug scenes – endemic heroin use and epidemic 'dance drug' use. In some respects the outcomes are quite similar and we can draw the following general conclusions.

Police operations which make socialisation of drug users difficult and disrupt retail and wholesale 'street markets' appear to be highly effective. However, to be effective in the long run, this nuisance policing must be continuous.

Drug dealing and using patterns are quite elastic. A good example of the situation is a balloon – police pressure at one point will make the balloon bulge elsewhere as users and dealers adopt displacement activities.

Displacement activities can open up a whole new can of worms for both police and policed.

Police operations, their outcomes and the use of media, alter public perception of both the nature and extent of the local 'drug problem'.

POSTSCRIPT

In July 1993, in a blaze of media publicity, Interdance lost their licence to run events at Sterns Night-club. At the hearing, the police stated Interdance's incompetent management had turned Sterns into 'a magnet and Mecca for drug dealers and users from all over the South of England'. The main evidence cited for this were the regular police arrests.

While Interdance appealed against this decision, the police were confident of its outcome. One could cynically suppose that the 'drug problem' had been solved by Sussex Police moving it outside their catchment area. Drug using ravers and dealers would agree with this – their pragmatic view was that it's 'business as usual'; the only thing that changes is the location. In August 1993, Interdance lost their appeal against the July decision, meaning that the club would now have to close at 11 each night. The company decided not to try for a final appeal, and Worthing is now, according to the authorities, rid of the menace of drugs. Doesn't all this have a sense of *déjà vu?*

NOTES

The authors are grateful to the South East Thames Regional Health Authority and South Downs Health NHS Trust, as well as police officers and anonymous informants.

REFERENCE

Fraser, A. and M. George (1988) 'Changing trends in drug use', *Drugs Arena*, 6, pp. 14–19.

Part II
Debating National Drug Policies

5 The Netherlands: Tightening Up of the Cafés Policy

Liesbeth Horstink-Von Meyenfeldt

In 1976, following a radical amendment of the Opium Act, the Netherlands adopted a drug policy based on two principles:

Drug use is considered to be primarily a public health issue rather than a judicial problem. The use of drugs is therefore not a statutory offence, although the possession of certain listed substances is prohibited.

A distinction is made between 'hard' drugs, which involve an unacceptable degree of risk (drugs such as cocaine, heroin and amphetamine are scheduled on the annex list 1 of the Opium Act), and hemp products, which are known as 'soft' drugs and scheduled on list 2. The penalties for possession of listed substances or for importing, exporting or trafficking in them differ accordingly as to whether the substance in question is a hard drug or a cannabis product. Possession of less than 30 grams of hemp, for instance, is a summary offence liable to a custodial sentence not exceeding one month, whereas possession of any hard drug is indictable.

The expediency principle gives public prosecutors in the Netherlands discretionary powers, and in certain cases the prosecutor can decide not to prosecute. To prevent a situation occurring in which each public prosecutor goes their own way and thereby endangers the uniformity of policy, public guidelines have been established for detecting and prosecuting different criminal offences.

The guidelines issued by the Public Prosecutions Department for the investigation and prosecution of drug offences under the

Opium Act are of course based on the same principles as the drug policy: highest priority being given to combating trafficking and lowest to cases of possession. In practice this means that, although the police do confiscate any drugs found in someone's possession, the Public Prosecutions Department will refrain from prosecuting – on the grounds of public interest – in cases that involve relatively small quantities (up to 0.5 grams of hard drugs or 30 grams of soft drugs), unless the offender is also suspected of dealing or another drug-related crime.

This quantitative distinction between offences involving hemp products and hard drugs is based on the assumption that soft drugs are less injurious to health than hard drugs. The principal aim is to separate the markets for these two categories in order to prevent young people who experiment with soft drugs from transferring to more dangerous substances.

Given that the law distinguishes between hard and soft drugs, the guidelines issued by the Public Prosecutions Department contain a special section on the retail trade in hemp products. By 1976, 'house dealers' selling soft drugs in youth clubs had become a common phenomenon, and so the guidelines recommended that the police were not to take action other than to prevent the display of advertising posters and to combat aggressive sales practices. They were also advised to review the social and administrative aspects of problems relating to drug use in youth centres together with the local public prosecutor and burgomaster and the head of the municipal police force. They have, for instance, raided a number of establishments, including *De Kokerjuffer* in Enschede, in connection with contraventions of the ban on advertising and drug pushing.

POLICY TRENDS SINCE 1976

So-called coffeeshops, the first of which opened in Amsterdam, soon took over the role of house dealers and youth clubs. Initially frequented by drug users, some of these establishments have gradually evolved into major retail outlets for hemp. Their main customers are foreign tourists who come to the Netherlands especially to buy drugs, which are known to be cheap and relatively easy to obtain. The practice has met with sharp criticism from abroad as well as from local residents, who frequently complain of disturbances in and around these coffee-shops.

To gain some measure of control of the trade in hemp, the Public Prosecutions Department in Amsterdam issued a police guideline in 1985, based on the national drug policy. On the grounds of the expediency principle the Department (in conjunc-tion with the burgomaster) agreed not to prosecute coffeeshop owners providing that they observed five rules: they were not to (1) advertise, (2) trade in hard drugs, (3) sell drugs to youngsters or, (4) sell drugs in quantities of more than 30 grams. Moreover, (5) they would be held responsible for preventing any public disturbance or nuisance on or in the vicinity of their premises. Failure to comply would result in closure.

As the coffeeshop phenomenon spread to other parts of the country, notably to border towns such as Arnhem, Venlo, Maastricht, Enschede, Breda and Tilburg, the local authorities decided to adopt the same policy as in Amsterdam, and in December 1991, the assembly of Procurators General voted to introduce the 'coffeeshop rules' as national policy.

In 1992 a report on drugs and public nuisance was published (Cremers: 'drugs and drug-related nuisance problems') under the auspices of the Assembly of Procurators General. It contained a number of recommendations envisaging an integrated policy, and proposed the introduction of local legislation, analogous to Venlo's public nuisance ordinance, which would enable munici-pal executives to establish a licensing system as a means of regulating the number and locations of all kinds of bars, pubs and restaurants, including coffeeshops. It should be emphasised that these are not licences to sell soft drugs; they merely entitle the holder to open a coffeeshop. A licence may not be issued to anyone with a police record (including those charged with the sale of drugs), and licence holders must also observe the five 'coffeeshop rules'.

Amsterdam, Arnhem, Maastricht and various other munici-palities are currently drafting legislation to provide for a licensing system. This will enable the authorities to prevent coffeeshops from clustering in certain parts of town, thus averting any excessive nuisance to the public. It also means that they will be able to stop coffeeshops from opening near schools or in residential areas. Moreover, besides reducing the coffeeshop phenomenon to manageable proportions, a restriction on the total number of establishments in any given municipality will be seen as a concession to critics abroad.

Amsterdam's municipal police also work in close cooperation with the Fiscal Intelligence and Investigation Department (FIOD), mainly to discourage the sale of drugs by removing financial incentives. The Ministry of Justice is strongly in favour of financial measures to combat the traffic in drugs, invoking for this purpose recent legislation which gives the police and Public Prosecutions Department wide powers to confiscate the proceeds of crime.

THE SITUATION BY THE MID-1990s

In practice, the policy described above has helped stabilise the number of cannabis users (at present between 500,000 and 600,000) and has led to a proliferation of coffeeshops. At present, several hundred are operating in Amsterdam alone, with dozens more in smaller towns such as Arnhem, Maastricht and, until recently, Venlo. The policy is considered a success by the Netherlands. In any event, it seems to have prevented cannabis users from making the transition to hard drugs. This emerges from numerous surveys carried out among users of soft drugs, and from the fact that relatively few cannabis users (some 21,000 to 23,000) are addicted to hard drugs.

Nevertheless, in my view, the situation at present is not what was envisaged when the policy was introduced in 1976. To judge by their numbers, coffeeshops must be 'successfully' providing not only for the local market but also for hundreds of foreigners who flock to the Netherlands to stock up on supplies. Over the last few years, moreover, some municipalities have been inspecting these establishments only after receiving complaints from the public rather than to ensure that they are not selling hard drugs. In fact many coffeeshop proprietors are involved in traffic in hard drugs, either directly or because contacts are made on their premises. Nor is it unusual for them to sell to minors and to sell larger quantities than the permitted 30 grams, mainly to foreign traffickers. Finally, the unsavoury practice of serving foodstuffs containing potentially harmful hashish to unsuspecting customers has tarnished the country's reputation.

Because of the Public Prosecutions Department's policy of not prosecuting coffeeshops which observed the five 'rules', the sale of cannabis has come to be seen as a semi-legitimate activity. The policy has had little effect as a deterrent. On the contrary, there are signs that the use of cannabis is increasing. A study conducted by the National Institute for Alcohol and Drugs (NIAD) (de Swart *et al.*, 1993) found that in 1984 4.8 per cent of schoolchildren aged 12 and over had used cannabis at least once; by 1988 the number had risen to 8 per cent and in 1992 13.6 per cent. The increase was thus greater between 1988 and 1992 than it had been in the preceding four-year period. Moreover, the average age at which children tend to experiment with cannabis is now lower than it used to be. Approximately 14 per cent of children aged 14 and 15 have used cannabis at some time. Those who took part in the survey were also asked whether they had used cannabis in the preceding four weeks. In 1984, 2.3 per cent of respondents aged 12 and over had done so; in 1988 the number was 3.1 per cent and in 1992 6.5 per cent. Here, too, the increase was greater between 1988 and 1992 than in the preceding four years.

A growing number of cannabis users have been seeking professional help. Some months ago, the Assembly of Procurators General recommended more stringent inspections of coffeeshops and requested the police authorities in a number of court districts to draft a plan of action.

Finally, the Netherlands has to be critical about the effects and results of the soft drug policy. It seems that the percentage of hard and soft drug users in relation to the total Dutch population is more or less the same as the statistics in Germany and Switzerland, although neither country has a coffeeshop policy.

CONTINUING DEBATE

During the first half of the 1990s, the Netherlands came under attack from the police and judicial authorities of other countries who had lost confidence in our approach. The way in which coffeeshops function in practice no longer reflects the official policy, and exercising the option not to prosecute has been seen as a failure to meet international commitments. In addition, local cultivation of a Dutch variety of marijuana known as *nederwiet* has flourished, partly due to lenient penalties and because statutory provisions which allow the cultivation of hemp for agriculture make it difficult for the Public Prosecutions Department and police to produce evidence of criminal activity in this area. Given that *nederwiet* seems likely to become an export product, the Netherlands could end up being regarded virtually in the same light as Morocco. Another point about which the Netherlands should be more concerned is the fact that the average THC percentage of *nederwiet* is very high – comparable with hash-oil, which is listed as a schedule 1 product.

The policy has been criticised not only by France and other EU countries, but also by the United Nations International Narcotics Control Board (INCB), which sent a delegation to the Netherlands in October 1992. Its annual report for that year was highly critical of the Dutch policy, mainly on the grounds that it violates international conventions and that its undesirable effects have spread to neighbouring countries. This refers primarily to the policy on soft drugs. Our Prime Minister responded unequivocally: the policy had proved successful and was therefore to be maintained. Nevertheless, the INCB's concern cannot be ignored, and measures must be taken to combat any negative side-effects.

At the beginning of 1993, in connection with the ratification of the 1988 Vienna Convention and the 1971 Convention on psychotropic substances, the Lower House of Parliament asked the competent political authorities to review the Dutch policy on drugs. In the debate that followed, the Lower House expressed broad support for the principles on which the policy is based. However, it emphasised the importance of enforcing the rules, particularly as regards the separation of the markets for soft and hard drugs, the prevention of public nuisance, and restrictions on the cultivation of *nederwiet*. On the other hand, proposals to liberalise the policy on soft drugs met with little support.

It was also suggested that a licensing system could be introduced to monitor the sales and quality of hemp in coffeeshops. The proposal was dismissed, however, as being impracticable and impossible to enforce. The Minister of Justice observed that a system of this nature would oblige the Netherlands to withdraw its consent from certain sections of international conventions, and warned of the possible repercussions. He also felt that such a system would exacerbate the crime problem in this country. Nevertheless, the outcome of the review was favourable, and the policy which the Minister of Justice and the Public Prosecutions Department had introduced in 1991 found broad support in Parliament.

The debate on legalising soft drugs goes back some years. The question was raised in the Lower House in 1976, when it was proposed that possession of less than 30 grams of hemp should no longer be a criminal offence. The Government observed that such a move would be in violation of the Single Convention on Narcotic Drugs, signed at New York in 1961, which requires the Netherlands, as one of the signatories, to prohibit possession of hemp products except for medical or scientific purposes. It was also agreed that legalisation would be incompatible with efforts to discourage drug use and inconsistent with the aim of criminal law as a deterrent. Moreover, criminal law provisions must be kept in place, it was urged, as they allow the courts to order an offender to seek professional help. In 1976, therefore, the government concluded that the Bill on which the present Opium Act is based had gone as far as possible within the scope of international law. The same arguments are still valid today, although 'drug tourism' has exacerbated the problems associated with soft drugs in this country.

Fine-tuning and monitoring the policy

It will be no easy matter for the Public Prosecutions Department, the police and the administrative authorities to enforce the policy outlined above and regain control over coffeeshops. In border regions they will have to enlist the help of the neighbouring country. The Ministry has opened negotiations with Belgium and France in a project known as the Hazeldonk Talks, to tackle the drug route between Rotterdam and Lille. Similar talks are also to be held with Belgium and Luxembourg. The Germans, too, have expressed an interest in working more closely with the Dutch police and judicial authorities.

An amendment to the Opium Act which is now being prepared will introduce a permit system for the country's almost negligible legitimate hemp production, thus making it easier for the authorities to act against illegal growers. The Ministry of Agriculture, Nature Management and Fisheries will be responsible for issuing such permits and enforcing the system.

In short, steps are being taken to tighten restrictions on soft drugs, since the measures now in place have proved insufficient to achieve the aims of this country's drug policy. Contrary to what has been suggested in some circles, it should be emphasised that these measures are not a response to the Netherlands' ratification of the Schengen Agreement or to the EU debate on drugs. In fact the opposite is true. In view of the growing drug problem, other countries have started to consider decriminalising drug use, and the Netherlands must formulate a measured contribution to this debate. After all, it is possible that other countries will adopt a similar strategy to ours, in which case the Netherlands would cease to be a Mecca for foreign drug addicts. Germany, for instance, recently decided – in line with Dutch policy – to adopt the expediency principle, which allows the authorities to refrain from prosecuting certain drug offences. The Schengen Agreement and the Maastricht Treaty are effective instruments for improving cooperation between the police and judicial authorities in their fight against wholesale drug trafficking. For the Ministry of Welfare, Health and Cultural Affairs, this is a challenge to cooperate more closely with its counterparts, as has been happening already at local level. Amsterdam, for example, is already building up a network of contacts in Germany.

Within the European Union the Drug Monitoring Centre has been set up to gather and analyse statistics on drug addiction in the member states. More research and comparability of statistics will contribute to a more professional discussion on the positive and negative effects of policies and will afford answers on many questions.

Given the lack of consensus among the public as well as in medical circles regarding the effects of using hemp, I do not see it being legalised in the near future. Nevertheless, the view that it is less harmful than hard drugs has certainly been gaining ground. The Netherlands should respond to these trends without opting for legalisation or even semi-legalisation. The Germans are in fact opposed to the Dutch coffeeshop system, and the German authorities would never go to the same lengths as the Netherlands in sanctioning small-scale drug trafficking. This is all the more reason to ensure that our system is properly monitored in the future. We need to regain the confidence of the international community, so that we may champion the many good elements of Dutch drugs policy with a greater air of authority.

REFERENCES

Amsterdams Bureau voor ondersoek en Statistiek (1993) *Drugstoerisme in de grensstreken.*

Swart, W. M. de, Mensink, C. *et al.* (1993) *Kerngegevens van het 3e Peilstationsondersoek naar riskant middelengebruik* (Utrecht: NIAD).

6 Sweden: Zero Tolerance Wins the Argument?

Leif Lenke and Börje Olsson

The theme of this paper is a modelling of Sweden's drug policy and its relationship to drug problems. Both the drug problem and the drug policy of a country have to be put into their broader contexts. Although claims have been made on behalf of the Swedish 'hard line' on drug users – successfully promulgated by the Conservative Party during their period in opposition – the basis of Sweden's relatively small heroin problem is the country's geographical position and its social and economic policies, not its drug-specific policies.

At the end of the 1960s Sweden shifted from its socio-medical drug policy to a clear law-enforcement approach, in which repression and formal social control predominated. Internationally, this has been seen by some as a particularly effective policy model. Over the years, repressive measures have become more and more prominent as drug use has been criminalised, stiffer penalties introduced, and treatment and rehabilitation budgets slashed. This drug policy can be understood in terms of Swedish alcohol policy traditions (discussed elsewhere)[1], but the post-War hardening of drug policy also has to do with the organisation of the police and, in a paradoxical way, with the relative strength of political parties – as we show in the latter part of this chapter.

Against this background, it has become important to analyse the scientific basis of Swedish drug policy. Is Sweden's relatively low level of drug problems a result of the repressive drug policy, or due to other factors? In this study, we use a comparative approach to discuss some factors which might be of importance for determining the level of drug misuse in a society. One such factor is unemployment, a high level of which can be expected to constitute fertile soil for the growth of demand for drugs. However, we do not think this factor alone is sufficient to explain the level of drug use. It is also important to consider the geographical location of a country, which may have substantial effects on its exposure to drugs.

POSSIBLE FACTORS IN DRUG PROBLEMS

Drug use and the role of unemployment

Youth unemployment in Sweden never exceeded 5 per cent throughout the 1970s and 1980s. No wonder, then, that unemployment has only been attributed minor importance in explaining the drug misuse which existed. However, it has been pointed out that the highest levels of drug use occurred in the early 1970s, when youth unemployment was allowed to rise for the first time since the Second World War, and that drug use was highest in the region which had the greatest increase in youth unemployment (Lenke, 1979).

From an international perspective, this relationship looks somewhat different. In a significant and methodologically well designed study in Great Britain, it was shown that heroin use increased in line with unemployment (Peck and Plant, 1986). The study also showed that drug misuse spread most markedly among adolescents whom – after a follow-up period – had not secured jobs. Many other studies clearly indicate that unemployment is very common among drug users.

To study the effect of unemployment on the level of drug use in various European countries, we have compiled different estimates of the number of drug users for the period 1985–90 (Table 6.1). We have chosen to use the number of known *heroin* addicts as an indicator of the drug problem in each country. There are several reasons for this. In almost all European countries, heroin is the most widely used drug among hard-core addicts and is the only drug type which is described in a fairly reliable way. Sweden is the only exception, where amphetamines have been the dominant hard drug. This unique Swedish drug pattern is an important reason for excluding amphetamines from the analysis, as we believe there are essential differences in the etiology of amphetamine use in Sweden and the use of heroin in other European countries: amphetamine addiction has been very strongly linked to an already existing criminal subculture (Änggård and Mossberg, 1978; Nilsson, 1993; Olsson, 1994). In descriptions of

Table 6.1 Heroin use and possible causative factors, selected countries, 1985–90

	Heroin use-rate	Unemployment rate (%)	Geographical position	Drug sanction rate	Restriction index	Left-wing influence
Austria	105	3	2	32	4	4
Belgium	50	11	2	5	3	2
Denmark	150	9	2	118	2	3
Finland	10	5	1	10	3	3
France	250	10	3	15	4	3
Germany	110	8	2	28	3	3
Ireland	100	17	1	*N.a.	0	0
Italy	260	10	3	1	0	0
Netherlands	125	10	3	13	0	2
Norway	75	2	1	47	5	4
Spain	235	15	3	*N.a.	0	3
Sweden	20	2	1	67	5	4
Switzerland	150	0	2	121	3	1
United Kingdom	215	13	3	41	2	1
	A	B	C	D	E	F

A. Rate per 100 000 inh. *Source*: WHO (Klingeman *et al.*, 1992) and Olsson (1993).
B. Unemployment rate, average 1980–1985. Computed from OECD, *Yearbook of Labour Statistics*.
C. Low value is given to peripheral nations.
D. Sanctions for drug crimes. Rate per 1000 000 inh. *Source*: Albrecht (1986) and *Narkotikasituationen i Norden* (1984).
E. See p. 110 for definition.
F. See p. 113 for definition.

drug addicts from other European countries, this connection is not as apparent or distinct as in Sweden (Council of Europe, 1987).

It could be argued that more occasional forms of drug use, and/ or the use of cannabis, ought to be included in the analysis, since a repressive drug policy is expected to deter people from using such drugs. But since proponents of the 'repression hypothesis' almost without exception adhere to the 'stepping-stone hypothesis' (i.e., heroin users are recruited from the group of occasional users), use of heroin could also function as an indicator of the effect of repression on cannabis and/or occasional use.

By using the frequency of heroin addiction as a measure of the level of a society's drug problem, we have conducted a regression analysis and calculated the statistical explanatory power of unemployment (five-year average during 1981–5 according to OECD) on heroin addiction. The correlation is statistically significant ($r = 0.47$, $F = 3.43$). This suggests that the level of unemployment does contribute to the level of heroin addiction. There are also other factors, we suggest.

Exposure to the international drug market

Another factor besides unemployment is exposure to the international drug market. By this we primarily refer to the geographical position of the nation in relation to the major drug routes in Europe. The nations can be categorised into three groups as regards market exposure: we have judged the strongest exposure as occurring in countries such as the Netherlands, Great Britain and Italy, based on the judgement of Interpol as well as the quantity of heroin seized;[2] the next group consists of Germany, Denmark, Switzerland, Belgium, France, and Spain; and in the last group we find Ireland, Norway, Sweden, and Finland.

When the factor 'market exposure' is added to unemployment in a multiple regression analysis, the correlation increases from 0.47 to 0.82, which gives a strong explanatory value of $r^2 = 0.67$, ($F = 11,25$). This means that unemployment and 'market exposure' together may account for much of the variation in heroin addiction between the countries examined here.

The role of repression

The aim of this study is not to find the best indicators for repression or to try to falsify the thesis that repression is an effective means of reducing drug use. Our purpose instead has been to stress two important structural factors that, in our view, define the space within which repression could eventually function.

To test the hypothesis that repression works, we have calculated the correlation between frequency of heroin users and a particular repression indicator. The chosen indicator is 'rate of convictions for drug offences',[3] and the result is a zero-correlation.

One could, however, argue that it is not repression *per se* that counts but the number of restrictions against drug use. To test this hypothesis, a 'restriction index' has been produced built on five different indicators as follows:

1. rate of criminal sanctions for drug offences;[4]
2. whether use of drugs is legal or not;
3. whether possession for own use is generally prosecuted;
4. whether the Drug Law distinguishes between 'soft' and 'hard' drugs;
5. whether methadone (or similar substances) is extensively used.

The value for each category is set at either 0 or 1. Each country will have an average between 0 and 5, indicating the degree of repression against drug users.[5] Other indicators could of course be used such as the length of sentence, but our assessment is that the outcome would not have been different. Regarding length of sentences as an indicator, we expect all countries to have rather similar maximum penalties (i.e., above 10 years imprisonment) as well as a shift in focus from drug users to traffickers.

Using this index, the correlation with 'heroin use'-rate increases to $r = -0.56$. This means that the more restrictive drug policy, the lower the rate of heroin use. However, if the Scandinavian countries with a peripheral position and low unemployment during the 1980s are excluded, the correlation diminishes and is not statistically significant.

This result necessarily invites us to search for scientific grounds for the strong interest in increasing repression against drug users. In Sweden's case, there is at least one probable explanation. The thesis of repression as being especially effective was promoted by the police medical officer, Nils Bejerot.

Police science

In his dissertation (1974) Bejerot tried to prove the thesis and used the prevalence of needle marks on arrestees in Stockholm between 1965 and 1970. His results have been criticised and refuted by Skog (1987), with the use of modern time series analysis (Box-Jenkins analysis).

Bejerot's strong influence on Swedish drug policy is therefore not a consequence of scientific support. A more important explanation is probably that he – as a police medical officer –

was given massive support and promotion by a police organisation that probably has no equivalent in Western society when it comes to its degree of centralisation and political influence in society. In contrast to the organisation of most other Western police forces, the Swedish force is centralised but at the same time – as is true of all Swedish authorities – independent of direct Parliamentary control (as in France). This organisation's central bureaucracy numbers over 1000 people, which constitutes a substantial force for lobbying due to its strong connections with the media, especially the tabloid press. This organisation has played a central role in the formation of Swedish drug policy and has systematically steered it in a repressive direction. The main function of police activities against drugs is to disturb street dealing, even if seizures are insubstantial. Or, as put by a coordinator of four local police groups in Stockholm:

'We are disturbing them [the users], standing in the way of their activities, threatening them with compulsory treatment and making life difficult for them. The more difficult it is, the more the other way of living stands out as a better alternative, that is a drug free life.'[6]

With reference to an 'ever increasing' drug problem, the organisation has been able to increase its forces by at least 1,000, a considerable reinforcement for a small country.

We turn now to the transmission of pro-repression sentiments into public policy.

CONSERVATIVE PARTIES IN OPPOSITION AND DRUG POLICIES

In spite of the fact that Swedish drug policy is built on a rather high degree of consensus, there are some considerable gaps between the political parties. The Conservative Party, *especially when it has been in political opposition*, has always put the drug question at the top of its political agenda. The party has – in concert with the police – systematically called for increased repression and expanded police resources.

The Social Democratic Party – most often in power in Sweden over the past fifty years – has constantly been on the retreat when it comes to the drug question (Nilsson, 1992). It has systematically tried to legitimate its repressive decisions by simultaneously increasing resources for drug treatment. As a consequence, Sweden has developed not only extreme repression, but also probably the most extensive drug treatment system in the Western world.

It is also possible to demonstrate this pattern in an international context. We suggest that it is no coincidence that we find the most liberal drug policies in countries dominated by conservative political parties. In countries like the Netherlands, Great Britain,[7] and Italy, the drug question has had a much lower profile in the political debate than in Sweden, Norway and Austria.

In fact, two general patterns of drug problem can be distinguished (see Figure 6.1).

Case A:

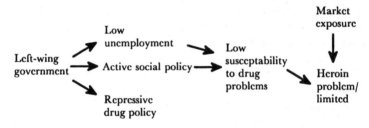

Case B:

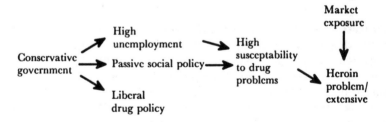

Figure 6.1   Two general patterns of drug problem

Comparative study of European drug policies and politics

The hypothesis that conservative parties tend to act more repressively against drug use when they are in political opposition, is rather paradoxical. In the light of their general 'law-and-order' profile this could be expected to extend to drugs even when in power. In order to understand this paradox, one has to take into consideration the fact that conservative parties have traditionally been rather liberal towards other drugs such as alcohol. They tend to see alcohol use as a question of 'freedom' or personal integrity.[8]

The rationale for conservative politicians' interest in the drug question must therefore be seen more as a potential and powerful party political tactic. The political influence of opposition parties is generally weak, but with one major exception. They have a considerable power for agenda-setting and placing their questions in a mass media forum. Conservative parties therefore tend to apply their law-and-order profile – which has traditionally been seen as compelling – to the field of drugs. Of course, the same option is open to left-wing parties. They, however, have generally not had a strong law-and-order approach, and when they do profile drug problems, they tend to underline the need for social and/or therapeutic measures.

To test the hypothesis that the degree of repression against drug users tends to increase with the degree of left-wing influence on government and legislation, the repression–restriction index used above is correlated with an indicator for political influence. The indicator for political influence has been difficult to quantify easily, as so many variations can be found regarding coalition governments and so on. A strong emphasis has been put on length of time in government as well as dominance in parliament during the 1970s and 1980s.[9] Again a classification on a scale from 0 to 5 has been applied: 0 means that a left-wing party has not had a dominant position in government and 5 that a left-wing party (parties) has dominated government over a long period of time.

As can be seen from the table overleaf, there is a positive correlation in Western European nations for strong left-wing political influence to be combined with a repressive drug policy. The correlation between the two indices is $r = 0.69$, which is rather strong and statistically significant.

One important 'outlier' in the analysis is Spain, a country that displays a relatively non-repressive drug policy in spite of a strong

	Left-wing influence	Repressive drug policy
Austria	4	4
Belgium	2	3
Denmark	3	2
Finland	3	3
France	3	4
Germany	3	3
Ireland	0	0
Italy	0	0
Netherlands	2	0
Norway	4	5
Spain	3	0
Sweden	4	5
Switzerland	1	3
United Kingdom	2	2

left-wing political influence during the latter part of the period 1970–90. If this country was omitted from the analysis, the correlation rises from 0.69 to 0.81, which is strong. Perhaps the case of Spain is not as incompatible with the hypothesis as seems if its special circumstances are taken into account. Authoritarian right-wing parties have had difficulties regaining influence after Franco's death. Perhaps the pressure on Spanish drug policy towards more repression in recent years (Zorilla, 1993) is an indication of a political offensive from the right-wing opposition.

Some clarifications of the interpretation are perhaps needed. What we are viewing is a tendency, rather than a rule, but the tendency seems to be rather strong. Furthermore, our interpretation is not mechanical and we do not even suggest which parties actually proposed or accepted policy changes. For example, if a conservative party pushed for drug restrictions when in opposition, the party would find it difficult not to implement the policy measures when it came to power. We also believe that conservative parties could very easily integrate the drug question into their 'law and order' profile for use when in office. So far this seems only to have been the case in the USA during the 1970s and

1980s. We see, however, signs of this by the Conservative Minister of Justice in Sweden as well as with the British government. Thus, the relationships shown above could quickly evolve if conservative parties find they need to relate to middle- and lower-class voters – a perennial problem for those parties. We see this pattern as a consequence of a political process where 'law and order' profiling is seen as a 'political innovation' (with roots in the US) and where drug policy is integrated into the 'law and order' programme.

Another analytical problem is when the analysis is applied to regions in federations of 'Länder' (Germany), Cantons (Switzerland) etc. The rule is, however, that general drug legislation is made on a federal level while restrictions and applications of the law are made by local attorneys and courts (see Chapters 3 and 10).

Acknowledging these difficulties, we hope that we offered food for thought on the link between political parties, their relation to power, and drug policies. It does seem possible that conservative parties in opposition seem rather good at getting their drug policies accepted into national policy.

CONCLUSIONS

Are repressive polices a significant factor in keeping down drug problems, as often claimed? One aim of the present study has been to look at a range of factors that potentially could explain the variations in European heroin misuse rates. These factors are taken to include unemployment and the geographical position of the country in relation to the flow of the European drug market. These factors account strongly for variation in heroin use, especially if compared to pure repression. However, the rate of criminal sanctions shows a zero-correlation when correlated to the rate of heroin use. Against this background, we suggest that the drug policy debate should not be reduced to a question of repression and restrictions.

Our second concern has been to explore the unexpected finding that, the stronger the influence of conservative parties, the less repressive the drug policy. This finding is rather paradoxical with regard to the strong 'law and order' profile taken by these parties. Our interpretation of this finding is that conservative parties have had a tendency to focus on the drug problem and the 'need for repression', especially when in opposition. For left-wing parties in the same position the demands have not been for repression but for social policy and treatment. If this relationship holds for the future, then any political shift that brings to power more conservative parties in Europe could tilt the balance of drug policies, away from repression and towards social integration of drug users. Correspondingly, if conservative parties lose power, we might see yet more repressive drug policies. But, of course, these are past tendencies rather than iron laws for the future – and history always brings its surprises.

NOTES

1. In an earlier article Lenke (1992) has described how the 19th century temperance movements reacted to a division of alcoholic beverages into 'soft' (beer and wine) and 'hard' (spirits). The radical temperance movements in Sweden, Norway and the USA never accepted such a division and called for an 'alcohol free society'. These movements applied the 'stepping stone' theory to alcohol and have included narcotic drugs in their modern theorems.

2. It could be argued that seizures should not be used as an indicator of market exposure, as it could also indicate the frequency of drug use. Other factors, such as the position of the 'mafia' in Italy, and Amsterdam as a world trading centre, must be seen as important factors for the size of the drug trade.

3. Source: Albrecht (1986) and Olsson (1993).

4. *Ibid.*

5. Leroy (1991), Nordnark (1991), and Albrecht and Kalmthout (eds) (1989) have been used as sources for this indicator.

6. *Aktionsgruppen mot Narkotika 1991*, p. 14, 'Vi ger oss aldrig!' (Stockholm: Socialdepartementet).

7. Downes and Morgan (1994, p.190) write that when the Conservative party came into power in 1979, the 'law and order' theme focused on union activities and greater police powers. The drug question is not even mentioned in their analysis of 'law and order' in Great Britain from 1970 to 1990.

8. The alcohol question used to be of the highest priority to liberal parties which had support from revivalist religious movements, who viewed alcohol as a 'sin'. See the reference to Lenke (1992).

9. Paloheimo, H. (1984) is one source for this indicator.

REFERENCES

Albrecht, H.-J. (1986) 'Criminal Law and Drug Control: A Look at Western Europe', *International Journal of Comparative and Applied Criminal Justice.*

Albrecht, H.-J., and A. van Kalmthout (eds) (1989) *Drug Policies in Western Europe*, Research Report 41 (Freiburg: Max Planck Institute for Foreign and International Penal Law).

Änggård, E. and D. Mossberg (1978) 'Missbrukskarriären', *Nordiska Samarbetsorganet för Drogforskning*, vol. 23.

Balvig, F. (1990) 'Narkotikakontroll i Schweiz', *Social kritik*, vol. 6, pp. 22–37.

Bejerot, N. (1974) *Narkotikamissbruk och narkotikapolitik* (Stockholm: Socialmedicinska institutionen, Karolinska Institutet).

Council of Europe (1987) *Multi-City Study of Drug Misuse* (Strasbourg: Pompitou Group/Council of Europe).

Downes, D. and R. Morgan (1994) 'Hostages to Fortune? The Politics of Law and Order in Post-War Britain', in M. Maguire, R. Morgan and R. Reiner (eds), *The Oxford Handbook of Criminology* (London: Clarendon Press).

Klingeman, H., C. Goos, R. Hartnoll and J. Rehm (1992) *European Summary on Drug Abuse. First Report 1985–1990* (Copenhagen: WHO).

Lenke, L. (1979) *Narkotika och förmögenhetsbrott. Rapport till Stockholms kommuns utredning om Social utslagning och ekonomisk brottslighet* (Stockholm: Stockholms kommun, mimeo).

Lenke, L. (1992) 'Dryckesmönster, nykterhetsrörelser och narkotikapolitik. En analys av samspelet mellan bruk av droger, brukets konsekvenser och formerna för deras kontroll i historiskt perspektiv', *Sociologisk forskning*, vol. 4 (91), pp. 34–47.

Lenke, L. and B. Olsson (1994) *Drug-related Police Interventions in European Cities. Report to the Pompidou Group* (Strasbourg: Council of Europe, Mimeo).

Leroy, B. (1991) *The Community of Twelve and the Drug Demand. Comparative Study of Legislations and Juridical Practice* (Brussels: Commission of the European Community).

Narkotikasituationen i Norden (1984) *Rapport till Nordiska kontaktmannaorganet för narkotikafrägor* (Socialdepartementet: Stockholm).

Nilsson, A (1993) *Injektionsmissbruk och kriminalitet.- en jämförelse mellan centralstimulantia- och opiatmissbrukare.* (Stockholm: Examensarbete vid Kriminologiska institutionen, Stockholms Universitet).

Nilsson, M. (1991) *Narkotikastrafflagen – en analys av lagstiftarens motiv* (Stockholm: Examensarbete vid Juridiska fakulteten vid Stockholms universitet).

Nordnark (1991) *Lagstiftnings och rättspraxis i narkotikamål*, Nordiska kontaktmannaorganet för narkotikafrågor (Regeringskansliets offsetcentral, Stockholm).

OECD (1991) *Yearbook of Labour Statistics.*

Olsson, B. (ed.) (1993) 'Narkotikasituationen i Norden – utvecklingen 1987–1991', *Nord*, vol. 2, Copenhagen.

Olsson, B. (1994) *Narkotikaproblemets bakgrund* (Stockholm: Department of Sociology, University of Stockholm).

Paloheimo, H. (1984) *Governments in Democratic Capitalist States. 1950–1983. A Data Handbook*, Studies in Political Science no. 8 (Turkku: University of Turkku).

Peck, D. and M. Plant (1986) 'Unemployment and illegal drug use: concordant evidence from a prospective study and national trends', *British Medical Journal*, vol. 293, pp. 929–32.

Scherer, S. (1978) 'The new Dutch and German Drug Laws: Social and Political Conditions for Criminalization and De-criminalization', *Law & Society Review*, vol. 12 (4).

Skog, O.-J. (1987) 'Sprøytenarkomani og kontrollpolitikk', *Nordisk Tidsskrift for Kriminalvidenskab*, pp. 97–119.

Zorilla, C. G. (1993) 'Drugs and Criminal Policy in Spain (1982–1992)', *European Journal on Criminal Policy and Research*, vol. 1 (2).

7 Italy: 'Mafia-dominated Drug Market'?

Ada Becchi

There is a view of drug trafficking, most strongly articulated in relation to Italy, but today also projected onto other settings such as eastern Europe, that a monopoly or cartel called 'the Mafia' controls drug markets, in terms of importation, distribution of drugs and, perhaps, even their retail sale. Of course, if true, then there may be considerable implications for legislation, policing and public order. But is there such a Mafia in Italy today?

ITALIAN CONCERN ABOUT DRUGS IN THE 1970S

As with other European countries, the spread of illegal drugs in Italy occurred gradually from the late 1960s onwards, and did not initially cause any particular concern. It was only with the news of spiralling deaths due to overdose in the early 1970s that the authorities reacted with the approval of new legislation: Law 685 (1975). While this law did not set out to punish users, it did impose more severe penalties on drug dealers and traffickers.

What had prompted the adoption of the new provisions was the view that 'mafia' organisations were heavily involved in the trafficking of drugs. Administrative steps were taken to coordinate enforcement, with the establishment of the Committee of National Coordination for Anti-Drug Action, the foundation of the Central Anti-Drug Services (SCA)[1] and a ceaseless monitoring of the drug 'problem'. Furthermore, the weakness of the existing anti-drug laws gave rise to a parallel debate (Arnao, 1985) as to the demand-related measures that should be taken in support of the already existing supply-related ones. On the one hand, the tendency to see policies which struck at drug supply as a part (possibly the most important part) of the struggle against the Mafia was thus reinforced. On the other, the user abruptly ceased being a 'victim' of drugs and rapidly became an accomplice to the mafia organisations, responsible for their enrichment and for their growth.

In hindsight, Law 685 did not live up to expectations. The modest quantity of drugs seized between 1975 and 1985 indicates a general sluggishness in the fight against the drug trade. In fact, it was only after the law was passed in the late 1970s that the Mafia actually moved into line as an albeit temporary pivot in the world heroin trade. This in itself would be enough to confirm the ineffectiveness of the new law. The point is hammered home by the fact that in the Italy of the 1970s and 1980s, and in some of its regions in particular, illegal narcotics could not only be circulated but also refined for the foreign and domestic markets with impunity, or with very little risk of being discovered. Fighting trafficking, linked as it became to the fight against the Mafia, soon became an arduous task.[2] Since the trafficking of drugs could not be easily halted, the authorities turned to discouraging consumption, through imposing detoxification treatment firstly for drug addicts detained in prison and secondly, through a new bill, for *all* addicts.

THE MAFIA DEBATE

Alongside anti-drug enforcement, market competition (as we shall see later) was also weakening the role of the American Cosa Nostra in the US narcotics market and consequently the role of Italian criminality in international trafficking. Gangs such as the Camorra, the 'Ndrangheta and the Sicilian Mafia tended more and more to supply the domestic market, even though some of them still tried to hold key positions on the international arena.[3] Besides trafficking, 'mafia' organisations were not only continuing their traditional illicit activities such as extortion and smuggling, but were also developing the level and broadening the range of the legal ones. Gaining public works contracts, and involvement in the public supplies industry in general, was found to be extremely remunerative. The details emanating from current judicial investigations are in keeping with this picture.[4]

In the meantime, the enforcement authorities were building up a much more sophisticated profile of both the mafias' activities and the drug scene itself, but this did not prevent people (until the spring of 1993) from seeing 'drugs' and 'the Mafia' as one and the same. The anti-prohibition movement demanded the legalisation of trafficking and accused the *status quo* of promoting organised crime through prohibition. The prohibitionists replied by stressing the need to punish users, and in turn accused the anti-prohibitionists of supporting the mafias. As for the police, they continued to emphasise the size, distribution and strength of the Mafia, representing them as hierarchically invincible (despite the many 'internecine' murders which gave the lie to this view) and portraying them as part of, or at the top of, a huge multinational drug corporation.

Penalties for drug users

These were the arguments employed by those wishing to strengthen the anti-drug legislation by introducing standard penalties against users.[5] This lobby became sufficiently powerful to force the passing of Law 162 in 1990, a law which had at its very heart the belief that traffickers could not be defeated as long as users were not pulled into the enforcement net and prosecuted. Moreover the argument went, drug users are not only a danger to themselves but also to others, and so society must work with the police in the task of identifying addicts. To cap this, not only heroin and other 'hard' drugs, but all narcotics were included in this judgement. Law 162 provided for a range of penalties. Users could avoid more severe punishments such as imprisonment by opting for detoxification treatment. They also incurred administrative penalties, such as the withdrawal of driving licences, and could be subjected to various constraints on their personal freedom.

Application of this law was fraught with difficulties. The 'compulsory treatment' aspect was stressed beyond the capacity to deliver, yet the judicial authorities, sceptical of the deterrence effect, often avoided sending drug addicts either to a treatment centre or to prison. At the same time, the bureaucracy inherent in such a law was placing a considerable workload on the police and the other enforcement agencies.

Next, decriminalisation

The criminalisation of users, therefore, soon became unpopular amongst the very people who had to implement it. In the summer of 1992, two years after its approval and one year after the end of the trial period, this unpopularity manifested itself in calls for revision. These calls led directly to the referendum of 18 April 1993, which, by 55 per cent to 45 per cent, supported decriminalising drug users.

Against this backdrop of a lessening of political and popular belief in the need for purely repressive solutions to the 'drug problem', it is possible to tell the story of anti-trafficking (and anti-Mafia) measures in the Italy of the early 1990s. From the outset, however, we must recognise that with the recent political upheavals, the drug question has declined as a major policy issue in Italy. The receding fears, however, can partly be ascribed to the equally recent successes against the Mafia and the emergence of the view that the Mafia's power is/was a consequence of political behaviour, rather than of economic opportunities, such as drug trade.

THE STRUCTURES OF POLICING

The enforcement of Italian anti-drug laws is now the responsibility of the Central Anti-Drug Services Directorate (DCSA). The main task of the Directorate is the coordination of investigations and intelligence, both at the national and international level. In particular, the DCSA:

> trains and instructs the Polizia di Stato (under the control of the Home Ministry) in the anti-drug field;
> coordinates anti-drug operations;
> monitors anti-drug operations performed by the police;
> carries out studies and research on the fight against drugs;
> directs international operations against drug trafficking.

Its international aspects seem to have been crucial in defining the effectiveness and performance of DCSA operations. Information obtained from foreign police forces represents the most important source of opportunities for intercepting narcotics shipments and for seizing drug consignments.

Although the fight against drugs could still be presented as one of the mainstays of the police's fight against the Mafia, the establishment of the Anti Mafia Investigative Directorate (DIA) in 1992 heralded a specialisation of tasks. However, as the fight against the drug trade is no longer the only front on which the Mafia is being pursued; trafficking has ceased to be seen as a 'Mafia problem', and has metamorphosised into a separate 'drug problem' all of its own.

Furthermore, two other enforcement agencies are involved in the implementation of anti-drug regulations, and carry this involvement out according to their own priorities: the Carabinieri (Defence Ministry) are engaged in the maintenance of public order and are widely established throughout the country, while the Guardia di Finanza (Public Finance Ministry) are principally responsible for the fight against tax evasion and smuggling. It is hardly surprising that this leads to a vast amount of overlap with the Polizia's work, often producing competitive rather than cooperative behaviour.[6]

THE STRUCTURES OF DRUG MARKETS

Conventional views

For a long time Italian drug trafficking was considered, and to a certain degree is still considered, as the major activity of the organised crime networks of the mafias. It is presumed that any lucrative criminal activity is inevitably an object of desire for these organisations and that they, for their part, control the illegal sector to such a degree that they can acquire control over the most profitable and/or the most coveted activities. This presumption is also tied to the international role these organisations are thought to play and with the identification of their domestic activities as a by-product of this role.

This view of the market is held first and foremost by the police, who consider the mafia-type organisations responsible to a very great extent, if not wholly, for Italian drug trafficking. The Sicilian Mafia, the argument goes, has reached an agreement with the Camorra and 'Ndrangheta to manage heroin trafficking alone and also deals with importing cannabis products. In the past, the Camorra held a preeminent role in cocaine dealing, while now all the organisations take part in it. 'Ordinary' people are often involved in dealing, and non-European immigrants in particular are frequently used for street dealing. In short, it is believed that there is a centralised organisation of supply operations which makes use of, and lays down the law to, local networks of wholesalers and dealers – something like the pyramid that Arlacchi and Lewis (1985) identified for the English market.

Research findings

This overall picture of supply is however in direct opposition to what has been reconstructed in studies on specific local markets (Arlacchi and Lewis, 1985, 1988 (with Turi), 1990a and b; Osservatorio sulla camorra, 1989; CNDT, 1988). The 'mafia' organisations are not involved at all in some local heroin markets, even amongst the importers (Verona). In other cases (Turin, Bologna) the role of these organisations is erratic and conflictual. In Naples, which is also a transit point, the Camorra has renounced any form of monopolistic control of drug dealing to devote itself to other (often legal) activities. Consequently we are not in the presence of a stable monopoly, because the Italian mafias prioritise other areas of activity and also because barriers to entry are particularly difficult to impose as long as 'the supply exceeds the demand' (Cesoni, 1992).

Besides, if the pyramid exists, the concentration of power at the top can hardly be pronounced since the police estimate that 10,000 people are involved at the highest levels (importers, distributors, wholesalers) and 65,000 in total (Istat, 1992).[7] Per capita income (1990) is estimated at between 160–300 million lire a year for traffickers and 34–52 million lire a year for dealers. Consequently dealer income corresponds to that estimated in research from other countries,[8] and that of traffickers is not extraordinarily high (estimated gains do not approximate net income, especially when financial backing is provided by third parties).

Put simply, the market seems to be overcrowded. Assuming that this view is correct, we are faced with a dilemma. If, as the police seem to believe, organised crime manages the drug trade as a monopoly, why is it forced to consent to or to promote overcrowding in the industry?[9] The answer can only be, either that organised crime is inefficient, or that it is forced to give a piece of the action to many other people and to redistribute trafficking proceeds on a large scale. This raises further questions.

Are overcrowding of the market, and the results of the local research investigations, at all consistent with the idea of a monopoly? Is the organisation that controls at least the upper levels of the pyramid of drug distribution in Italy really a monopolistic organisation? If it is not, this would suggest that Italian organised crime does not fit into one of the categories of Schelling's classic essay (1980), since it would indicate that it is not essential to hold a monopolistic position in order to intervene in a sector such as drug dealing. If it is, another of Schelling's categories would fall, namely that which states that a monopoly guarantees the disciplined order of the market.

If the definition of an organised crime monopoly is something that disciplines the market, then it is all too evident that this control does not exist in the Italian market. How, then, can organised crime be said to be involved in Italian drug trafficking?

Monopoly versus competition

In fact, drug markets (each specific market, by area and by substance) are not monopolies, not only because there are a great many dealers but also because there are large numbers of importers and wholesalers working in competition with one another. Even if criminal organisations do intervene, they do not do so in a unitary fashion – the mafias are well known for its infighting. There may be a temporary agreement over the division of the spoils but such arrangements do not generally last. In short, drug markets are ruled by disordered competition where entry is free and change continual.

This leads to the tentative conclusion that the reason why drug markets are not taken over by a criminal monopoly is simply because the potential monopolist, the Mafia in Italy's case, is too disorganised and inefficient to stop competitors, attracted by the high profits obtainable for a less costly organisation, constantly penetrating the market. If so, it is possible that the symptoms of serious disorder we read about daily in Italian newspapers stem precisely from this competitive confrontation. Furthermore, even if the traditional picture of a quasi-monopolistic Mafia-dominated market were correct, it would not be applicable to the whole country but only to the areas in which the mafias thrive.

The main data sources for judging the extent of the mafias' role in drug trafficking are the proceedings of the great Mafia and

Camorra trials, although they are concerned primarily with the participation of these criminal organisations in *international* drug dealing and tell us less about their role in the national context. As far as they go, however, they do confirm that (a), the mafia-type criminality has limited managerial talents at its disposal, and (b), its strength lies in the opportunities for making use of wide networks of complicity which strengthen their bonds the more they intertwine with those other networks of relationships going under the name of 'territorial and familial control'. Again, this demonstrates that Italian mafia organisations can operate successfully in drug dealing only when they are protected by 'the environment'.

This argument is consistent with the fact that the Italian mafias have proved to be only rarely successful when operating in the international market. Quoting Lewis, Ruggiero reports that the Italian (or Sicilian–American) Mafia tried to penetrate the British drug market but did not succeed because it lacked experience concerning the 'rules of English import-export'. Recent studies (Cesoni *et al.*, 1992) do not even indicate a viable Italian role in supplying Europe's various outlet markets. Police estimates concerning transit towards other European countries refer only to heroin and quantify it as being, at best, 'modest' (Calzaroni, 1992). Nothing supports the idea that Italian criminal organisations play a prominent role in drug dealing towards the Northern European countries. In fact, until the events in Yugoslavia, Northern Italy was crossed by the Balkan Route and Italian organised crime drew its supplies from there. This merely confirms the fact that Holland, Belgium and Spain are much more important and that the Italian mafias are creatures of habit, a fish out of water when floundering in the shallows far from home.

The other peculiar aspect of Italian drug dealing (which draws the peninsula closer to the United States than to other European countries) is to be found in the final links of distribution. The retail trade in Italy is very overcrowded (Ruggiero speaks of criminal 'massification') as opposed to the specialisation that characterises distribution in Britain. Unlike America, however, it would be difficult to correlate this overcrowding to the conditions of the youth labour market. Such a massification of criminal labour stems less from the conditions of the labour market (one can hardly say that unemployment is worse in Turin than in Liverpool) than from the disorderly set-up of the industry, a set-up with serious consequences from the point of view of user health protection.

CONCLUSION: NO MORE MAFIAS?

The role of Italian organised crime in international drug dealing was considerably reduced during the 1980s. The Sicilian Mafia is no longer an important supplier to the United States market, as it was from 1978 to 1982. During the early 1980s, according to the then Attorney General, 80 per cent of the heroin that reached the East Coast of America depended on the 'Sicilian Connection' (President's Commission, 1986). Now US sources speak of a share of around 5 per cent (Falcone and Padovani, 1991). During the last few years only a few Cosa Nostra families, specifically those based in New York, have continued dealing in heroin and their role has progressively diminished (Savona, 1992).

Furthermore, information from the Mafia trials reveals that when Italian criminal organisations were involved in the international heroin market, primarily directed towards the United States, they relied on La Cosa Nostra there for distribution, while their own tasks were limited to specific operations (especially refining) and/or to financial participation. This arrangement has lapsed for a number of reasons, the principal ones being: (a) refining has moved to the drug-producing countries; (b) financial speculation in drug dealing has proved to be liable to heavy risks; and, (c) the ties of some mafia members (rather than mafia families) to La Cosa Nostra were probably one of the main causes of the mafias war that broke out at the beginning of the 1980s and degenerated into a bloody battle against the Italian state.

These observations seem to be strengthened by the changes which have occurred over the last year in the police's view of the various roles played by criminal fraternities in the drugs trade. The ethnography of drug trafficking recorded in the last official report (DCSA, 1993) shows the huge number of criminal organisations involved in the Italian trade, such as Italian mafias, foreign mafias and urban gangsters. If the Italian mafias are defined as dealers whose areas of origin are the four Italian regions of Sicilia, Calabria, Campania and Puglia, they represented only a third of arrests in 1992, while foreigners made up 15 per cent. More significantly, two-thirds of the heroin seized in 1992, 60 per cent of the cocaine and 58 per cent of the cannabis was confiscated while arresting foreign criminals.

Why then do the police continue to identify drug dealing with the Mafia? There are various possible reasons. On the one hand there are unquestionable advantages in representing drug dealing in this way. The enemy is more easily identifiable by a public which knows how difficult it is to defeat the Mafia. Therefore citizens can be asked both for greater financial contributions and greater renunciation of their own personal liberties. On the other hand, this picture has possibly been stressed because it was thought to be the one preferred by the public or, more pointedly, by the political elite.

NOTES

1. The Service was set up with staff chosen from the three police forces, and its leadership alternated between representatives from each. Recently the SCA became the Central Anti-Drug Services Directorate (DCSA).
2. Official sources justify the poor results in the fight against the Mafia (and consequently against drugs) in the late 1970s and early 1980s as the consequence of the priority given to defeating terrorism (Becchi and Turvani, 1993).
3. Camorra and 'ndrangheta are names used for mafia-type organisations based in Campania (Naples) and Calabria.
4. The research quoted in this article (Arlacchi, etc.) is also based on the results of the judicial investigations. The data which can be drawn from these investigations can sometimes be complemented by other data obtained from the health services or from the police (CORA, 1992).
5. Other measures introduced between 1990 and 1992, such as the money laundering ones, are not considered here, as they were not conceived as anti-drug measures *per se*, but as tools to fight general economic crime (Savona, 1993).
6. The growth of the three police forces has been rapid (about 2 per cent a year) over the last decade, but it can only indirectly be related to the fight against drugs. It is usually associated with more general motivations such as the fight against the Mafia and the maintenance of public order.
7. The average numbers arrested by the police annually are 5,000 for trafficking and 35,000 all told.

8. Reuter's research (1991) in Washington estimated the monthly income of a fulltime dealer to be $3,600, comparable to the income of an Italian dealer.
9. Ruggiero (1992) has also diagnosed the overcrowding of the industry, with reference to the Turinese market, albeit approaching the question with different premises and different ambitions to the author of this paper.

REFERENCES

Arlacchi, P. and R. Lewis (1985) *Camorra, contrabbando e mercato della droga in Campania* (Rome: Antimafia Commission, Mimeo).
Arlacchi, P., R. Lewis and R. Turi (1988) *Il mercato della droga a Crotone* (Municipality of Crotone).
Arlacchi, P. and R. Lewis (1990a) *Imprenditorialità illécita e droga. Il mercato dell'eroina a Verona* (Bologna: Il Mulino).
Arlacchi, P. and R. Lewis (1990b) 'Droga e criminalità a Bologna', *Micromega*, vol. 4.
Arnao, G. (1985) *Il dilemma eroina* (Milan: Feltrinelli).
Becchi, A. and M. Turvani (1993) *Proibito? Il mercato mondiale della droga* (Rome: Donzelli).
Bompiani, A., Minister of Social Affairs (1992) *Problemi delle tossicodipendenze* (Report to the 12th Commission, Chamber of Deputies, 2 December, Rome).
Calzaroni, M. (1992) *Schede analitiche per le singole attività illegali* (Rome: Istat, Mimeo).
Censis (1989) *Il peso dell'illecito sul paese Italia* (Milan: Angeli).
Cesoni, M. et al. (1992) *L'Italie* (Paris: Editions Descartes).
Centre National de Documentation sur les Toxicomanies (CNDT) (1988) 'Special Italie', *Bulletin*, vol. 14.
CORA (1992) *Osservatorio delle leggi sulla droga*, vol. 6 (Rome: Millelire).
Direzione Centrale Servizi Antidroga (DCSA) (1993) *Attività del Ministero dell'interno nel settore degli stupefacenti. Anno 1992.*
Ehrenberg, A. (ed.) (1992) *Penser la drogue. Penser les drogues* (Paris: Editions Descartes Collection Science Humaines).
Falcone, G. and M. Padovani (1991) *Cose di cosa nostra* (Milan: Rizzoli).
Lewis, R., R. Hartnoll and S. Bryer (1985) 'Scoring Smack: The Illicit Heroin Market in London, 1980–1983', *British Journal of Addiction*, vol. 80 (3), pp. 281–90.
Osservatorio sulla camorra (1989) *Persone e luoghi della droga a Napoli* (Naples: Sintesi).
President's Commission on Organised Crime (1986) *Report to the President and the Attorney General. The Impact: Organised Crime Today* (Washington DC).
Reuter, P. et al. (1991) *Money from Crime: A Study of the Economics of Drug Dealing in Washington DC* (Santa Monica: Rand).
Rey G. M. (1992) *Analisi economica ed evidenza empirica dell'attivita illegale in Italia* (Rome: Istat).

Ruggiero, V. (1992) *La roba. Economie e culture dell'eroina* (Parma: Pratiche Editrice).

Savona, E. (1992) 'The Organised Crime–Drug Connection: National and International Perspectives', in H. Traver and M. Gaylor (eds), *Drugs, Law and the State* (Hong Kong: Hong Kong University Press).

Savona, E. (1993) 'Mafia Money Laundering versus Italian Legislation', *European Journal on Criminal Policy and Research*, vol. 1 (3), pp. 35–6.

Schelling, T. (1980) 'Economics and Criminal Enterprise', in R. Andreano and J. Siegfried (eds), *The Economics of Crime* (New York: Wiley & Sons).

Senato della Repubblica (1993) *Elementi di documentasione sulla questione della punibilità per l'uso di stupefacenti, dossier 47, January.*

Stajano, C. (ed.) (1992) *Mafia. L'atto di accusa dei giudici di Palermo* (Rome: Editori Riuniti).

8 Denmark and the Nordic Union: Regional Pressures in Policy Development

Lau Laursen

In the three Scandinavian countries, Sweden, Denmark and Norway, the discovery of the drug problem can be localised fairly precisely to 1966. Before the middle of the '60s, drug use reported by the authorities as being problematic was linked to either deviant or criminalised groups or persons engaged in the health services.

In both Denmark and Norway drug use had been fairly limited and confined to amphetamine, barbiturates and morphine-like drugs. In Sweden the situation was different. From the end of the 1930s, the illegal use of amphetamine preparations increased dramatically; and from the beginning of the 1950s, this problem was shifting over into an intravenous use of central stimulants.

From 1966, the authorities in all three Scandinavian countries increasingly reported a radical shift in drug use patterns. Use of cannabis and then LSD increased among young people, cannabis breaking through earlier in Denmark and Sweden (around 1965–6) than in Norway.

This new phenomenon started a fierce and often emotional public debate, a debate that took on the character of a moral panic. The mass media's sensational descriptions of the phenomenon, the recurring debates in the Scandinavian parliaments, the ever-larger amounts of money invested in control of illegal drug use among young people, and the establishment of Nordic, national and local coordination agencies, indicated that Scandinavian society really felt this new phenomenon to be a threat to its well-being.

The result of the discursive maelstrom in the period 1965–75 was a heavily changed and extended control system in all the three countries. The strong societal reaction to an unacceptable

131

behaviour was expressed most clearly by the inclusion of the offence of illegal handling of drugs in the penal codes of Norway and Sweden in 1968 and of Denmark in 1969 with high maximum penalties. The powers of the drug police were expanded in order to enforce intensified action against 'organised drug crime' – a new term, full of power (Laursen, 1992).

Societal and individual attitudes to (and control over) the use of alcohol and other drugs vary widely within Scandinavia. As Jepsen (1992, p. 34) notes, the Scandinavian countries exhibit differences in their traditions of official reaction to social deviance. These are most striking in the field of alcohol control: Norway and Sweden have highly controlled alcohol production and distribution, based on state monopolies, while Denmark allows nearly free production and distribution. But these manifest differences across the region are equally well reproduced in the field of drug control too.

In the debate on Nordic drug control policy, it has been a central conclusion that the Nordic countries today agree on the prohibition policy, first and foremost through their homogeneous view of the totally prohibited drugs. They also agree on a strict penal attitude to drug crimes, especially the serious and professional ones. However, these common viewpoints have been consolidated over time, because, even on these central questions consensus has not always existed among the Scandinavian countries.

But once the general principle of control is accepted, Scandinavian consensus ends. In almost every other field there are great formal and informal differences between Denmark on the one hand and Norway/Sweden on the other. The central areas are the attitude towards the user, the criminalisation of use and court procedure in drug cases. In the treatment field, the use of methadone maintenance or compulsion stand as ready examples of divergence. Court sentences in Denmark and in Norway/Sweden vary greatly for almost any kind of drug crime. At certain times in the last 25 years, this has caused an extraordinarily intensive debate and controversy among the Scandinavian countries.

THEME AND TEXTS

The character of the public debate has had a different appearance and content in Denmark as opposed to Norway/Sweden. This essay attempts to localise differences in the drug discourse in Denmark, Norway and Sweden. It is given a historical perspective, in order to try to uncover some original discursive paths in each country, and to show what connection there is between the drug discourse and the drug control policy of the countries in question.

In the second part of the essay the discursive differences are related to each other on a Scandinavian level in order to examine how the national discourses and control policies have influenced each other. In this connection focus will be on whether the overall Scandinavian discourse has influenced the Danish drug discourse and control policy.

It is the intention to analyse central texts of the Scandinavian drug discourse in the period 1968–70 and 1980–2. News articles and editorials in newspapers together with parliamentary debates form the most important texts in my illustration of the connection between discourse and control policy. This is due to the fact that these types of texts and their producers (journalists and politicians) are some of the most important actors in creating ideological and cultural understanding of the drug phenomenon. The mass media forms an important arena for various other drug policy actors, including the agents of the control system, first and foremost the police and the judicial system. It is an arena where the actors accept and legitimise a certain control policy before it is implemented in the political and institutional arena.

Scandinavian drug policy has been modelled by two waves. The first wave took place in 1968–9, the second between 1980 and 1982. In both periods a strong discursive concentration can be found, which stressed comprehensive policy evaluation in the Scandinavian parliaments, press and central administrations, and also preventative responses towards drug addiction.

THE FIRST WAVE

Roots of disagreement 1968–9

Three parliamentary debates, one from each Scandinavian country in 1968–9, have been exposed to content analysis. These debates all cover intensified penal code initiatives. Relevant media materials will be included in the analysis.

As mentioned above, in 1968 and 1969 the Scandinavian parliaments accepted the use of more severe penalties, applying mainly to illegal trade and trafficking.

Norway

In May 1968 the Norwegian Parliament introduced a totally new section of the Norwegian penal code, a section which raised the maximum penalty for professional drug crime to six years imprisonment. Twenty-one MPs participated in this debate (Stortinget, 1967/68, pp. 386–99) which was characterised by an overwhelming consensus on the need for penal code initiatives. The central theme was that punishment, with its associated preventative effect, was the most important means of control. Even users were to be punished. Only a few speakers differed from this line, by mentioning that information and treatment, rather than punishment, would be best for users. Restrictive control policy was never put to discussion, and legalisation was brought up only when a few speakers fiercely ruled out any such proposals that had been put forward in the public debate.

Despite surveys showing only a small prevalence of cannabis use, and despite the fact that Norwegian police had not yet produced clear evidence of international drug crime activity on Norwegian territory – in spite of these two facts, everybody regarded the situation as extremely threatening, in fact so threatening that quite extraordinary measures were called for by the authorities. During a question debate in 1967 a speaker, Erling Engan, maintained that the persons who 'inconsiderately profit by the drug victims are enemies of society and must be treated as enemies of society' (Stortinget, 1967/68, pp. 386–99).

Drug stories in *Dagbladet*, a large Norwegian daily, have been analysed from the three months up to the parliamentary debate of 1968. It is remarkable that 90 per cent of the drug articles in this period were placed on the front page, and no debate articles were found. Almost all front page articles describe police cases that reveal drug leagues trying to smuggle drugs into Norway. The cases are always described in great detail.

The Norwegian discourse was marked by an obvious character of moral panic. The Swedish and the Danish discourses were somewhat different.

Sweden

A couple of months before the Norwegian Parliament, Sweden's Parliament introduced stricter legislation with a doubling of the maximum penalty for drug crime from two years imprisonment to four years. The Swedish parliamentary debate was an odd debate (Riksdagen, 1968, Nr. 10, pp. 120–37). There were few contributions, but they were long, and the majority of these showed a modified, analytical and technical attitude to the drug problem. One reason for this might be the atypicality of the debate in question. However, a comparison with other Swedish parliamentary debates about drugs from a year earlier and a couple of years later shows that this is not the case. Some debates had the same objective character, while other debates had a character more of trench warfare rather than of reasoned political debate. These many shifts in the character of parliamentary debates are very typical in the Swedish drug discourse during 1967–9. A reading of the large Swedish paper *Dagens Nyheter* confirms this picture.

The debate's main point was the question of how to deal with users, and a central theme was whether the user should only be treated, within the Swedish compulsory treating system, or whether their behaviour also should be criminalised. Agreement was reached on raising the maximum penalty for serious drug crime, but almost no comments of a 'Norwegian' character were heard (e.g. about drug dealers being enemies of society). One can trace a predominant optimism with the treatment philosophy, and all the speakers spent a long time detailing practical–technical solutions for control within the treatment system.

Denmark

In May 1969 – a year after the corresponding legislation had been introduced in Norway and Sweden – the Danish Parliament inserted a new section in the Penal Code which allowed for up to six years imprisonment for serious drug crimes. There were 20 contributions in the Danish parliamentary debate (Folketingstidende, 1968/69, pp. 3150–71), and they took many different directions. The debate can best be described as pluralistic and liberal in the political sense of the word. Only on the question of severe punishment for hardened professional dealers was an almost unanimous agreement reached. The demand for harsh generic penalties is therefore doubly difficult to understand. A Danish belief in the general preventative effect of punishment was conspicuous by its absence relative to that found in Norway.

The question of upholding the existing legal situation (non-criminalisation of use) was central to the Danish debate. One MP, Mrs Else-Merete Ross, expressed precisely the viewpoint which had come to be Danish practice. She said:

'If the use is small, the police ignores it and concentrates rightly on the bigger assignments. In many cases, small scale dealers who use drugs themselves must, for reasons of treatment, not be criminalised.'

(Folketingstidende, 1968/69, p. 3156)

The differentiation between cannabis and other drugs, first and foremost heroin, was another important point of debate. Because of a considerable uncertainty in the Danish debate about the harmful effect of cannabis, quite a few MPs said that cannabis should be left out of the penal code. Their view was that cannabis trafficking should be kept in the somewhat milder Euphoric Drugs Act, with a maximum penalty of two years. A significant minority of participants in the debate said that the total legalisation of cannabis should be seriously considered. However, very few demanded immediate legalisation.

Again, copies of a Danish paper with a high circulation, *Politiken*, have been studied from the three months up to the parliamentary debate. The drug problem is treated regularly and in many different types of articles. During the month before the debate, the problem was headlined in 32 articles, 9 of which appeared on the front page. From a discourse-analytical viewpoint, these articles give an impression of a multi-faceted debate, a debate which at the same time is rather blurred and which has the same character as the parliamentary debate. Nonetheless, it has to be conceded that the Danish front page articles are of the same type as the Norwegian ones. They are agenda-setting, built around sensational drug cases, and represent clearly formulated wishes for expansion of the control apparatus. But, actually, this illuminates the discrepancy in the Danish drug discourse at that time. With a large majority in favour, the legislators chose to mould the *theory* of the law to the Norwegian and Swedish model. In practice, though (in the good old Danish manner), a compromise was reached which secured flexible and adaptable implementation through guidelines to the prosecution. This clearly took an accommodating standpoint on the use, trade and import of cannabis, and on the use and small-scale dealing of other drugs, such as heroin. These guidelines have since become very controversial in Denmark and have met with a lot of criticism, first from Norway and then from Sweden. By the standards of the other two Scandinavian countries, the guidelines are regarded as the definite document exemplifying wishy-washy Danish liberalism in the field of drug use prevention.

At the annual session of the Nordic Council in 1971 (Nordiska Rådet, 1971, pp. 261–78), several Norwegian politicians fiercely attacted Danish drug policy during a debate on cooperation in the fight against drugs. The Norwegians criticised Danish court practice and stressed Denmark's Nordic obligation to conduct a more repressive control policy. 'Denmark makes up the southern boundary of Scandinavia, and the Danish attitude spoils Norwegian control policy', they claimed.

The Swedish politicians kept in the background during this debate but they later came into the open: from the mid-1970s the criticism against Denmark was advanced in Sweden as well as in Norway.

Discussion of the first wave

It has been the aim of the first part of this paper to illustrate the differences in control policy between the Scandinavian countries. The review of parliamentary debates and media coverage from the late 1960s in the three countries clearly shows the discursive differences – especially between Norway and Denmark. The roots for the differences in Scandinavia's current drug control policies can be found in the diverging policies developed at the end of the 1960s.

In Norway, the overall policy and the views behind it have not changed much since. In fact, the policy seems to have become even more Draconian. From early on, Norway moved into a fundamendalistic discursive framework, marked by a moralistic attitude to drug users as well as dealers. Drug use has always been criminalised with a relatively high level of punishment, as with first-time offenders. There has never been a serious attempt to distinguish between different drugs or between recreational use and heavy addiction. Norwegian control policy has followed a restrictive path since the end of the 1960s, a path later substantiated by moral panics in which the main discursive features are rhetorically powerful declarations of war. The attitudes of the Norwegian enforcement authorities, politicians and the public have always been concurrent.

Sweden was very indecisive at the end of the 1960s, but soon hardened its resolve and approached the Norwegian view on drug policy.

Finally, Denmark has not radically changed its formal control policy since the beginning of the 1970s, but it must be stated that Danish control practice has come close to that of Norway and Sweden. The present chapter is particularly preoccupied with the development of the Danish drug discourse. As already mentioned, around 1970 the Danish discourse dissociated itself markedly from its Norwegian counterpart.

The public debate became characterised by conflicts between different viewpoints all acceptable within a common framework. Whereas the Norwegian and Swedish debates may be termed 'fundamentalist-moralist', the Danish discourse was originally pluralistic and politically pragmatic. The decision of the Danish parliament to instruct prosecutors to take a soft line when enforcing the law against users is the best example of the Danish capacity for pragmatic compromise. As mentioned above, this decision was to form the basis for the Norwegian and Swedish criticisms of Danish drug policy throughout the 1970s and 1980s.

THE SECOND WAVE

Nordic alarm

The developments in Scandinavia during the early 1970s just outlined (with clear discursive and political differences between Norway/Sweden and Denmark) was continued and intensified into the 1980s. Around 1980 Sweden swung into a restrictive course and became the dynamic centre for the formulation of restrictive and penally-dominated drug policies in Scandinavia. Today, Norway and Sweden can be found at the head of the group of European countries with the most restrictive enforcement policies.

Believing that between 1975 and 1981 'an enormous increase of cannabis and other drugs had taken place' (Nordiska Rådet 30, session, 301) Norway and Sweden sought to support a more intensive Nordic effort against drug abuse.

At the Nordic Council session in 1981 the preparation of a common Nordic action programme was proposed, a programme which some years later was passed by the Nordic Council of Ministers (with the Danish signature) under the illuminating title 'Action Programme for a Drug Free North'. This idea was adopted by the Social and Environmental Committee of the Nordic Council and put forward as a Recommendation at the session in March 1982. The proposal contained three points:

1. Each Nordic country should be actively prevented from accepting any kind of drug use, unless for medical reasons.
2. The resources for police and customs should be increased, and Nordic cooperation in the fight against drug use and drug crime should be intensified.
3. A harmonisation of Nordic drug legislation should be supported.

In 1977–9 various indicators pointed to the spread of drug misuse in Scandinavia. Due to this development, within a couple of years Norway and Sweden started to reinforce drug control and police efforts against drugs.

Penalties

Today, Norway has the highest maximum penalties in Scandinavia, and sentences illegal traffickers more harshly than its neighbours (Thunved, 1991, p. 1). The maximum penalty for serious drug crime was extended in 1981 to 15 years, and in 1984 to 21 years imprisonment. In 1984, the maximum penalty for use was doubled, from 3 to 6 months (Hansen, 1988, pp. 25–34). On both occasions, the increase was based on morally-grounded arguments that society has to make its views known by applying stronger sentences.

As has been shown by Christie and Bruun (1985), Swedish developments have been more shifty. The battle between various political views on drugs has been hard-fought in Sweden. Earlier Swedish parliamentary debates were characterised by a broad discursive framework. Well into the 1970s, after the breakthrough of heroin in the drug market, it was accepted that a distinction could be made between cannabis and heroin. Police activity was largely directed towards commercial drug crime. The user was met with treatment.

This strategy changed radically around 1980 with a heavier stress on the theme 'Without users, there's no use'. As early as 1979 Sweden gave up the liberal legal practice of not pursuing charges in cases of possession for own use (Laursen, 1992, p. 81). The Drug Criminal Act was reconsidered in 1981, and raising the maximum penalty for serious drug crime was discussed (though without a resolution). It was chosen, however, to demonstrate a restrictive resolve by raising the *minimum* sentence for major drug crime to 2 years and the *maximum* sentence for minor cases to 3 years. Control policy was further tightened up in 1983, 1985 and 1988. Among other things criminalisation of use in 1988 has to be seen as the definitive change in Swedish drug control policy (Solarz, 1987, pp. 25–33).

This sketch of the development in control policy in Norway and Sweden indicates that the views which became established in Northern Scandinavia during the 1980s would have consequences for future Nordic cooperation as well as for Danish drug policy. From the end of 1980 until the beginning of 1982, the criticism of Danish drug policy played an important role in the tightening up of enforcement policies in both Norway and Sweden, and opposition to the liberal Danish policy became crystallised around the symbol of Christiania in Copenhagen. This so-called 'Free City' was founded in 1971 in a disused military barracks by a group of people who through social experimentation were looking for a new way of life. Since then, the Free City has often become the issue for debates of an exaggerated and ideological nature.

WARFARE AGAINST DENMARK

During the last two months of 1981 and the following period of media coverage which lasted until the March 1982 Nordic Council session, the authorities in both countries judged the drug situation to be threatening.

In November, the Norwegian Parliament approved a supplementary grant of almost 18 million Nkr. to combat drug use, of which 9 million was allocated to an extension of police and customs enforcement (Stortinget, 1981/2, p. 761).

In December, the Swedish Parliament specifically debated the 'Danish threat', under the title 'Initiatives against the spread of drugs from Denmark' (Riksdagen, 1981/2, No. 43, p. 63). This debate was a practice run for the passing in May 1982 of a number of initiatives against alcohol and drug abuse (Riksdagen, 1981/2, No. 153. p. 153).

The messages of the Norwegian politicians are very clear and unambiguous. As in the early 1970s, the attitude to Denmark's drug policy was used as a tactical weapon in the Norwegian drug strategy. There were 24 contributions in the Norwegian parliamentary debate of 1981. Christiania and Danish drug policy are mentioned directly or indirectly in about half of them.

The Swedish discourse was even harsher than the Norwegian when it came to condemning Denmark. There were 17 contributions in the Swedish Parliamentary debate. Esse Petersson, the MP who had called for it, set the tone:

'The drug hole of Christiania is a stinking abscess that spreads infection to a large area of the region. . . .The free handling of drugs in Christiania is not only a Danish problem, but a matter for the entire North. It is first and foremost cannabis trade for the Nordic market which is channelled out to an increasing extent through Christiania.'

(Riksdagen, 1981/2, No. 43, p. 66).

Once set up, this discursive framework was latched onto by other speakers. The criticism was overwhelming and concentrated on the following points:

1. The idea of legalisation gains ground because of the lack of anti-cannabis arguments.
2. Not only cannabis, but also so-called hard drugs can be found in Christiania.
3. Denmark breaks international agreements by allowing the sale of cannabis in Christiania.
4. The Danish attitude towards drugs is too liberal, and authorities accept the use of drugs.
5. 80 per cent of all cannabis in southern Sweden comes from Christiania.
6. Danish customs control in the Baltic is too weak.

7. Denmark is too lenient in drug cases.
8. Denmark does not believe like Sweden, that cannabis is the stepping stone to heroin use: Denmark only makes the broad distinction between cannabis and 'hard drugs'.

It becomes clear that the Swedish Parliament was directing a very serious – and in its tone, very emotional – criticism towards Denmark's drug enforcement policy.

The Scandinavian war on drugs

The parliamentary debates in Oslo and Stockholm were a clear prelude to the passing of the recommendation of the action programme 'A Drug Free North' at the Nordic Council Session in March 1982. In the Nordic Council's debate, the Norwegian and Swedish censure of Denmark's policy was equally unanimous, though somewhat more subdued. This may be due to the fact that the Danish Government – with a few verbal reservations – had accepted the ideas behind the Recommendation document at a meeting of the Nordic Ministers of Social Affairs and Ministers of Justice on 19 February 1982.

The reservations implied that the Danish Government was in favour of a harmonisation of minimum and maximum penalties, although it did not believe that more rigorous penalties had any preventative effect (the Danish Minister of Justice, Ole Espersen, Nordisk Rådet, Session 30, p. 315). This was reflected in Denmark's voting pattern at the Nordic Council session: half the Danish MPs voted in favour of the Recommendation, while the other half voted against it. The Recommendation, however, was passed by a large majority, as all Norwegian, Swedish, Finnish and Icelandic delegates (except one) voted in favour (Nordiska Rådet, Session 30, p. 317).

The mass media in Sweden and Norway supported the action of their Parliaments and Governments in pursuit of a more restrictive drug policy. In the six-month period up to the Nordic Council, the Norwegian daily *Dagbladet* frequently commented on the 'Danish problem', and set out its stall in a leading article at the time of the Norwegian parliamentary debate:

To the North, Christiania is a market place for free trade of narcotic drugs. This depressing fact not only concerns Denmark. Everything indicates that many of the narcotic drugs being traded in Norway, as well as in Sweden, come from Christiania, and therefore it is time for authorities and public opinion in these countries to become aware of this.

(Dagbladet, 26 November 1981)

The editorial ends with a strong appeal for the case to be taken up at the Nordic Council session. The discursive highpoint was reached during the Council itself. A leading article in *Dagbladet* (6 March 1982) had the last word on the Danish problem, especially over the question of harmonisation of legal practice and attitudes to cannabis:

Denmark still represents a low point in relation to drug penalties in the North. . . . Therefore it is natural that Denmark now changes the legal practice in such cases.

There is an obvious correlation between the picture of the Danish problem as given in the Norwegian *Dagbladet* and the Swedish journal *Dagens Nyheter*. The high coverage of both Danish drug policy and Christiania is encapsulated in two leading articles. On the day after the debate in the Swedish Parliament on the spread of drugs from Christiania, *Dagens Nyheter* commented on the drug problem. The phenomenon was a symptom of 'rottenness in Denmark', and the argument was that the drug trade not only began in Christiania, but that the entire North had become a market place for drugs (*Dagens Nyheter*, 5 December 1982).

In its editorial after the debate in the Nordic Council, the paper concluded that the agreement on harmonising legal practice was directed against Denmark. The following argument was used, which restates the essence of the criticism against Denmark:

It is obvious that authorities in Denmark do too little, and that the relative passivity has to do with the Danish attitude to drugs.

(*Dagens Nyheter*, 5 March 1982)

The Nordic Council's Recommendation was an expression of the fact that the war against drugs in Norway and Sweden had been raised to a Nordic level by 1981. In Norway and Sweden, Governments, Parliaments, the press and the public thought that the restrictive precautions already taken could only be sustained and further developed if Denmark changed its attitude on fundamental issues of drug policy. Though the content of the Recommendation was directed towards all five Northern countries, the emphasis was clear. The rather liberal Danish attitude towards cannabis and towards the use of drugs in general would have to be tightened up. Penalties for handling illegal drugs, from individual use to large-scale smuggling, should be raised to a Norwegian and Swedish level. The control system of the police should be extended, and cooperation between the Nordic countries intensified.

Danish reactions

As in Norway and Sweden, the drug debate flared up in Denmark during the years 1980–2. The authorities could demonstrate a serious increase in seizures, arrests and users in treatment. Thus, from 1980 to 1981, the police registered a substantial increase both in trafficking offences and in the cases of minor dealing and possession for own use (*Rigspolitichefens Arsberetning*, 1981, p. 43).

An attempt now is made to gauge how the Norwegian and Swedish discourse affected the Danish debate on control policy, legislation and legal practice.

In the period November 1980 to June 1982, Folketinget (the Danish Parliament) had nine debates on drug policy, in which the political right proposed a more restrictive policy. In March 1982, a debate was also held on the 'Free City' of Christiania. Most of the proposals were voted down, although a Bill put forward by the Social Democratic minority Government, which recommended a new section in the Penal Code on proceeds from drug trafficking, was passed.

Along with the intense discourse in Parliament, the drug problem received extensive coverage in the Danish media. The number of articles on the drug problem increased dramatically during the period 1979–82 (*Dansk Tidsskriftsindex 1975–82*). Drugs also occupied a prominent place in the news coverage of social problems. This becomes apparent through a quantitative content analysis of the *Dagbladet Politiken* for the period 1 October 1981 to 1 May 1982, a period corresponding to that applied for the analysis of Norwegian and Swedish media and also to the discursive peak in Danish parliamentary debate during these years. The news coverage alone comprises of 111 articles on drugs, 12 of which led on the front page. The headlines of these front page articles appear as follows:

He got 46 years in Thailand (01.12.81)
Cocaine in the Danish market (28.12.81)
Too few to stop drugs (06.01.82)
She knew too much (09.01.82)
Hash hidden in gutter (15.01.82)
Hard drug sentences (16.01.82)
Cocaine the big problem (20.01.82)
Car with hash-load chased (21.01.82)
Accused of hired murder of drug hooker (05.02.82)
Extra drug squad in Kastrup Airport (06.03.82)
Life for hired murder (03.04.82)
Drug catch of kr. 5m at Kastrup Airport (20.04.82)

The headlines focus on the work and results of the control system. Thus, there is not much to indicate that Danish society, as represented by the media, has less interest in or weaker attitudes towards drug addiction and enforcement. On the contrary, the Danish media image appears to be tougher in this respect than its Norwegian and Swedish counterparts.

And so the Swedish and Norwegian criticism coincided with an unusually heated Danish climate of debate. In several cases, this criticism was taken up by the right-wing opposition in Parliament, and the criticism forced the government and the left-wing opposition into a defensive position, from which it became more and more difficult to question enforcement policy. Among other things, this led to two small socialist parties voting in favour of a new section in the Penal Code (section 191a on drug 'fencing') in spite of their critical attitude towards a further penal tightening (Folketingstidende, 1981/2, pp. 5561/8).

In March 1982, Folketinget debated the future of Christiania. This took place just after the aforementioned session in the Nordic Council.

It would be natural to deal with these two debates together. They share many common features which show that it was not a coincidence Christiania played such a central role in the debate at the Nordic Council session of March 1982.

At the Council session, the Danish Minister of Justice Ole Espersen outlined Denmark's drug policy, while at the same time explaining his country's attitude to the Recommendation and the Norwegian and Swedish criticism. Denmark could accept in principal the Recommendation's first point on rejecting the acceptance of drug use, but it was felt unnecessary to do so. No political party had legalisation in its programme, and 'there is no responsible person in Denmark who would think of accepting any kind of drug use which was not justified by medical reasons' (Nordiska Rådet, 1982, p. 314).

Regarding the Recommendation's second point on increasing resources for customs and the police, Ole Espersen referred to three facts. First, in the last few years, Denmark had increased the drug squad by 100 officers, which had caused a substantial rise in the number of serious cases. Second, Denmark preferred to focus more on the risk of arrest as a preventative factor, a policy which had quadrupled the number of minor cases in the last few years. Third, Denmark had assigned more money to police educational/information work in schools.

The Recommendation's third point on standardised legal conditions in the North was met with two objections. First, it was thought that tightening maximum and minimum penalties for serious drug crime would not have any criminal preventive effect. Second, the Minister of Justice rejected a general tightening of penalties towards users. However, the Norwegian and Swedish criticism elicited a promise from Denmark that it would reexamine the law which allowed for legal possession of 100 grams of cannabis for own use.

Moving on to the Danish parliamentary debate on Christiania, which was prompted by a government white paper on the future of the Free City (Folketingstidende, 1981/82, p. 3091). The battle-lines were clearly drawn up during this debate on 16 March 1982. The right-wing opponents of the Government's policy instantly demanded the closure of Christiania, largely because of its open hashish market. The criticism of the Nordic Council, therefore, came at a critical point for the Danish opponents of Christiania. The main speakers for the five opposing parties all referred to the Nordic condemnation of Christiania, while the proponents of government policy either refuted the criticism or did not mention it at all.

Ole Espersen rebutted this argument while commenting on the criticism from the other Nordic countries. His statement represented the view of the parliamentary majority. He reported that hashish seizures at Christiania in 1981 amounted to no more than 4–5 per cent of all hashish seizures in Copenhagen. It was stressed, however, that Christiania would have to be considered one of the focal points of trade in hashish in the city, but primarily as a retail market – as indicated by the almost uniformly small seizures there. As for the Nordic criticism, the Minister of Justice conceded the view formulated at the Nordic Council that a coordinated and consistent policy of targeting dealing should be pursued across Scandinavia. He found the criticism of Christiania and Denmark valid as far as this point was concerned, and indirectly accepted the point that in future the police would concentrate more on the open hashish dealing in the streets of Christiania.

But at this point, the Minister's concessions came to an end. He went on to say that 'there is no basis for the view that Christiania might validly be considered a unique centre for crime among the Nordic countries, as had been maintained in parts of the daily media, in particular in the other Nordic countries' (Folketingstidende, 1981/2, p. 3720). The national Chief of Police, according to the Minister, had clearly indicated that the large seizures of drugs on which the police had concentrated their efforts in 1981–2 had by-passed Christiania. With this in mind, Ole Espersen concluded that the criticism at the Nordic level indicated 'that the other Nordic countries have met with quite considerable difficulties, that they have great difficulties in solving the problems and that consequently some politicians apparently try to gloss over their own social problems by pointing to special conditions in our country' (Folketingstidende, 1981/2, p. 3721).

DISCUSSION

The Nordic drug control discourse, as demonstrated above, was expanded and radicalised considerably between 1980 and 1982. The review of Scandinavian parliamentary debates and the Nordic Council sessions has uncovered the discursive background to the 'retooling' of control policy in all the countries, both in the form of an expanded legal basis and a more restrictive enforcement practice.

It seems reasonable to conclude that Norwegian and Swedish criticism of Danish drug policy, specifically directed towards Christiania, had far-reaching consequences for Danish drug policy. The Nordic criticism played an important role in the already heated Danish debate, in which the hawks had launched an offensive against the relatively liberal doves of Danish control practice. This led to indirect Nordic support for the arguments of the proponents of a more restrictive drug control policy. Those politicians who wanted to preserve liberal practices, or even to expand on liberalisation, were forced into defending the status quo, and only with partial success.

The Nordic criticism thus led to a series of new restrictions in Danish drug control, although it must be admitted that a police clampdown was already under way independent of the Nordic criticism. The unanimous passing of the penal code amendment on drug 'fencing', however, seems considerably influenced by Scandinavian opinion. Court practice in relation to possession of cannabis for own use was also tightened as a direct consequence of Nordic criticism, and the amount accepted for own use was considerably reduced. In the same manner, in order to modify Nordic criticism, Ole Espersen allowed the police to intensify their efforts against open hashish street dealings in Christiania. It should be acknowledged, however, that the majority of the Danish parliament only accepted the Recommendation of the March 1982 Nordic Council session with strong reservations.

The events of 1982, in the wider perspective, had significant consequences for changes in Danish drug policy throughout the 1980s. Finally, we will therefore look at three characteristic examples which indicate Danish concession to Nordic demands after the polemic discussions of 1980/2.

1.   During the 1985 session of the Nordic Council, all Danish parliamentarians backed the final proposal from the Nordic Council of Ministers for a 'Nordic Action Plan against Drugs' (Nordic Council Report, 1985, p. 379) which (on the initiative of the Conservative group within the Council) had been proposed at the 1983 Council meeting. This action plan is based upon a goal of 'A drug-free Scandinavia', a goal which has later proved itself to be a strong ideological foundation for restrictive measures of drug control.

The Nordic Council decided to apply the 1982 Recommendation (including the item on working for a harmonisation of the legal situation in the drugs field) as a basis for the Nordic plan of action. But as the thesis of the 'drug free society' has limited adherence among the Danish public, their politicians chose a pragmatic 'policy of the ostrich' and evaded making the usual reservations. This is revealed in a 1984 parliamentary debate on a ministerial statement on the drug problem, in which the Nordic plan of action is not mentioned once (Folktingstidende, 1983/4, p. 4155 in statement, and p. 5798 in debate).

2. At the end of the 1980s, the Danish police changed its drug control strategy and began, particularly in Copenhagen, to use more resources in street actions. This demand-reduction strategy emanated at the Nordic level from Swedish deliberations in the early 1980s. Copenhagen's Chief of Police, Poul Eefsen, has referred to the Swedish police manifesto '*Head-on attack on drugs*' and says that 'it will be necessary to attack the problem at street level, that is, to make sale of drugs to users difficult by dispersing the market, making it visible and trying to prevent deals from being made' (Eefsen, *Information*, 30 October 1993).

3. In September 1993, following police reports that male Somalian refugees were increasingly using the drug, the Danish Minister of Health placed 'khat' on the list of totally prohibited drugs. Opinions differ as to the harmfulness of the drug. With this prohibition Denmark was the only country in the European Union which prohibited khat until Sweden and Finland joined the EU in January 1995. Furthermore, the drug is not even on the international list of prohibited drugs. The initiative for this prohibition came from the police, who felt that as Norway and Sweden had banned the drug, a similar prohibition was necessary in Denmark (*Politiken*, 5 September 1993).

The Nordic discourse and the Norwegian and Swedish criticism of Denmark on a number of levels has considerably influenced Danish drug policy. This criticism had direct consequences in 1982, and has since had an indirect affect on the development of Danish opinion while pushing Danish drug policy in a more restrictive direction. Whether this criticism reflected a real Danish threat to Norway and Sweden or simply served to veil the latters' own limited capacity to deal with their own problems can only be posed as a question, as the matter has not been under scrutiny in the present study.

REFERENCES

Christie, N. and K. Bruun (1985) *Den gode fiende* ('The ideal enemy') (Oslo).

Dagbladet (Norwegian daily newspaper) (1/3/68–1/6/68; 1/10/81- 1/4/82) (Oslo: Universitetsforlaget).

Dagbladet Politiken (Danish daily newspaper) (1/11/68–1/2/69; 1/10/81–1/5/ 82; 5/9/93) (Copenhagen).

Dagens Nyheter (Swedish newspaper) (1/1/68–1/4/68; 1/10/81–1/4/82) (Stockholm).

Dansk Tidsskriftsindex 1975–82 (Index of Daily Newspapers, Danish Index to Periodicals) (Copenhagen).

Folketingstidende, *Forhandlingerne* (Danish Parliament Report) (1968/9; 1982/2; 1983/4) (Copenhagen).

Hansen, M. T. (1988) *Narkotika* (Oslo: Institutt for Kriminologi og Strafferett).

Information, 30 October 1993 (Copenhagen).

Jepsen, J. (1992) 'Drugs and social control in Scandinavia', in H. Traver and M. Gaylord (eds), *Drugs, Law and the State* (Hong Kong: University Press).

Laursen, L. (1992) 'Sammenhold på afveje. Træk af nordisk narkotika kontrolpolitik 1965–85', in *Nordisk Alkoholtidskrift*, vol. 9 (2), pp. 73–85.

Nordiska Rådet (Nordic Council) (1971; 1982; 1985) *Sessions* (Stockholm).

Rigspolitichefens Årsberetning *Annual Report of the National Chief of Police* (1981) (Copenhagen).

Riksdagen, *Førstekammarens Protokoll (Swedish Parliament, Report of First Chamber)* (1968; 1981/2) (Stockholm).

Stortinget, *Kongeriket Norges Stortingsforhandlinger* (Norwegian Parliament Report) (1966/7; 1967/8; 1981/2) (Oslo).

Solarz, A. (1987) *Narkotikakontrollens utveckling i Sverige* (The development of drug control in Sweden) (Stockholm: CAN).

Thunved, B. (ed.) (1991) 'Lagstiftning och rättspraxis i narkotikamål' (Legislation and court practice in drug cases), *Nordnark*, 1991: 1 (Stockholm).

Part III

Contesting Styles of European Policy Making

9 The EU, Home Affairs and 1996: Intergovernmental Convergence or Confederal Diversity?

Nicholas Dorn

The following pages attempt to locate the options for the future development of drug enforcement policies (at local, national and pan-EU levels) in the context of development of the European Union along either intergovernmental or confederal[1] lines.

This investigation throws up some perspectives that may, at first, appear paradoxical. The hypothesis advanced is that development along confederal lines would lead to continuing (indeed probably increasing) variety and volatility in drug enforcement policies and practices. Such a situation has been described in relation to drug policies at local, provincial or canton levels within those countries which have a federal structure (see Fahrenkrug, Chapter 10). The present chapter simply projects this situation onto a possible future for the whole EU.

This would result in a higher level of citizen involvement in policy-making, and more democratic legitimation at local, provincial and Union levels. But, there might also be dangers, in terms of the possibilities of intolerance towards social groups, extremes of policy from one place to another, and volatility in drug control. Oversight by the European Court of Justice might soften some of these potential problems but, as is well known, controversy surrounds the possibility of an EU criminal jurisdiction in which the Court would play a role.

BACKGROUND

So far, the balance of forces in drug policy-making has resulted in a surprisingly high level of diversity in local, regional and national settings in European countries, but a clear convergence in intergovernmental policies and policing actions against trafficking. In the middle of this user-control diversity and trafficker-control convergence sits the 'mixed case' of policies on open drug scenes, where users and supplier meet, and where policies can become quite volatile. If this picture is the past, then what about the present? Will diversity continue, or will convergence prevail?

Diversity of policies on drug users

During the early and mid-1990s, drug control policies in Europe continued to be diverse and also somewhat volatile. In some countries there has been increasing social reaction against users (for example, in France) – but in other countries, there has been more decriminalisation (Italy in 1993). It even seems that one can have a tightening-up and a slacking-off alongside each other. In Britain, for example, public reaction and police responses towards users of cannabis became more relaxed in the late 1980s and early 1990s but, at the same time there were waves of public anxiety and police targeting of users of 'crack' cocaine.

Of course, national trends are only part of the picture. Cities and other local administrations vary considerably in the ways in which they interpret national policies. In many countries, they may have considerable powers to make policies themselves, in the fields of public order, public health and welfare – as illustrated by Chapters 1, 3 and 10. Certainly, law controls on *drug users* seem to be rather variable, and contingent on domestic political climates and concerns: there is no pan-EU trend.

So, if one were to predict the future on the basis of the drug *user*-control trends of the 1990s, then one might suggest more diversity in drug policies within the EU. But there are also drug *trafficker*-control trends to consider, and there things have been rather different.

Convergent policies on drug trafficking

In relation to European laws, policing practices and cooperation against *drug trafficking*, there has been a convergence in policies, as a result of close intergovernmental action. The direction of convergence in relation to anti-trafficking measures has been clear. Some call it a necessarily firm response to a major threat, others call it repressive and a danger to human rights. Indeed, some observers have linked trends in anti-trafficking measures, and general trends in police cooperation in Europe, to a broader argument about the nature of the EU – that the Union represents a new form of centralisation and authoritarianism (that is the view of some radical criminologists).

It has also been said that:

> the danger exists that the combination of a powerful 'law and order' rhetoric and the absence of a mature package of constitutional control mechanisms or of significant democratic pressure to develop these will mean that the legitimating foundation of the new institutions become even narrower and less securely grounded.
>
> (den Boer and Walker, 1993, pp. 3–27)

Such concerns lead some observers, including some members of the European Parliament, to ask awkward questions:

> Sooner or later the question will be asked concerning the need to have a European criminal law . . . [and] the (con)federal, Parliamentary and judicial context which would be necessary in order to achieve this.
>
> (Van Outrive, 1994)

This opens either a can of worms or, depending on one's view, the window to the future. Either way, it is clear that the future of drug policies and drug enforcement in the EU member states will be inscribed within the broader future of the governance and structuring of Justice and Home Affairs in the EU.

That future, in turn, will form a part of the broader development of the Union. We therefore ask: will the future development of the EU facilitate convergence (as has been the case on the trafficking side) – or will it facilitate diversity in drug policies (as has been the case so far in relation to policies on drug users)?

A possible tie-breaker: 1996 and the IGC

One pivot for the EU will be around the year 1996. It is then there are some foreseeable events with considerable relevance for the general development of the Union (and so for drug policies). 1996 sees an Inter-Governmental Conference (IGC) of European Union member states. This 'Maastricht Review' conference will examine the possibilities for reform of the institutions and decision-making procedures of the EU. Already in 1993 and 1994, as this book was being compiled, political parties in member states, the mass media, in the European Parliament, and in COREPER (the secretariat of the European Council) were developing their positions for the 1996 conference. The changes in (or consolidations of) structures cannot be predicted – but it is possible to identify two (interlinked) arenas in which change is on the agenda:

1. Enhancements of the influence of the European Parliament, the Committee of the Regions and Local Administrations throughout the EU (which might be associated with a development of communitarianism, federalism or confederalism in the EU, see below).
2. Changes in the purview of the Court of Justice, which may have implications for the governance of police cooperation against pan-European drug trafficking (discussed in the second half of the chapter).

The future of EU drug policies is inscribed in this larger drama of the future of the EU.[2]

QUESTION 1: ARE DOMESTIC EU DRUG POLICIES GOING TO BE HARMONISED?

Throughout the 1970s and up until the middle or late 1980s, the dynamic towards economic, social and possibly political integration of the EU seemed unstoppable. But it is clear that, since the late 1980s, there has been a resurgence of pro-sovereignty feelings in many countries. In the early and mid-1990s, domestic political changes in some countries, notably Italy, shifted the balance somewhat towards an EU characterised by relations between national governments, and away from the more confederal EU previously foreseen by many. If the pro-sovereignty trend continues or gathers force, then it will manifest itself (perhaps strongly) in many EU policy areas, including in drug policies.

But, on the other hand, there seems to be some public support for some powers to be transferred from the member states to the European Parliament. A Eurobarometer poll revealed that:

> more EU citizens would like to see MEPs gain [more] power than not [44 per cent for, 33 per cent against]. The Danes (18 per cent) followed by the British and Irish were least in favour of MEPs having more say in decision-making, whilst countries bordering the Mediterranean (Italy, Greece, France and Spain) were the most supportive.
>
> (European Commission, 1994, p. 1)

This division of political opinion is part of the broader debate on communitarianism, federalism and confederalism, versus inter-governmentalism and sovereignty of nations. Its resolution will have consequences for drug policies, as this chapter aims to show.

Confederalism and the European Parliament: formula for diversity in local policies

The European Parliament (EP), understandably, has been to the forefront of the debate on the 'democratic deficit' of the EU. This deficit is said to arise because of the allegedly bureaucratic mode of operation of the European Commission, the rather private mode of operation of the Council of Ministers, and the historically limited powers of the European Parliament itself.

Until the mid-1980s, the EP was widely regarded as a mere talking shop, neither being consulted by the Commission as the latter drew up draft EU legislation, nor having any right of review of such legislation before it was discussed and decided upon by the Council. This situation shifted somewhat as a result of the Single European Act, after which the 'cooperation procedure' gave the EP the power to offer amendments to Council legislation in limited areas; and the 'assent procedure' was instituted, giving the EP the right to veto EU foreign treaties. Following the Treaty of Union signed at Maastricht, the assent procedure was extended to important budgetary measures, and to legislation on citizenship issues (including residence rights). The EP has expressed interest in the possibility of extending the assent procedure to wider areas (*EP News*, 1994, p. 4). Also as a result of Maastricht, the 'co-decision procedure' was instituted, giving the EP the right to amend proposed EU legislation in development policy and some areas of social policy and public health. The EP would like to extend this to some areas of Justice and Home Affairs (*ibid.*). Several of the EU's assent and co-decision areas touch on aspects of drug policies. For example, foreign treaties such as Association Agreements with external states increasingly often include references to control of trafficking. Development policies *vis-à-vis* developing countries may include measures directed at crop substitution. EU social policy and public health cover aspects of management of drug users. Justice and Home Affairs covers drug addiction (i.e. drug users and related matters) and also police cooperation against drug trafficking (Treaty of Union, Title VI, Article K.1).

Greater involvement of the European Parliament in such matters would obviously boost the influence of MEPs and of the diverse political constituencies that they represent. This is not an attractive prospect for [some] member states as represented by ministers in the Council of Ministers. And, according to some observers, the principle of subsidiarity as set out in the Maastricht Treaty shows that this argument has been settled in favour of the member states and inter-governmentalism. But this is only one viewpoint amongst many about the way in which subsidiarity can and should be understood:

> For the UK, it [subsidiarity] was a way of curbing the centralising trend in Europe which it so hates. For the [German] *Länder* it was a way of achieving both this and the promotion of the downward evolution of power to the regions. For the regional movements themselves it was seen, together with the Committee of the Regions and the initiates on cultural and linguistic identity, as the beginning of regional input into the Community process.
>
> (Green, 1994, p.297)

Now, it is not possible to speak of any of the proponents of these various positions as being right or wrong, since they are arguing not so much as to how things *are* but, how things *ought* to be. Nevertheless, if subsidiarity has become the issue, then its epistemological background (Catholic) surely would support the idea of a radical devolution of responsibilities downwards – not just to the member states, but through them, to regions, localities, social groups, and families. A historically informed perspective suggests that:

> [T]he principle of subsidiarity is not only to be invoked in order to resolve the respective spheres of action of the Community and its Member States, but also. . . it concerns the internal structure of the Member States (decentralisation, for example) and systems of political control (the role of the State, social partnerships, non-governmental organisations, etc). [And it] would imply that the Member States commit themselves, more and more, to the path of decentralisation and of citizens' rights.
>
> (Ranjault, 1994, pp. 49–52)

As the arguments during the run-up to the 1996 Inter-Governmental Conference again demonstrate, the levels of decision-making for many aspects of policy in the EU are still 'up for grabs'. No predictions can be made (Green, *op. cit.*). On the one hand, the member states presently hold most power and, if their internal politics and relations with each other allow, may hang on to it. On the other hand, considering the general development of Europe, there are strong *regionalist* movements and pressures which, in the long run, are more likely to result in alliances 'up' to the EP, and 'down' to the localities, than with the member states (Scott *et al.*, 1995, p. 60 *et seq.*). So, on the face of it, and taking the long-term view, the prospect of the EU developing along such a confederal, decentralised path must be taken as seriously as the EU taking an inter-governmental, relatively centralised, Council-led path.

We therefore ask, what would be the implications for drug policy, in a European Union either characterised by more confederalism, or by sovereignty and intergovernmentalism?

A reasonable hypothesis, we suggest, would be as follows:

> more diversity in the confederal scenario, since this style of politics emphasises the taking of decisions at various levels, including regional, city or local levels;
>
> more uniformity in drug policies in the intergovernmental scenario, because, in this case, the prerogatives of the member states are most likely to be preserved, and top-down control would be strongest.

Before arguing this case, we wish to stress that we are not equating member state decision-making with 'hard' repressive measures, nor are we equating community decision-making with 'soft' tolerance. Uniformity of policy, as defined by EU member states, might indeed result in harder measures (as was the general trend throughout the 1980s). Alternatively, it might result in decriminalisation, following the lead of several states in the early 1990s; this is the scenario that so many Norwegians and Swedes feared in the run-up to their entry into the EU. As for confederal diversity, this would not necessarily imply liberality or tolerance, as we explore below.

Why should a more federal system for the EU favour diversity in local drug policies?

> First, because a higher profile for the European Parliament means that MEPs will have greater influence (especially over matters central to the Treaty of Rome – pillar 1 of The Treaty of Union).
>
> Second, because MEPs are much more accountable to their grassroots than is the Council of Ministers (the members of which being more accountable to their governments).
>
> Third, because the diversity of social circumstances and political responses facing MEPs in their constituencies is very great – and likely to get greater as the EU widens.
>
> Fourth, because sensitivity to provincial and city-level political forces will be reinforced by the Committee of the Regions (Scott *et al.*, 1995). What this adds up to is a Parliament of Diversity.

Unable (and also possibly unwilling) to impose any top-down *dicta* upon 'lower' political structures, the EP is likely to adopt the strategy of presenting itself as politically sensitive to political organs and population groups below it. So, the confederal road for the EU can be expected to be relatively open in diversity in responses to drug problems at provincial, city and local levels. Where the focus is on users, it might either define them as persons to be helped through provision of low-threshold social welfare and health services *or* as patrons of the drug trade, as persons to be punished. At local level, there might be a willingness to provide basic services to all in need *or* a reluctance to support services for non-local drug users from local taxes. Open drug scenes might be seen within the framework of anti-trafficking policy, or public order, or public health, or there might be oscillations between these frameworks.

The impact of diversity resulting from a process of federalisation might go beyond the management of local drugs scenes, and have implications for policing priorities towards the middle, distribution level of drug markets. Already, even in non-federal Britain, police and policing authorities vary their anti-distribution strategies. During 1993/4, the London Metropolitan Police drugs strategy working group prepared a draft (internal, unpublished) strategy document. This envisaged a de-emphasising of targeting of kilo-level cannabis traffickers (distributors). The objective would be to redirect anti-trafficking resources towards heroin and cocaine distributors and retailers. Limitations on police resources mean that such targeting would be facilitated by a focusing away from cannabis distributors – cannabis being considered to cause relatively few problems in relation to crime, public order or health. So, just as a country can decide to tolerate a retail trade in cannabis (the Netherlands), so a city police agency might decide to de-emphasise the distribution trade in cannabis, when it has much more pressing targets. In the event, the Metropolitan Police 'stalled' on their proposal, due to the volatile political situation on crime control in Britain. But any weakening of top-down controls on policing would open up the possibilities of greater variety in city-level anti-trafficking policies, in response to local circumstances.

QUESTION 2. WHO WILL POLICE THE POLICE?

As far as relations between the Council and other EU institutions are concerned, that between the Council and the European Court of Justice is perhaps the most sensitive. Judicial powers, once given to the Court, cannot be taken back (at least, not without great difficulty). The *acquis communautaire*, the legal basis of the Union, not only impacts upon existing national legislation (which may have to be amended), but also circumscribes the powers of member states to legislate in future in areas covered by the Treaty of Rome, the Single European Act, the Treaty of Union and derived Directives, Regulations and Court judgments. For this reason, those who are concerned to maximise sovereignty are ill-disposed to granting the Court further powers. But they face the difficulty that they might at some future date wish to use the Court to 'bring into line' *another* member state. Let us for instance imagine a future situation in which member state X refused to implement present EU agreements on police cooperation against trafficking, or on public health. In such circumstance there would be no formal recourse other than to the Court.

Member states' ambivalence towards the Court can be seen in the Treaty of Union, in the title on Justice and Home Affairs, and in drafts of the Europol Convention. There, the member states contemplate the possibility that future EU conventions on justice and home affairs

> may stipulate that the Court of Justice shall have jurisdiction to interpret their provisions and to rule on any disputes regarding their application. . .
>
> (Article K.3(c) of the Treaty of Union).

This might appear to open up the possibility of Europol, or a future operational arm thereof, being subject to direction by the Court. This makes some sense, insofar as international and EU bodies require some kind of mechanisms for judicial oversight, interpretations of powers, and guidance in the case of uncertainty or disputes. Of course, not every circumstance can be anticipated and taken care of in the founding Convention. If such judicial oversight is to be carried out, by whom else other than the European Court of Justice? But, for those with a strong pro-sovereignty disposition, this prospect raises difficulties; police cooperation should continue to be the subject of arrangements between the sovereign states.

In the two years in which this book was being prepared for publication, the debate over how to provide proper oversight and control of Europol continued to be lively – as successive drafts of the 'Europol Convention' indicate. The first draft, debated by the Justice and Home Affairs ministers in 1993, followed on from the Treaty of Union (extracted above) and foresaw the Court taking the oversight role:

Judicial Control
1. Each High Contracting Party which considers that another High Contracting Party has failed to fulfil an obligation

under its responsibility in accordance with the present Convention may bring the matter before the Court of Justice. Under the same conditions, the Europol Management Board may bring the matter before the Court of Justice.

2. The Court of Justice has sole jurisdiction to hear and determine disputes regarding the legality of decisions of Europol Management Board. Each High Contracting Party may appeal in this matter on the grounds of lack of competence, infringement of an essential procedural requirement, infringement of this Convention or misuse of powers.

3. The Court of Justice shall have jurisdiction to give preliminary rulings on the interpretation of the present Convention as well as on the validity and interpretation of the Management Board's decisions. (European Council, 1993a *draft* – not corresponding to final text)

But a year later, in Autumn 1994, this section had been considerably redrafted, in a way that brought in the Court only *after* the JHA Council itself had a chance to resolve any problem.

Judicial Competence
All disputes between Member States or between Member States and Europol having to do with the implementation or interpretation of this Convention shall be dealt with by the Council with a view to reaching a solution. If the Council does not reach an agreement within a period of six months, or if Europol cannot resolve the issue within the same period, then a case can be taken directly to the European Court of Justice. (European Council, 1994, Article 37, paragraph 1, September *draft* – not corresponding to final text)

This contrasts with the earlier draft's granting of 'sole jurisdiction' to the Court. In addition, the September 1994 draft nowhere made mention of any role for the Court in interpreting the Europol Convention or assessing legality of decisions of the management board. However, no agreement was reached. The next Justice and Home Affairs Council meeting, in November 1994, considered yet another text, in which three options were offered – conflicts between member states regarding Europol would either go direct to the ECJ, or to an arbitration process, or to a qualified majority vote in Council – but again no agreement could be reached. Instead, some window-dressing was announced by the European Council.

It is clear that, in the process of tightening up the draft Europol Convention, there have arisen questions of judicial and political oversight and control which are not purely technical. In reaction to a confederalist section of the Treaty of Union, foreseeing the possibility of an important role for the Court in regulating police cooperation in the EU (where cooperation against drug traffick-ing is a leading element), there has arisen an intergovernmental response, reasserting the privileges of the member states. At the time of writing this somewhat awkward situation had not been resolved.

Judicial control: from Europol to national police agencies?

History suggests that, in general, once the jurisdiction of the Court has been established in any area of law, so the boundaries of that jurisdiction have tended to widen somewhat, through its own decisions. So, maybe any establishing of the Court's jurisdiction in relation to juridical control of Europol could become the channel through which its influence will spread to other aspects of criminal justice. For example, since Europol by definition works together with national police agencies, the boundaries between EU cooperation and national policing will become somewhat blurred.

Thus, the surprising possibility exists that inter-governmental police cooperation and the Europol Convention may turn out to the Trojan Horse through which, bit by bit, the European Court of Justice gains powers of judicial oversight. In the first place, such oversight would be restricted to pan-European police intelligence and cooperation. But it could then spread to cover national police intelligence units, and regional/Lander/Canton units, and city-level policing organisations. (After all, these are not hermetically sealed levels of intelligence and operation, but are and must be inter-linked – as the police acknowledge.)

Of course, the chances of this happening would depend in part on the extent to which Europol develops an operational capacity (in addition to its intelligence tasks) and begins to work at operational level with national, regional or city-level police forces.

Some members states oppose such developments, but others, notably Germany, have seemed in favour of going in this direction. In 1992, Commander Jurgen Storbeck, the then head of the international bureau of the Bundeskriminalamt (BKA), said

'We feel that eventually Europol will become an operational agency. Of course there are important legal differences between the countries, but it should be possible for Europol to carry out arrests in conjunction with local police and according to local judicial regulations. To be realistic, I don't see this happening before the end of the century, but certainly Germany and one or two other countries would like it much earlier.'

(reported by Kirby, 1992)

In 1994, Mr Storbeck had been appointed as the head of Europol. It remains impossible to predict whether the developments which he foresees will in fact come about before the end of the century. What we can say is that the more the member states and their national policing agencies speak of the threat posed by international and pan-European drug trafficking, so they strengthen the case for more cooperation against this threat. This has a knock-on effect, insofar as some parties to the discussion begin to perceive more of a need for judicial oversight of the collective response. At the end of the day, there is only one body that could fulfil that function, and that is the European Court of Justice. But, as much as member states and policing agencies want a Europol of some kind, many are concerned to retain an inter-governmental framework, and to keep the Court out of these matters. This has caused something of a contradiction, a Catch 22 situation, and much awkwardness and delay in the development of police cooperation.

As we went to press, EU member states signed the Conventions on Europol, the Customs Information System (CIS) and the Protection of Financial Interests (against EU fraud), subject to ratification by national parliaments. In relation to Europol, however, the European Council could not agree.

Fourteen Member States have stated that, after a period of six months [in any dispute on the interpretation or application of the Europol convention], they will automatically take the dispute in question before the Court of Justice. The United Kingdom has refused to rally to this position. (Agence Europe, 1995)

As Reuters (1995) reported, this running debate 'foreshadows a complicated discussion in [the 1996] inter-governmental review of the EU's working on whether the Court should take on increased powers'.

Knowledge brokers: the Monitoring Centre and Europol

From the late 1980s onwards, and following a proposal by President François Mitterrand, the Commission began to innovate in the area of drugs, with a series of feasibility studies for what became, in 1994, the European Monitoring Centre for Drugs and Drug Addiction. The EMCDDA is a EU institution rather like the European Environmental Agency. Its role is to collect (i.e. in many cases to design monitoring systems for collecting) information relevant to the formulation of EU drug policies. Activities which the EMCDDA will perform include collection and analysis of existing data; improvement of data-comparison methods; dissemination of data; cooperation with European and international bodies and organisations and with non-Community countries.

The initial area of interest of the EMCDDA focused upon drug users, reflecting pre-Maastricht limitations in competence, historical conceptions of drug problems, and availability of professional expertise in many European countries. From 1994 onwards it applies itself to a much broader field, reflecting the new span of competence (just about everything except anti-trafficking measures in the narrowest sense of policing). The Priority Areas of the EMCDDA are: (1) demand and reduction of the demand for drugs; (2) national and Community strategies and policies; (3) international cooperation and geopolitics of supply; (4) control of trade in narcotic drugs, psychotropic substances and precursors; (5) implication of the drugs phenomenon for producer, consumer and transit countries.

From the start, the Monitoring Centre attracted the suspicions of some member states concerning matters of sovereignty. Britain amongst other states became concerned that the Commission/ EMCDDA might be getting too involved in matters of strategic intelligence, which should be left to the member states and their policing agencies. It should be remembered that this was the period when Europol was being set up, yet still lacked a clear legal basis for its operational activities (the Europol Convention still being redrafted in late 1994). So there was and remains much sensitivity over who 'owns' what information – the EMCDDA/Community, or Europol/Member States?

This question may be particularly sensitive in relation to information about regional or city-level drug markets, where *aggregated* information on drug problems and policies would seem to fall within the purview both of Europol and of the EMCDDA. The situation necessarily becomes complicated, because a *balanced overview* of what is going on in Europe would depend on 'top down' information about major trafficking routes and development (Europol competence), and on 'bottom up' information about local drug markets and patterns of drug use (EMCDDA competence).

In theory, Europol offers an excellent opportunity for national policing agencies to improve the quality of their strategic intelligence. But it is possible that this opportunity may be missed, as ambitious and competitive national policing agencies and agents, conscious of short term rewards, cannot resist the chance to play the same old professional games on a bigger stage. When it comes to their construction of strategic intelligence, police agencies have a tendency to exaggeration – since the bigger and more spectacular the threat which police intelligence 'reveals', the bigger the claim on the media's attention and on the state's resources. This unfortunate aspect of the relationship between policing, media and politics can result in 'flavour of the month' enthusiasms in police thinking. This tendency may well turn out to be as true of Europol as of national policing agencies. If so, then there could be demands for its *strategic information role* to pass to other agencies, for example those governmental organisations and NGOs at local, regional and national levels who collate drugs information and pass it to the EMCDDA.

In the view of the author – considering the complexity of drug phenomena and the fact that no one seems to have a monopoly of wisdom on appropriate policies – multiple sources of information or intelligence for policy-making seem better than just one source. It follows that cooperation, between police information providers (such as Europol) and civil information providers (such as the

EMCDDA), would be preferable to non-cooperation. The question arises, in what context is such cooperation likely to be most meaningful? Not, it is suggested, in a purely inter-governmental EU, since then the policing agencies would be too isolated. In a confederal EU, the formulation of policies on drug enforcement on local, regional and other levels no doubt would be more complicated, since so many more voices would be heard. But the greater the transparency of decision-making, the better its quality.

CONCLUSION

This chapter has examined two paths for development for the EU and has suggested potential implications for drug policies and policing.

1. A more federalised EU would involve devolving of powers to smaller units of government: a greater emphasis on the roles of Regions and City administrations. Already, in many continental EU member states, decisions are taken closer to the citizen than is the case in Britain. This tendency would be enhanced in the case of a 'deepening' of the EU. The consequence would be considerable diversity of locally determined drug enforcement policies.

At the same time, a more deeply federalised EU would involve the strengthening of its key institutions, in particular the European Court of Justice and the European Parliament. In which case, the ECJ might be equipped to oversee the administration of drug enforcement, at the levels of pan-European cooperation, member states and localities. This might be helpful, in order to rein in any local extremes in policy, and to improve the quality of the administration of policing.

2. Inter-governmentalism, in contrast, would emphasis the policy-making prerogatives of the member states, especially where these are already stronger than regional or local administrations. The European Parliament would be able to carry on issuing reports on matters relating to drugs, and the Committee of the Regions could do likewise – but the practical consequences might not be very great. As for the European Court of Justice, its remit would not extend to the juridical oversight of Europol. In short,

the balance of powers would remain rather similar to that described in preceding chapters in this book.

In these circumstances, the 'map' of drug enforcement in the EU would become a quite simple aggregation of different, but relatively stable, national policies (Netherlands + Italy + Sweden, etc.).

3. Finally, a few words about the bright idea of 1994, the possibility of a 'variable geometry' Europe (much discussed during the time this chapter was being drafted). This would involve the development of concentric 'rings' of cooperation, with only the central 'core' of the EU being closely linked to the development of the European Parliament, the ECJ and the *aquis communitaire* of the Treaty of Rome. Broader rings would be essentially intergovernmental in character.

The consequences for drug enforcement could be quite paradoxical. In the inner, more federalised core, there could be locally determined policies, and hence greater diversity in drug policies and enforcement. Meanwhile, in the outer 'ring', intergovernmental relations could result in more convergence in drug policies and enforcement. These speculations raise many questions about the intergovernmental conference of 1996 and the longer-term future of Europe.[3]

NOTES

1. The use of the term 'confederal' deserves explanation. Other contributors use a variety of terms, with which I wish to link the present discussion. Fijnaut (Chapter 11) refers to communitarian institutions of the EU and to communitarianism. Both Alpheis (Chapter 3) and Fahrenkrug (Chapter 10) use the terms federal and federalist (that is to say, as in German, Swiss or other systems of government, also the EU to some extent). The present writer mentions these terms and also, more commonly, confederal; for a verb, federalise is used. Van Outrive (1994) 'splits the difference' linguistically speaking between federal and confederal by writing (con)federal, but this device is a little clumsy for repeated use. All these terms as used here refer to an EU in which decision-making is somewhat dispersed from the national level to other levels of the Union. Apologies to those who feel that this conjoining blurs important distinctions.

2. The development of domestic drug policies may also be linked to the development of EU foreign policies. In Chapter 14 the author explores external/trade policies and Common Foreign and Security Policy ramifications. These, it will be argued, have the potential to impact upon domestic policies.
3. The author thanks Svanaug Fjær and Simone White for expert commentary on drafts of this chapter.

REFERENCES

Agence Europe (1995) 'EU: signature of text on Customs Information System, Protection of Financial Interests', *Reuters Textline*, July 28.

Boer, M. den and N. Walker (1993) 'European policing after 1992', *Journal of Common Market Studies*, vol. 31 (1), pp. 3–27.

European Commission (London office) (1994) *This Week in Europe* (WE/22/94, 9 June), Eurobarometer survey of public opinion at the time of the June 1994 elections to the European Parliament.

European Council (1993) Unpublished draft Act of the Council regarding establishment of a European Police Office [Europol], November.

European Council (1994) Unpublished draft Act of the Council, as considered at the Berlin meeting of the JHA Council, September.

EP News (election special, 1994), (Brussels: European Commission, DG for Information and Public Affairs).

Green, P. (1994) 'Subsidiarity and European Union: Beyond the Ideological Impasse? An analysis of the origins and impact of the principle of subsidiarity within the politics of the European Community', *Policy and Politics*, vol. 22 (4), pp. 287–300.

Kirby, T. (1992) 'Pressure Grows for an EC-wide Detective Force', *Independent*, 20 April 1992.

Ranjault, P. (1994) 'On the Principle of Subsidiarity', *Journal of European Social Policy*, vol. 2 (1), pp. 49–52.

Reuters European Community Report (1995) 'France struggles for accord on Europol', *Reuters Limited*, June 20.

Scott, A., F. Peterson and D. Millar (1995) 'Subsidiarity: A Europe of the Regions versus the British Constitution?' *Journal of Common Market Studies*, vol. 32 (1), pp. 60 *et seq.*

Van Outrive, L. (1994) 'La Fraude Communautaire: une approach équivoque', *Deviance and Société*, vol. 18 (2), pp. 211–14.

10 Drug Control in a Federal System: Zürich, Switzerland

Hermann Fahrenkrug

To many foreigners the image of Switzerland is not only linked to beautiful mountain areas, delicious chocolate, cheese fondue and safe bank accounts but also to the disturbing existence of large open drug scenes in cities like Zürich and Berne. The 'Platzspitz needlepark', an open drug scene with thousands of drug dealers and users right in the centre of Zürich caught the attention of an international audience and has become a metaphor for the terrible drug situation the small alpine country must be facing. That the Platzspitz was closed to drug users in 1992, renovated and given back to traditional park goers the following year (let alone the fate of the 'needlepark goers') has probably escaped the notice of the international public.

Media images of drug issues and their fallout are constructions guided by 'news-making' imperatives like sensationalism and dramatisation, imperatives which will not be treated here (for the Swiss media coverage of drug problems, see Widmer and Zingg, 1993). But any attempt to report the drug situation in Switzerland finds itself confronted by the powerful Platzspitz needlepark image. It is clear that we need better 'constructions of reality' in order to understand the Swiss drug situation than the media glance at the tip of the iceberg can offer us.

Here, a 'thick description' (Geertz, 1973) of the social discourse on drug problems and drug policy in Switzerland is attempted. The intellectual effort and method consists of interpreting 'a multiplicity of complex conceptual structures, many of them knotted into one another, which are at once strange, irregular, and unexplicit and which he (the ethnographer 'interpreter') must contrive somehow first to grasp and then to render' (Geertz, 1973, p. 10). If the task of 'thick description' is generating

171

interpretations of 'matters already in hand' the elements to be rendered intelligible in our case are newspaper articles on drug problems and drug policy, policy statements from the state, cantons or communities, official drug statistics, primary data on drug problems from a recent cantonal health authority survey, and the results of a plethora of scientific studies on Swiss drug issues.

SWISS DRUG PROBLEMS: TACKLING THE ICEBERG

In a recent European overview of the drug situation (Klingemann *et al.*, 1992), between 1985 and 1989 Switzerland appears to be at the top of nearly all the 'drug problem indicators' compared with the other European countries. Based on many data sources, the country report for Switzerland found increases in heroin and cocaine consumption, multiple drug use and drug-related AIDS cases. On top of that, the number of annual drug-related deaths registered by the police grew from 120 to 248 persons over the 5 year period (see Figure 10.1). But what really frightened the public (and health authorities) was the rapid growth in the drug-related AIDS cases (see Figure 10.2).

A look at more recent mortality statistics shows that the number of drug-related deaths registered by the police climbed continuously from 248 to 419 cases between 1989 and 1992 (see Figure 10.1). The regional distribution of these cases and the calculation of a death rate per 100,000 inhabitants (see Figure 10.3 and Table 10.1) indicates a highly variable situation with higher death rates in the large Swiss-German cities (Basle, Zürich and Berne) and the north-eastern and north-western Swiss-German regions (see Figure 10.3 and Table 10.1) compared to the French-speaking parts of the country and the smaller cantons in the central and eastern parts (Institut Universitaire, Zürich, 1993; calculations based on slightly lower number of cases). While the latter experienced an increase in their relatively small number of drug-related deaths over the investigated three-year period, the north-eastern area of the country (the canton and city of Zürich) faced a spectacular downturn in its relatively high number of drug fatalities. Over the last few years, drug-related mortality seems to be rather stable in the French and Italian-speaking western and southern parts of the country.

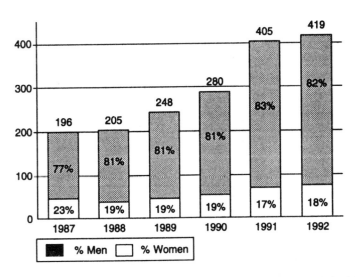

Source: Bundesamt für Polizeiwesen, Berne (1993), *Schweizerische Betäubungsmittelstatistik.*

Figure 10.1 Number of drug-related deaths in Switzerland, 1987–92

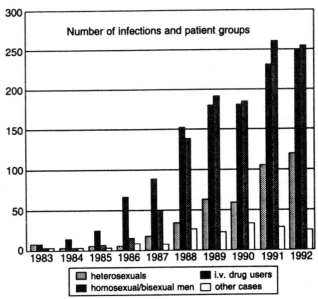

Source: Bundesamt für Gesundheitswesen (1993), *Bulletin 28.*

Figure 10.2 Intravenous (i.v) drug users and AIDS cases in Switzerland, 1983–92

North-west

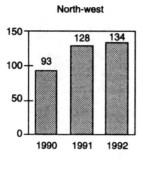

West and south

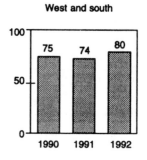

North-east

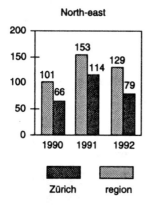

Central

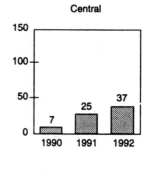

Zürich   region

Source: Institut für Sozial and Präventivmedizin (1993) Epidemiologische Analyse der Drogentodesfälle (Zürich: ISP).

Figure 10.3   Number of drug-related deaths in Switzerland, 1990–2, regional pooled data

Only a more detailed analysis of the causes of the changing patterns of drug-related deaths would allow for the conclusion that, in recent years, there has been a real displacement of drug problems from the Swiss-German cities to the more rural German-speaking part of the country. Even more difficult to prove would be the linkage of the indicator 'drug-related mortality' with regional drug consumption patterns and changing reactions to drug problems in the areas concerned. Swiss drug epidemiology is currently unable to furnish the necessary data to look into these questions, but the case of Zürich will be treated later.

Table 10.1   Crude death rates, drug-related death per 100,000 inhabitants
regions and selected cantons, 1990–2

Regions of Switzerland	1990	1991	1992	1990–92
North-west	4.45	6.05	6.29	5.60
North-east	4.84	7.27	6.07	6.07
Central	1.08	3.77	5.48	3.47
West/south	3.89	3.78	4.04	3.91
Total CH	4.09	5.55	5.50	5.05
Selected cantons				
Berne	6.03	6.32	4.72	5.69
Basle-City	9.39	10.73	12.21	10.79
Zürich	5.74	9.90	6.82	7.48
Geneva	7.71	5.24	7.29	6.75

Source: Institut für Sozial und Präventivmedizin (1993) *Epidemiologische Analyse der Drogentodesfälle* (Zürich: ISP).

Other information relating to the general Swiss drug situation can be found in a recent cantonal health authority survey covering the period 1990 to 1993 (BAG, 1993). Although they cannot base their estimates on any kind of epidemiological evidence, the cantonal health and police authorities confirm the above-mentioned tendencies towards an increasing consumption of hard drugs (heroin and cocaine) in the vast majority of the cantons. A large number of cantons also identify a growing proportion of young beginners and second generation immigrants among the drug using population.

Based on figures given by the 26 cantons and other sources, it can be estimated that in 1993 there were 30,000 regular heroin and cocaine users in Switzerland (SFA, 1995). The previously published Swiss cantonal drug report (BAG, 1991) had suggested the figure of 25,000 hard drug addicts (heroin and cocaine) for 1989. Obviously it would be dangerous to deduce from this an increase of 20 per cent in hard drug use between the two years, but the minimum educated guess we can advance is that the prevalence of hard drug use has 'not decreased' in the early 1990s in Switzerland.

This picture of the demand side of the Swiss drug situation is confirmed when one looks at the supply side data. The aforementioned cantonal sources consider heroin (in 20 cantons) and cocaine (in 21 cantons) as being available on a larger and cheaper scale now than before 1990 (BAG, 1993). Although police seizures of illegal drugs are not a very reliable indicator of the drug market's development, the cantonal impressions are corroborated by a growing quantity of seized heroine and cocaine over the last few years (Bundesamt für Polizeiwesen, 1993).

Summing up the limited empirical evidence on drug use in Switzerland, we can say that although the media image of the 'Platzspitz needlepark' has focused too much upon the epiphenomena of certain visible urban drug scenes and is therefore 'dramatically' biased, a number of direct and indirect indicators show us that the country undoubtedly has drug problems which at the current state of play resemble an iceberg and are difficult to encapsulate.

The concern with this 'drug problem iceberg' is repeatedly expressed in opinion polls by up to 75 per cent of the Swiss population. Only recently has unemployment outstripped the drug problem as one of the primary causes for public concern (for population attitudes, see Leuthold *et al.*, 1993). It is against this background of the recent drug situation that the latest drug policy developments in Switzerland have to be understood.

SWISS DRUG POLICY: DEALING WITH THE RUSSIAN BABUSHKA DOLLS

Switzerland has a federalist political system, functioning through the principle of subsidiarity (Krisi, 1980). One of the main characteristics of this principle is the general reticence of the members of the Swiss confederation, the 26 cantons, to delegate competencies and tasks guaranteed to them by the constitution to the federal state.

Applied to drug policy, this basic feature of Swiss politics accounts for the fact that although a Federal Swiss Drug Act exists (dating back to 1924) and which has been reformed several times (1952, 1975) there is no unified Swiss drug policy (see Schultz, 1989 for more legal details on the Swiss Drug Act). In fact, federal competencies in drug matters are legally limited to the areas of research, documentation and information (e.g. collection of cantonal data on the drug situation and the elaboration of a drug report).

As the application of the Federal Drug Act falls on the cantons, the executive competencies in the areas of prevention, treatment, care and enforcement are fixed at the cantonal level. The federal state only has a supporting role in these matters and has kept a rather low profile in political and practical terms until recently. The overall drug policy situation is therefore highly complex and varies from canton to canton. The dictum of the famous Swiss artist Jean Tanguely given at Switzerland's 700th anniversary, 'La Suisse n'existe pas' (Switzerland does not exist), might well apply to whatever entity one would like to call 'Swiss drug policy'.

In many cases the need to recognise drug policies at the cantonal level has to be taken further to the community level. Although Swiss communities do not enjoy any formal legal competencies in drug policy matters, urban communities like Zürich and Berne with large centralised drug markets, more or less open drug scenes and visible drug use and related problems, already developed in the early 1980s their own strategies to deal with drug issues in their territory (see the contribution of Eisner in a recent book on Swiss drug policy by Böker and Nelles, 1992). As cities and communities are responsible for their own health services and police forces (the issues of health care, social welfare and safety) specific drug intervention measures have a rather local feel to them (see Malatesta *et al.*, 1992).

Drug policy in Switzerland is therefore best described through the metaphor of a set of Russian Babushka dolls, one inside the next. In the largest federal state doll is hidden the smaller but more influential cantonal doll; and inside that are found a set of even smaller dolls, representing the city and community levels, which often carry most of the responsibility for dealing with the drug problem. Drug policy analysis is therefore constantly forced to switch between different interacting levels of federal state, cantonal and community/city.

Federal drug policy in the early 1990s: calling out a tugboat to tackle the iceberg

In February 1991 the federal government – with policy-making and intervention measures at the forefront of its mind – announced a special package of measures to address the country's urgent drug problem. A few months later, the increasing number of hard-drug addicts in a progressive state of psycho-physical and social deterioration prompted the first National Drug Conference (an extraordinary event where federal, cantonal and community officials met for the first time to discuss drug issues, see BAG, 1991a, Nationale Drogenkonferenz). At the same event, the government restated its wish not to reform the predominantly repressive Swiss Drug Act in a more liberal direction (e.g. decriminalisation of drug use) as had been suggested in 1989 by its own Federal Drug Commission (BAG, 1989, Bericht der Subkommission 'Drogenfragen').

As an initial measure, the federal government allocated more money (6–8.7 million Swiss francs per year until 1996) and personnel to the Public Health Office (the staff of the Section for Drug Questions grew from 1.8 to 10 posts), in order to reinforce its own forces in the fight against drugs. A standing group on 'the drug question' was established, allowing for a better coordination of government activities between departments. Besides creating a commission charged with the study of possible revisions to the Swiss Drug Act (decriminalisation of drug use and higher minimum sentences for dealers), the government demanded the development of new drug research guidelines. Finally, the federal government gave orders to prepare the necessary judicial steps in order to ratify several international drug treaties – the Convention on Psychotropic Substances (1971), the Protocol amending the Single Convention on Narcotic Drugs (1972) and the UN Convention against Illicit Traffic in Narcotic Drugs and Psychotropic Substances (1988).

The central targets of the federal drugs package were formulated rather ambitiously:

Stabilise the number of heroin- and cocaine-dependent people in the country by 1993;
Reduce the number of drug addicts by 20 per cent by 1996.

The specific measures to be taken fell into two groups: 'larger measures' and 'accompanying measures'. Within the framework of the existing Swiss Drug Act, the first group comprised of measures of prevention, care, counselling, 'survival help' and treatment for drug dependent persons. The accompanying measures included the development of projects in the areas of professional training, research, evaluation and documentation/ information services all of which were described in great detail at the conference (BAG, 1991b). Moreover, the whole package was planned to be strictly evaluated.

In 1992 the perceived urgency to address the country's drug problem came to such a pass that the federal government gave an additional annual credit of 3 to 4 million Swiss francs in order to finance care facilities for drug users (Nachtragskredit I/92).

Based on this package of measures and its related financial resources, the state re-entered the drug policy scene, or as one commentator said 'sent a tugboat to the cantons' support'. In particular, the Federal Office of Public Health and its Section for Drug Questions with its newly engaged personnel became main players in the confederation's treatment of drug problems. A new dynamic was brought to the drug discussion not only by the office's role as 'initiator' and 'catalytic agent' for drug projects on the cantonal and community level, but also its own measures – such as annual confederation-wide AIDS and drug prevention campaigns and its willingness to cofinance a highly controversial scientific trial of opiate distribution to drug addicts.

But supporting canton and community efforts to reduce drug problems and strengthening the dialogue between the different drug policy levels was not the only federal aim. In order to implement the package of measures, the Public Health Office asked for an 'optimal interplay' of the drug policy partners and a strategic consensus (BAG, 1991b). The federal state saw itself more in the role of the leading coordinator in the fight against 'the drug iceberg', a role that had no precedent in the existing drug legislation. The tugboat might yet turn out to be a camouflaged destroyer.

The director of the Public Health Office clearly expressed the wish of the federal state to coordinate drug policies:

'From the Confederation's point of view, a strategic and central element is the cooperation and coordination of all the efforts undertaken at the different levels (communities, cantons and Confederation) and in different concerned organisms, be it of repressive or therapeutic character.'

(Zeltner, 1992)

Therefore, what characterises federal drug policy in the early 1990s is not only the new material/financial input into the country's drug discourse and measures but also a new form of intervention in the fight against drugs, which in the Swiss political context might be termed 'soft federal centralism'.

Cantonal drug policies: preparing slowly for the rising drug tide

A detailed analysis of cantonal drug policies in Switzerland would need the elaboration of 26 different case studies. What can only be given here are general drug policy trends, again based on the results of the health authority survey (SFA, 1995). Canton officials answered a set of questions – in the form of crude dichotomous policy indicators – on a variety of possible 'drug policy targets' on each canton's agenda. We do not attempt here to break down the answers according to the canton's share of the country's drug problem. Although a canton like Zürich with an estimated 7,000 to 8,000 hard-drug addicts (making up a quarter of Switzerland's estimated total) certainly has a stronger influence on the drug policy options discussed and applied in Switzerland than the canton of Uri with less than 100 addicts, it is evident that this 'country-wide' policy influence is difficult to assess and in no way binding on the cantons' self-government in the drug arena.

The best example of how difficult it is to influence the cantons' autonomy in drug matters is the fate of the above-mentioned 'soft federal centralism'. When the survey of health authorities asked whether the new federal policy orientation had had any direct influence on cantonal drug policies in 1993, only 7 out of 26 cantons confirmed such an influence. Another 4 cantons left the answer open, but 15 cantonal health authorities clearly denied any impact from the federal state level on their own drug policy (SFA, 1995). For the time being, the majority of cantons seem to be determined to maintain their self-government on the drug front.

Table 10.2 gives an overview of how many cantons developed drug policy statements at all, what forms were chosen and what directions were taken.

As can be seen from the answers, no Swiss canton is left without an official board or commission dealing explicitly with drug issues. In 17 of the 26, these groups have elaborated a policy to deal with the cantonal drug problem, 11 of which did so after 1990. Another 4 cantons were in the process of doing so at the time of the survey.

Table 10.2   Cantonal drug polices, 1993

Drug policy goals	Number of cantons
A cantonal drug commission exists	26
A 'concept' to fight drug problems exists	17
	(+ 4 in preparation)
Development of survival-aid and harm-reduction measures	20
Increasing AIDS prevention	20
Liberal revision of Swiss Drug Act	12
Repression of all drug use	10

Source: Schweizerische Fachstelle für Alkohol- und andere Drogenprobleme (SFA) (1995) *Illegale Drogen in der Schweiz 1990–93. Im Auftrag des Bundesamtes für Gesundheitswesen.*

The next step from concept elaboration to the establishment and application of a cantonal 'drug action plan' was taken by only 11 cantons, which leads us to the conclusion that conceptual deliberation is rarely transformed into coherent drug policies, let alone practical measures. Political conflicts and financial problems were often cited by the authorities as the cause of inactivity.

As for the content of the drug policies, three targets received agreement from 20 cantonal health authorities, even a few of those without a concept or action plan on drug issues: 'the development of survival aid measures' for drug addicts, a general 'harm reduction orientation' for the cantonal drug policy and 'the intensification of AIDS prevention' for drug users. The commentaries appended to the survey revealed that the expected rising tide of miserable drug addicts and AIDS-infected users were the origin of these policy decisions.

Only 10 to 12 cantons endorsed the more fundamentalist drug policy statements in the questionnaire – 'repression of any kind of drug use', a policy drafted round abstinence and prohibition, and 'a liberal revision of the Federal Drug Act' (i.e. decriminalisation). This shows that the cantonal drug priority is geared towards realistic problem-solving and practical harm reduction approaches.

The specific problem-solving mix coming under the headline of 'survival aid/harm reduction' is far from identical across the cantons. While in some Swiss-German cantons, survival aid and harm reduction include a rather generous distribution of injection materials, the opening of day care centres and injection rooms for safe drug use and even the participation in the controlled federal distribution of opiates (in 5 cantons), a larger number of German-speaking cantons and nearly all of the French-speaking Roman cantons restrict themselves to basic medical care, traditional drug treatment/methadone maintenance and social welfare measures. Again, only a detailed canton-by-canton analysis could disentangle the actual cantonal arrangements of the dominant policy trend towards individual survival aid and societal harm reduction.

It should not of course be forgotten that this orientation does not exclude more or less repressive components of demand and supply reduction in the cantonal drug policy mix. Asked in the survey whether their canton still took the strict line on prohibition of use (the Swiss Drug Act approach), 18 of the 26 confirmed that position. A rising number of infractions against the federal drug law shows that the practice of a harm reduction approach may well go hand in hand with a traditional 'blaming-the-user' criminal policy (see below). But the Zeitgeist of Swiss drug policy at the beginning of the 1990s is definitely more on a public health-oriented harm-reduction side.

Decentralising drug problems and drug help: 'drug-ridden' communities strike back

A more specific harm-reduction development in Swiss drug policy was determined by the highly centralised structure of drug markets and scenes, and the infrastructure of drug care institutions. Until recently drug users tended to concentrate in the visible 'tip-of-the-iceberg' scenes in cities like Zürich, Berne, Basle, St Gallen, Lucerne and Olten. Based on a cheap drug supply offered by well-organised markets and sustained by tolerant local drug policies, world-famous Swiss open drug scenes like 'Platzspitz' in Zürich and 'Kocherpark' in Berne appeared around 1986. With hundreds or thousands (in Zürich) of hard drug users concentrated in one place, the need for medical and social support structures (especially under the banner of AIDS prevention) became evident. Very rapidly, local communities found themselves in the avante-gardist role of establishing low-threshold institutions for AIDS prevention, survival aid and harm-reduction measures. The liberal city councils felt that drug addicts in an 'addicted society' should not be considered as 'criminals' but as 'ill people' with a legitimate right to societal tolerance, health care and social welfare measures. Other voices – at that time in a minority – advanced the view that these terrible drug scenes needed to be closed as quickly as possible, since they were illegal 'junkie paradises', where people were artificially maintained in a state of addiction. Open drug scenes were nothing but breeding-places for crime which attracted ever more drug consumers. For these hard-liners only repressive solutions could stop the hell at Platzspitz.

A trip to Zürich: Platzspitz and after

The Platzspitz example of a once popular park in the middle of Zürich being transformed into an open drug scene, can stand as a model for the processes outlined above (Eisner, 1993; Grob, 1992). Between 1987 and 1992, when the park was finally closed by the city authorities, the Platzspitz was not only the 'cash, carry and shoot' drug supermarket depicted in the media but also the central outreach point for drug aid and especially AIDS prevention. Zürich city council took a deliberately medico-social approach to drug use and its related problems, which stemmed from the conviction that people do not lose their entitlement to medical and social assistance just because they use drugs. A whole citywide network of low threshold services, survival aid and harm reduction was gradually built up and its funding base legitimised by two popular votes.

In 1988 a joint federal, cantonal and community project on AIDS prevention, called 'ZIPP Aids' was set up in the Platzspitz and began a process of internationally esteemed preventive work (Grob, 1992). Zipp Aids managed – with police protection against the aggressive elements of the drug scene – not only to exchange 10,000 sterile syringes for drug injectors each day, but also to help thousands of users through its outreach work with services such as Hepatitis B vaccination, safer sex guidelines and general health measures (Hornung *et al.*, 1991). The project ended in 1991 and its services are now largely carried on by the Zürich municipal health service.

From the beginning of this 'Platzspitz adventure' (which indeed took on unexpected dimensions with the macabre spectacle of dying and suffering drug addicts in the streets) the political opposition against the needlepark was strong. But only in 1991 was there a change in city drug policies, brought about by demands for better neighbourhood security and by economic pressure groups fearing for their commercial interests and the status of Zürich as an international banking centre. This led to a less tolerant and more repressive approach by the city authorities towards the Platzspitz open drug scene. The main aims were to move the drug users from the city centre, thereby making them 'invisible' to the public eye, and curbing the crime associated with drug use.

The ten drug policy guidelines which Zürich city council published in 1990 proposed two important modifications to the general harm-reduction framework adopted earlier. Guidelines 7 and 8 announced the transfer of the city's survival aid and care structures into the hands of other 'community or private' or 'cantonal' institutions. Although guideline 9 stressed that an 'open, supervised drug scene in the city of Zürich has to be tolerated for the moment' (i.e. in 1990) the city authorities decided on several measures 'to reduce the attraction of staying in the drug scene Platzspitz' and thereby to limit an 'effect of attraction' for drug users to frequent it. Measures were taken in this vein, including the banning of camping and of drug-stalls, the restriction of food for drug users and 'a higher presence of police forces in uniform undertaking more identity controls' (10 Drogenpolitische Grundsätze, 1990). Obviously the decentralisation of the supply and demand sides of the drug scene, together with the restrictions placed on the drug aid infrastructure, could not be carried out without the support/repression of the police.

It was in this context that the decision to close the Platzspitz park gradually was announced in the autumn of 1991 and put into practice in February 1992. This move to a stricter policy of 'decentralisation' (quite literally) became yet another incentive for the Swiss cantons with no open drug scenes to think about their own 'hidden' drug users, often exported to Zürich or other centralised urban drug scenes, and to prepare the help they could get once they were sent 'back home'.

Although it was first hoped after the closure of the park that drug users would deliberately stay away from their 'central' Zürich drug scene and look for 'decentralised' help in their home cantons, this expectation turned out to be false. Drug users and the usual swarm of dealers did not leave the city centre but dispersed, 'guerilla-like', into several densely populated neighbouring districts, paradoxically creating a much higher level of social disorder than before. The reaction of the resident population, fearful of seeing their neighbourhood turning into a 'Bronx', was to form a social movement which together with the political anti-drug lobby became a real political threat to the city council. This coalition was strong enough to force the responsible officials to take decisions in order to get the 'addicts and the dealers from the street'.

The city council of Zürich bowed to the pressure, and – with the cantonal authorities – ordered a joint municipal–cantonal police initiative which applied an even stricter control policy in order to meet its original decentralisation targets. But after months of an unproductive 'cat-and-mouse game', with drug users and dealers being chased around the city centre, a new 'settled' open scene formed itself in the Lettensteg area in the spring of 1993 and had to be tolerated. Again, thousands of drug users and suppliers gathered in a permanent and visible way at a former train station only a few hundred metres from the old Platzspitz area. The targets of displacing them and motivating them to find aid and treatment in their home communities by 'constructive coercion' were obviously not reached. Neither the drug addicts themselves, not to mention the drug dealers, nor the cantons and communities were willing or practically prepared to follow Zürich's decentralisation policy at the time.

In the summer of 1993, whether as an unrelated secondary measure or a tactical move to put even more pressure on the drug users to leave and on the surrounding cantons to take their fair share of the drug problem, Zürich council decided to reduce aid and care for drug users and to restrict them to Zürich citizens alone. Scientific studies on the Platzspitz dwellers (Künzler, 1990) had already established that only 35 to 40 per cent were actually citizens of Zürich and therefore legally entitled to receive aid. Systematic police controls around the Lettensteg scene ('Operation Falcon') concluded that only 18 per cent of those identified were citizens of the city of Zürich (another 22 per cent coming from the canton of Zürich) and that over 56 per cent of identified drug users had their origins in the other Swiss cantons (only 4 per cent came from other countries). Zürich was simply no longer willing or able to carry the burden of half of Switzerland's drug problems, and limited drug services to its own citizens. In addition, more police were employed to fight illegal drug trafficking. This war against the dealers has lately taken on a rather xenophobic tone, with accusations – based on police arrest statistics – that 'most' drug dealers are 'false political asylum seekers'.

Despite the serious deterioration of their living conditions (less support for their basic needs and greater stress getting their drug supply) very few drug addicts actually left the scene or were willing to move into treatment, as a recent study of the drug users after the Platzspitz closure indicated (Sozialamt Zürich, 1992). Most of them preferred to struggle along, adapting to the new 'hassles' the decentralisation approach brought to their lives.

The latest development in this spiral of 'forced decentralisation' is the creation of a 'triage and repatriation centre' in a Zürich suburb, which has a capacity for 100 people and where drug users taken into custody on the open drug scene can be detained for 24 hours under the law of 'involuntary civil committal' for persons in need of urgent psychiatric help. Within this period of time (planned to be extended to 72 hours) the person's identity has to be established and the cantonal or community authorities informed of the immediate repatriation of the user. However, the first experiences in the autumn of 1993 show that although the cantons and communities have started to build up better care and treatment infrastructures, the latest 'decentralisation-by-forced-repatriation' approach does not seem to work any better than earlier attempts. For the large majority of the repatriated persons, it leads to a rather expensive 'revolving door' with many drug addicts returning after a short stay in their communities to the place where they find the best and cheapest drug supply, namely Zürich.

Although it is not possible to generalise from the experience of Zürich's attempt at decentralisation, it is symptomatic of the tendency of some other 'drug-ridden' Swiss communities (Berne, Lucerne, St Gallen) to close their open drug scenes, making them less attractive for drug users and dealers and to shift the burden of help and treatment for non-citizens back to their 'home cantons'. The strategy of 'forced repatriation' of drug users under the 'involuntary civil committal' procedure is, however, rare (advocated by only five cantons, among them Zürich and Berne, in the cantonal health authorities survey, SFA, 1995). But it still gives an indication of the growing awareness that there is a 'problem' and the attempt at a practical redistribution of the financial and social burden at the cantonal level.

Harm reduction and policing: a case of strange bedfellows?

The total number of all police-notified infractions against the Swiss Drug Law increased nearly fourfold between 1980 and 1992 (from approximately 8,000 to 31,000), indicating rather vividly the level of repressive activity by the police over the last decade. The relationship between the percentages of 'offender categories' prosecuted has not changed very much between 1980 and 1991: 'drug consumption only' (65 per cent in 1980; 72 per cent in 1991); 'drug consumption and drug dealing' (23 and 31 per cent) and 'drug trade and smuggling only' (3 and 5 per cent) (Bundesamt für Polizeiwesen, 1992). Seen on the national level most of the police activity is directed against the 'drug consumption only' category. The Federal Swiss Drug Act is based on a prohibitionist legal framework concerning drug use and the police must therefore enforce it.

Looked at on a cantonal level, large differences in the offender structure become visible and point to highly variable applications of the repression principle by the cantonal police authorities. While in Zürich and Basle with their urban drug scenes the 'drug consumption only' category comprised 57 and 65 per cent and the mixed 'drug consumption/dealing' type amounted to 29 and 33 per cent, the Swiss German canton of Aargau (neighbouring Zürich) and the French-speaking canton of Vaud show a 90 per cent and 7–9 per cent relationship between 'consumption only' and 'consumption/dealing' offenders (Bundesamt für Statistik, 1994).

A specific indicator for the intensity of police prosecutions of drug law infractions can be taken from Figure 10.4 showing the cantonal rate of drug law-related police notifications per 100,000 inhabitants.

Among the five most repressive cantons we find two cantons with larger visible open urban drug scenes (Zürich and Basle), one urban canton without a visible urban drug scene (Geneva) and one rural canton without any visible drug scenes (Aargau).

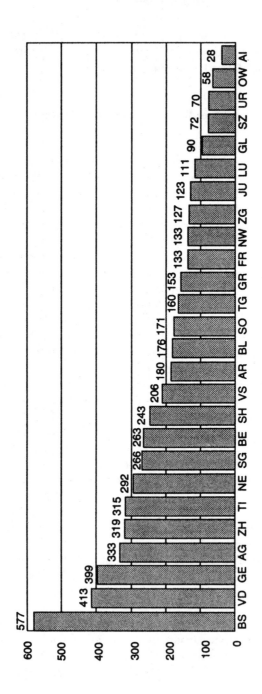

Source: Bundesamt für Gesundheitswesen, Berne (1991) *Bericht der Kantone Über die präventiven und therapeutischen Massnahmen im Drogenbereich 1986–1989.*

Figure 10.4 Cantonal rate of drug law notifications; per 100,000 inhabitants, 1990

The police strategies on demand/consumer or supply/dealer reduction are obviously not guided by the fact of existing drug scenes and their problems, but by other factors of a primarily political nature. As a recent study (Malatesta *et al.*, 1992) shows, it is the complex cantonal drug policy mix of public health-oriented and public order/safety-oriented elements that determines the relative role of the police and their activities. The cases of Basle, Zürich and Aargau with high notification ratios also make it clear that a repressive control approach to drug use and drug dealing is not the preserve of the traditionally repressive French-speaking Roman cantons but can be used by Swiss-German cantons with a rather liberal drug policy image.

In order to avoid a canton-by-canton investigation of the policy imperatives relating to drug control, another overview of the canton's answers from the recent health authorities' survey (SFA, 1995), this time concerning their policing activities, is given in Table 10.3. It can be seen from the results that except for 'prevention activities', which seem to be a main police task in nearly all the 26 cantons, the overwhelming majority of the cantonal police authorities characterise their priorities in the traditional areas of 'fighting the drug trade' (23 cantons), 'notification of drug use' (20 cantons) and 'impediment/dissolu-

Table 10.3   Police activities related to drug problems, 1993

Type of police activity		*Number of cantons*
Drug prevention by policemen		24
Fighting the drug trade	high-level	23
	low-level	21
Notification of drug use		20
Impediment/dissolution of open drug scenes		20
Cooperating with social and health services		17
Protecting the population against drug crime		16
Deterring beginning drug users		15
Fighting the drug-related white collar crime		14

Source: Schweizerische Fachstelle für Alkohol- und andere Drogenprobleme (SFA) (1995) *Illegale Drogen in der Schweiz 1990–93. Im Auftrag des Bundesamtes für gesundheitswesen.*

tion of open drug scenes' (20 cantons). Slightly more than half the cantons extend their policing to the tasks of 'protecting the population against drug crime' (16 cantons), 'deterring new drug users' (15 cantons) or 'fighting drug-related white collar crime' (14 cantons). A high number (17 cantons) also mention police cooperation with the canton's health and social services authorities.

The following excerpts from the answers given to a questionnaire completed in 1992 by 13 Swiss city administrations give a more tangible impression of low-level policing (Schweizerischer Städteverband, Drogenplattform, 1992).

Question: What kind of measures are being taken to deal with drug scenes in your city? [Answers selected with respect to police activities]

Basle – Swiss drug delinquents: notification to legal authorities; foreigners: notification to foreigner's police and extradition; daily police controls, no tolerance of large open drug scenes; arrest of high-level dealers

Berne – notice to home community of drug delinquent; referring of non-residents to home community; extradition of illegal foreigners; notice to federal political asylum authorities; notice to traffic authorities concerning driving licenses

Biel – regular police presence and controls on the drug scene; observation of the scene; report to local political authorities

Geneva – police repression

Lausanne – permanent police pressure against drug users

Lucerne – more police presence and control; notice of young drug users to their parents and district youth attorney; statistical inquiries in the drug help institutions

Olten – notification of non-resident drug delinquents to home community for repatriation; special police actions against drug dealers

Schaffhausen – cooperation of city council with police organs

Solothurn – daily police controls; tolerance of local drug users

St Gallen – police measures in combinations with notice to home community

Winterthur – consequent prosecution of drug offenders

Zürich – repatriation of non-resident drug users to home communities; police controls and repression of consumption and dealing on the drug scene.

Although several cities have highlighted cooperation between police, social services and health authorities, the traditional control tasks mentioned above underline the impression already established from our study of Zürich; namely, that the political decision to combine harm reduction measures with the repression of open drug scenes and to make local drug services inaccessible and unattractive to non-resident drug users, has allowed the police to regain a prominent role in the Swiss approach against drug problems.

While in a first 'optimistic' harm reduction phase the policing consisted of observing and controlling open drug scenes, and protecting the outreach drug help and AIDS prevention services, the following phase of 'forced decentralisation' called for a return to the traditional repressive role of police drug control. In the drive to eliminate the visible drug scene, the police are brought back to the fore, identifying drug users in order to send them back to their home communities and harassing and prosecuting users and user-dealers.

With the latest turn in a few cantons to 'coercive drug treatment', the police are given the role of foisting unwilling patients onto treatment facilities. Whether this can still be seen as a 'legitimate' relationship between a health-oriented harm reduction approach and a control-oriented police one seems rather doubtful (see Chapter 2).

CONCLUSION

It is notoriously difficult to assess the Swiss drug problem in the absence of unequivocal scientific data on the number of drug users or the extent of drug-related problems.

Nevertheless, some epidemiological indicators, such as the rising number of drug-related deaths, accompanied by the fears of the Swiss people and politicians of a drug epidemic and spiralling drug-related AIDS cases, puts the country in a certain state of alert. This situation and the general feeling that 'something must be done', provides us with the background to the recent drug policy initiatives at federal, cantonal and community levels throughout Switzerland.

The legal framework of the Federal Swiss Drug Act is geared in practice to the cantons. It is up to the cantonal authorities to organise the repression of demand for and supply of drugs, and to provide the care and treatment facilities for drug addicts. According to the drug policy of the canton in question, the situation on the ground is, however, highly inconsistent and incoherent. The federal state has recently launched a major public health 'package of measures to reduce drug problems' and thereby begun to play a new centralising and coordinating role, directing the cantons' autonomy in the drug field towards a harm reduction approach. Without changing the essentially repressive regulations contained in the Swiss Drug Act, the federal state now advocates and supports more and better survival aid and treatment facilities for drug users in need of assistance.

Besides this 'soft federal centralist' pressure on the cantons to face their own drug problems and provide better drug aid, another move from a few urban communities with large 'centralised' open drug scenes works in the same direction. Under the banner of 'decentralising' the drug scenes and the aid infrastructure built around them, more repressive measures are being taken (the extreme being the use of 'involuntary civil committals'). By restricting the survival aid and care infrastructure to local drug users, the pressure on addicts to look for help in their 'home canton' is increased.

Whether these new tendencies in Swiss drug policy of tackling the 'drug iceberg' from the top down with a federal centralist harm reduction package and from the bottom up with a repressive redistribution of the drug problem burden will succeed, remains to be seen. It does at least open up a productive and more flexible 'third way' between the traditional 'repressive–prohibitionist' and 'liberal–addiction maintenance' methods of dealing with the drug problem.

REFERENCES

Albrecht, H.-J. and van Kalmthout, A. (1989) *Drug Policies in Western Europe*, Criminological Research Report, vol. 41 (Freiburg: Max Planck Institute for Foreign and International Penal Law).

Böker, W. and J. Nelles (1992) *Drogenpolitik wohin? Sachverhalte, Entwicklungen, Handlungsvorschläge. 2. Auflage*, publikation der Akademischen Kommission der Universität Berne (Berne: Paul Haupt).

BAG/Bundesamt für Gesundheitswesen, Berne (1989) *Aspekte der Drogensituation und Drogenpolitik in der Schweiz. Bericht der Subkommission 'Drogenfragen' der Eidgenössischen Betäubungsmittelkommission.*

BAG/Bundesamt für Gesundheitswesen, Berne (1991a) *Bericht der Kantone. Über die präventiven und therapeutischen Massnahmen im Drogenbereich 1986-1989.*

BAG/Bundesamt für Gesundheitswesen, Berne (1991b) *Nationale Drogenkonferenz, Massnahmen des Bundes zur Verminderung der Drogenprobleme. Ein Grundlagenpapier des Bundesamtes für Gesundheitswesen.*

BAG/Bundesamt für Polizeiwesen, Berne (1993) *Schweizerische Betäubungsmittelstatistik.*

Bundesant für Statistik (1994) *Drogen und Strafrecht in der Schweiz*, Heft 19, Berlin.

Eisner, M. (1992) 'Drogenpolitik als politischer Konfliktprozess', in W. Böker and J. Nelles, *Drogenpolitik wohin? Sachverhalte, Entwicklungen, Handlungsvorschläge. 2. Auflage*, Publikation der Akademischen Kommission der Universität Bern (Berne: Paul Haupt).

Eisner, M. (1993) 'Policies towards open drug scenes and street crime; the case of the City of Zürich', *European Journal on Criminal Policy and Research*, vol. 1 (2), pp. 61–75.

Geertz, C. (1973) *The Interpretation of Cultures. Selected Essays* (New York: Basic Books).

Grob, P. J. (1992) 'The Needle Park in Zürich; The Story and the Lessons to be Learned', *European Journal on Criminal Policy and Research*, vol. 1 (2), pp. 48–61.

Hornung, R. (1991) *Das Zürcher Interventions-Pilotprojekt gegen Aids für Drogengefährdete und Drogenabhängige (ZIPP-AIDS): Zwei Jahre Aids-Prävention am Züricher Platzspitz (1989-1990)* (research report).

Institut für Sozial und Präventivmedizin *Epidemiologische Analyse der Drogentodesfälle* (Zürich: ISP).

Klingemann, H., C. Groos, R. Hartnoll and J. Rehm (1992) *European Summary on Drug Abuse. First Report (1985-1990)* (Copenhagen: WHO).

Künzler, H. P. (1990) *Analyse der offener Drogenszeve 'Platzspitz' in Zürich. Sozio-ökonorische und medizinische Aspekte*, Zürich.

Leuthold, A., M. Cattaneo and F. Dubois-Arber (1993) 'Die Schweizer Bevölkerung und das Drogenproblem: Problemsicht und Lösungsvorschläge', *Sozial- und Präventivmedizin*, vol. 38 (4), pp. 206–16.

Malatesta, D., D. Joye and C. Spreyermann (1992) *Villes et toxicomanie. Des politiques urbaines de prévention du sida en Suisse. Rapport de recherche no 99.*

Schultz, H. (1989) 'Drugs and Drug Politics in Switzerland', in H.-J. Albrecht and A. van Kalmthout, *Drug Policies in Western Europe.*

Schweizerische Fachstelle für Alkoholprobleme (SFA) Université de Lausanne/DEEP-HEC Lausanne (1992) *Soziale und präventive Aspekte des Drogenproblems unter besonderer Berücksichtigung der Schweiz.* Im Auftrag des Bundesamtes für Gesundheitswesen.

Schweizerische Fachstelle für Alkohol- und andere Drogenprobleme (SFA) (1995) *Illegale Drogen in der Schweiz 1990–1993. Im Auftrag des Bundesamtes für Gesundheitswesen* (Zürich: Seismo Verlag).

Schweizerischer Städteverband (1992) *Zusammenfassung des Fragebogens der Drogenplattform des schweizerischen Städteverbandes.*

Sozialamt der Stadt Zürich, Forschungsstelle der Fachstelle für Drogen- und Obdachlosenhilfe/Suchtfragen (1991) *Die zehn drogenpolitischen Grundsätze als Rahmenbedingungen von städtischen Drogenhifseinrichtungen. Eine textwissenschaftliche Analyse.* Forschung und Dokumentation Nr 4.

Sozialamt der Stadt Zürich, Forschungsstelle der Fachstelle für Drogen- und Obdachlosenhilfe/Suchtfragen (1992) *Auflösung der offenen Drogenszene am Platzspitz in Zürich. Auswirkungen auf die Lebensumstände von betroffenen Dorgenabhängigen. Ergebnisse einer Befragung im Rahmen der Evaluation der Massnahmen zur Auflösung der offenen Drogenszene.* Forschung und Dokumentation Nr 8.

10 Drogenpolitische Grundsätze des Stadtrates von Zürich (1990). Informationsstelle der Stadt Zürich.

Widmer, J. and P. Zbinden Zingg (1991) *Discours sur la drogue dans les médias suisses. Résultats de deux recherches sur la presse écrite d'octobre à décembre 1991.*

Zeltner, Th. (1992) Manuscript read to the FDP, Schweiz. Drogentagung Luzern.

11 Intergovernmental Cooperation on Drug Control: Debates on Europol

Cyrille Fijnaut

Over the last thirty years international police cooperation has become a major focus of debate within Western Europe. From time to time this debate has been completely reoriented by the unpredictability of political processes. The three most important landmarks are: the establishment of TREVI in 1975–6, the incorporation of cooperative mechanisms in the Schengen Treaty (1985) and the Schengen Convention (1990), and the recommendation of the Treaty of Union (signed in December 1991 at Maastricht) to found Europol within the framework of the European Union (Busch, 1988; Fijnaut, 1987; Le Jeune, 1992).

Although each of these initiatives can be related to the 'fight against drugs' to a greater or lesser extent, the foundation of Europol is undeniably the most relevant one for our purposes. Whereas TREVI was established to further international police cooperation vis-à-vis the containment of political violence, and the relevant arrangements in the Schengen Treaties are meant to serve a much wider purpose than the enhancement of international police cooperation in the drugs field, Europol's primary function is to organise the exchange of information on drugs at a Community level.

First, we need to analyse the provisions of the Maastricht Treaty in relation to Europol. This analysis will show that the foundation of Europol is – from several viewpoints – a remarkable institutional achievement in Western Europe. One of the most peculiar aspects of Europol is the limited involvement of the European Parliament in its organisation and functioning. And this is why this chapter also sets out to examine the extent to

195

which Europol, as conceived in the Maastricht Treaty, meets the expectations and proposals which have been voiced in the European Parliament with regard to the institutionalisation of international police cooperation. For it should become clear that Europol could become a very controversial issue at the European Union level if the European Council of Ministers and the European Parliament take opposing standpoints on its institutional position, its tasks and, maybe, powers.

So, no attempt at all is made in this chapter to give an overview of the different forms of international police cooperation which over the years have been devised to improve the effectiveness and efficiency of the Western European police forces. For such an overview I refer the reader to the existing reviews of this general development (Benyon, Davies and Willis, 1990; Home Affairs Committee, 1990). Equally, cooperation between the European police forces and the American police will be left aside. It would take too long to discuss here their entwined relationship in the 'war on drugs' (Nadelmann, 1993).

THE TREATY OF MAASTRICHT WITH RESPECT TO EUROPOL

The relevant provisions in the Treaty and the actual situation

At first sight the establishment of Europol is one of the minor points of the Treaty. Only in Title VI, relating to cooperation in the fields of Justice and Home Affairs, and particularly in Article K.1, point 9, is it stated that police cooperation for the purposes of prevention and combatting terrorism, unlawful drug trafficking and other serious forms of international crime . . . in connection with the organisation of a Union-wide system for exchanging information within a European Police Office (Europol), is one of the questions of common interest for member states of the European Community. The fact, however, that a Declaration on Police Cooperation has been annexed to the text of the Treaty itself, shows that this form of cooperation received more political attention than the provision in Article K.1.9 suggests. This declaration contains a summing up of the functions which Europol sooner or later may fulfil:

support for national criminal investigation and security
  authorities;
creation of databases;
central analysis and assessment of information;
analysis of national prevention programmes; and measures
  relating to further training, research, forensic matters and
  criminal records departments.

In addition to these statements on the tasks of Europol, it is very
important to look at the provisions in the Maastricht Treaty
which define to some extent the position of this new cooperative
mechanism in the European Union. On the basis of the general
provisions in Title VI, it can be concluded that not only the
European Council but also the European Commission and the
European Parliament will be involved in Europol's decision-
making processes. Indeed, excepting the provisions on the right of
initiative (only for the member states) and the Committee of
Senior Officials (of the member states), Article K.4.2 clearly states
that the Commission will fully participate in all the activities with
respect to the field of Justice and Home Affairs. And Article K.6
regulates the participation of the European Parliament: the
Commission has the duty to inform it regularly about activities in
this field, the Chair is obliged to consult it on the most important
aspects of cooperation concerned, and the Parliament gives up the
right to ask questions of the European Council and to make
recommendations to it. For the rest, the institutional position of
Europol will be clarified in a specific convention between the
member states as was decided at the Lisbon Summit in June
1992.[1] So, we're still waiting for further details on this crucial
issue.

In the meantime, the real construction of Europol has already
started. At the same summit the European Council agreed upon a
proposal to establish a project team that would facilitate the
creation of a European Drugs Unit, the first stepping-stone
towards Europol. This team began work on 1 September 1992 in
Strasbourg. At their special meeting in Brussels, on 18 September,
the ministers instructed the ad hoc group 'to redouble its efforts to
ensure that Europol is put in place quickly and in particular to see
that the first phase, the Europol Drugs Unit, is in place by
January 1993'.[2] In other words, even if the Treaty of Maastricht
was not to be implemented as a whole, the Treaty would have

played a central role in the restructuring of international police cooperation in the European Community. As was stated in the conclusions of the Edinburgh Summit, 11–12 December 1993: 'the European Council looks with interest for the quick foundation of the Drugs Unit of Europol'.[3]

The institutional and functional framework of Europol

In order to get a clear picture of the institutional and functional framework of Europol it is necessary to return to the origins of Europol: the German debate started in the 1970s on the necessity of restructuring international police cooperation within Western Europe (Fijnaut, 1993, pp. 81–5). The participants in this debate – politicians, senior police officials, presidents of police associations – agreed that restructuring was necessary. Their opinions, however, greatly differed as to whether Europol should be established within the framework of Interpol or within the framework of the European Community. Whereas leading police officers, notably the successive heads of the Bundeskriminalamt, declared themselves in favour of Interpol, important federal politicians defended the opposite view. Their opinion found its clearest expression in 1989–90 when the Federal Minister of the Interior, W. Schaüble, explained in detail the tasks of such a Europol: the gathering and analysis of information; the training of police officers; the common administration of forensic facilities, etc. He left aside at the time, however, two essential questions. The first one was whether Europol should be a Communitarian affair or an intergovernmental issue for the member states (see Chapter 9). And the second was whether Europol, or at least its members, would not only have supportive tasks but also executive police powers to empower it to investigate, on its own initiative and/or in close cooperation with the police of the member states, international organised crime. On this last point, he differed markedly from the view expressed by the Federal Chancellor Helmut Kohl, who in 1988 and again in 1989 argued in favour of the establishment of a real European FBI (Federal Bureau of Investigation).

This provocative German debate never got much attention in the rest of Western Europe. In the other member states it did not bring about anything like a continuing public discussion on the way the problems in this field should be settled. But the Schengen Treaty of 1985 – signed by Germany, France and the Benelux countries – already made clear in which direction the Community was proceeding. In its annexes the proposal was made that with a view to the fight against the trade in illegal drugs a central information exchange should be instituted. In other words, Interpol was already being passed by, as early as 1985. The TREVI working group 'Europe '92' undeniably reinforced the impression that this would happen. In its so-called 'programme of action', a confidential discussion paper presented at the Dublin Summit in 1990, it was clearly stated (paragraph 3: 'combatting drug traffic') that in this area all the member states of the European Community would cooperate as follows:

> by intensifying the regular exchange and permanent updating of detailed information relating to drug trafficking, the methods used for its prevention and law enforcement, and all the data pertaining to the drugs phenomenon, through the channels of appropriate national bodies and departments;
> by establishing in the member states a network of liaison officers familiar with drug-related matters;
> and by reinforcing and coordinating surveillance at their external sea, land and air frontiers.

In addition, those member states which do not already have drugs intelligence units, the document continues, shall examine the methods whereby such units can be established. Member states would then conduct a study on the need for and the conditions under which it would be possible to set up a European Drugs Intelligence Unit (EDIU). The European Council, however, was not willing to wait for such a study and took the decision at Dublin to establish the EDIU. And although it was clear, from the 'programme of action' itself, that this Unit would only fulfil a supportive role and have no executive powers, the institutional position of EDIU within the European Community was not elucidated. But it goes without saying that the EDIU was almost certainly conceived as an intergovernmental institution and not a Communitarian one.

Anyway, as for the original German debate on the restructuring of international police cooperation in Western Europe, the Dublin decision to establish an EDIU shows that the other member states

would no longer totally reject a restructuring along intergovernmental lines. And so it is no wonder that the German delegation
at the Luxembourg Summit got the impression that the gap
between Germany and the other member states on this point
could be completely bridged. At the summit's end, the Germans
sprung a proposal to establish a Central European Investigation
Bureau (Europol) on the other delegations. The timetable for the
institution of Europol's functions was to be as follows: in the first
resort a bureau will be founded for the exchange of information
and experience (up to 31 December 1992); thereafter, in the
second phase, executive powers will be assigned, also within the
member states; the Commission as well as the individual member
states reserve the right to submit proposals.

In comparison to the later provisions in the Maastricht Treaty,
this proposal differs on a number of crucial points.

From a functional viewpoint it is clear that the German
proposal covered the complete spectrum of ideas put forward by
leading German politicians: Europol should have supportive tasks
as well as executive powers. The Maastricht Treaty, however,
displays the general opposition of Europe's political leaders to the
foundation of such an all-embracing Europol. They were only
willing to assign supportive tasks to Europol. Of course, this was a
very disappointing experience for the German architects of this
new institution (Rupprecht, 1991; Rupprecht and Hellenthal,
1992, pp. 248–81).

From an institutional viewpoint the German initiative already
revealed the mixed character of Europol. On the one hand the
delegation clearly designed Europol as an intergovernmental
affair. On the other hand, it linked this institution to the
Community – in the strict sense of the word – by giving the
Commission a right of initiative. So, when one reads the relevant
general and specific provisions in the Maastricht Treaty, one can
only come to the conclusion that in Maastricht the Communitarian character of Europol has been strengthened, in particular
by involving the European Parliament to some extent in the
policy-making process. Nevertheless, one may not lose sight of the
fact that the Europol provisions in the Maastricht Treaty are part
of its Title VI – the foundation of Europol is included in the so-
called 'third pillar' of the Treaty, ie the 'pillar' of intergovernmental cooperation between member states. In other words,
Europol has not been conceived as a Communitarian affair.

Europol, Interpol and TREVI: towards new arrangements

If we are to understand the position of the European Parliament, we need to underline the fundamental differences between the most relevant existing institutional arrangements in this field – Interpol and TREVI.

Interpol and TREVI are still permeated by the informal and confidential character that has always typified police cooperation in Western Europe (Fijnaut, 1987). The organisation, mission and duties of both institutions are not based on unambiguous international treaties and their operation is still guarded from the general public, let alone the subject of independent review, external control or democratic accountability. What is more, both institutions only represent intergovernmental cooperation, although on this point, the institutional position of Interpol is very different from that of TREVI. Whereas Interpol functions more or less as a fraternal international police association, TREVI forms a real intergovernmental cooperative mechanism between member states of the Community, though completely extraneous to its established institutions.

With this institutional picture of Interpol and TREVI in mind, it can be seen that the foundation of Europol and the 'Communitisation' of international police cooperation in Western Europe is an important step towards the democratisation of this form of cooperation (see Chapter 9).

At present, for the first time in the Community's history, all member states are now in the position of having to conduct international police cooperation in a formal manner. This means that in the future, national parliaments will have no excuse to abstain from control of 'their' police forces abroad. Parliaments can make use of their new power to call their governments to account and, in so doing, will also have an opportunity to fill the so-called 'democratic gap' in the European Community. In addition, the European Parliament will gain a consultative position in this field from which it can not only complement the activities of the national parliaments but can also coordinate them to some extent.

As for the privileged position of Europol, it can be expected that in the long run this new police institution will not only complement Interpol, but will take over the tasks of Interpol as far as the European Community is concerned (Mletsko and Mletsko, 1992, p. 486). The fact that the European Drugs Intelligence Unit has been renamed the Europol Drugs Unit and that this Unit is not lodged in Interpol, clearly marks the beginning of a development in which Interpol will end up merely as the global counterpart of Europol.

Being embodied in the Maastricht Treaty, within the framework of intergovernmental cooperation, it is obvious that the governments involved have to arrange, one way or another, the governance of Europol. The most natural solution to this problem would be the fusion of TREVI and Europol, in such a way that the political and official 'superstructure' of TREVI is imposed on Europol, as is foreseen in Maastricht. Parallel to the reordering of the relationship between Interpol and Europol, such a development would also considerably reduce the confusing complexity of international policing in Western Europe. Whatever happens, it seems clear that (as in the United States with the federal police services) an eventual realignment of relationships will be a very sensitive and complicated operation (Rachal, 1982).

THE EUROPEAN PARLIAMENT AND EUROPOL

Since the early 1980s, the European Parliament has developed an interest in the way international police cooperation is structured at the European level. Most of the time this interest has been allied to other issues: fraud against European Community funds, the containment of terrorism, the fight against prostitution, the content and role of the Schengen Treaties and, indeed, the 'war on drugs'.

It goes without saying that we shall limit ourselves here to an analysis of the most important initiatives of the European Parliament with respect to the drugs issue. Two enquiries will be taken into consideration: first, the 1986 *Report Drawn up on Behalf of the Committee of Enquiry into the Drugs Problem in the member states of the Community on the Results of the Enquiry* (Rapporteur: Sir Jack Stewart-Clark), and second, the 1992 *Report Drawn up by the Committee of Enquiry into the Spread of Organised Crime Linked to Drugs Trafficking in the member states of the European Community* (Rapporteur: Patrick Cooney).[4] Moreover one can not overlook the recent

Report of the Committee on Civil Liberties and Internal Affairs
on the Establishment of Europol (Rapporteur: L. Van Outrive).[5]

The reports on the drugs problem and organised crime in the member states

The report on the drugs problem in the member states covers a lot
of related issues. But it is clear that the committee in question paid
a lot of attention to law enforcement in general and international
police cooperation in particular. Its main idea in this field, which
can be linked to the Europol initiative, amounts to the proposal
that a European Community Drugs Task Force (ECDTF) should
be set up, to be modelled on the existing United States Task Force
Programme and adapted for Community use with all possible
improvements. The aim of such a Task Force would be to improve
coordination and the efficiency of all law enforcement agencies
involved with drug trafficking across the Community. Its
establishment would not go hand in hand with a reduction of
the role of Interpol in this matter. In fact, the relevant
department of Interpol should be expanded, reorganised on the
basis of a number of principles and recommendations suggested in
the report and given financial backing.

As for the debate on the development and organisation of
Europol, these suggestions raise several important issues. It must
be acknowledged, though, that it already contained the basic
ideas which were later included in Dublin's TREVI action
programme. On the other hand, the suggestions shed no light on
the main political issues at stake in the Europol discussions.

First, the institutional position of such an ECDTF has to be
considered, and yet the committee paid no attention at all to this
central problem. Nevertheless one might have expected that when
its members were of the opinion that the establishment of an
ECDTF should be a Communitarian affair, they would have
formulated solid arguments for this option. Otherwise one can
only assume that they were very naïve as to the willingness of the
member states to transfer an important part of their sovereignty in
the field of policing to the supranational Community overnight.
The most reasonable explanation of the committee's proposal,
therefore, is that it took the view that an ECDTF would be an
intergovernmental institution. In the light of this conclusion it is
rather astonishing that the committee in no way considered the

future relationship between an ECDTF and Interpol, the more so as it suggests reinforcing Interpol's position in relation to the member states of Europe. This lack of clarity can only point to the conclusion that the committee was unaware of the institutional ramifications of its proposals.

Second, one can only be struck dumb that the committee completely overlooked the problem of whether the members of an ECDTF should possess executive powers or not. Its unconditional reference to the United States Task Force Programme suggests that the committee was of the opinion that the members of the ECDTF would make use of executive powers to investigate drugs trafficking networks, because the participants in the American task forces have always preserved such powers. On the other hand, one can hardly imagine that the committee really believed this should be applied at European Community level in Western Europe. If it did, one would expect the committee to have defended such a position in explicit terms, if only to defend itself against charges of gross naïvete. For it is clear that member states would have kicked up a fuss at cross-border operations by foreign executive policemen. So, we give the committee the benefit of the doubt, reaching the conclusion that in its opinion the adaptation to Community use of the United States Task Force Programme includes the suggestion to withhold executive powers from the members of the ECDTF.

As far as the 1992 report is concerned, a distinction must be made between the majority and the minority opinion of the Committee of Enquiry in question. The majority expressed its doubt as to the feasibility and desirability of Europol as proposed by the German delegation at the Luxembourg Summit: as the report was to say, the idea 'is premature because there does not yet exist a corpus of European criminal law in which such a police force could act across national frontiers'. The majority also highlighted the difficulties of coordinating Community-wide police operations, due to the multiplicity of police forces among the member states. Despite these reservations, it failed to come up with a clear conclusion in relation to the establishment of Europol. On the contrary: the majority merely stated that 'the most appropriate proposal which is currently under discussion concerns the establishment of a European Drugs Intelligence Unit (EDIU) which should be staffed by police and customs officials from the various member states and include drugs liaison officers from key non-Community countries'. This Unit should be based in Lyon, so that it can integrate its activities with Interpol. It should be politically responsible to the European Council of Ministers or to a specific body in the Council created for that purpose. The European Parliament must have the right to question the Council on matters pertaining to European drugs policy, and the President of the European Parliament and its Legal Affairs Committee should receive an annual report from the Council on such matters. For the EDIU to function efficiently it must be able to count upon effective relay units in the member states.

In the minority report no mention at all is made of Europol. And as far as the EDIU is concerned the members in question agreed upon the need for such a Unit but were of the opinion that it can only be established 'if mechanisms have been agreed upon to guarantee democratic control of the activities of the Unit'. What this condition precisely means, however, remains unclear, because the minority only repeat the suggestions made by the majority.

It is rather astonishing that a parliamentary committee set up to enquire into drugs-related organised crime pays little or no attention to Europol. The reason for this is not clear. For even if the committee only wanted to discuss the establishment of an EDIU, one might have expected that it would have been informed about the stepping-stone theory behind the EDIU in relation to Europol. Anyhow, one may come to the conclusion that the committee largely agreed upon the way in which Europol would be embedded in Communitarian as well as intergovernmental structures of the Political Union – but leaving the European Commission out in the cold.

Likewise it is remarkable that the committee didn't go into the relationship between such an EDIU/Europol and Interpol. It is particularly difficult to understand what the institutional integration of both these bodies really means. As stated before, the intergovernmental position of Interpol is completely different from the institutional position that an EDIU/Europol would eventually occupy. So inevitably a lot of legal, organisational and political obstacles have to be removed before anything like operational integration of Interpol and EDIU/Europol can take place. One may, in my opinion, reproach the committee that it totally overlooked this complicated issue.

Lastly, it can be deplored that the committee took no position at all on the question of giving executive powers to an institution like EDIU/Europol, as it might have led to a more sophisticated debate on this issue. By relating the EDIU/Europol to Interpol the committee suggested that only the first is empowered to support national investigation authorities. On the other hand, the committee assigned this institution such an active and activating role in the fight against the drugs trade that one can hardly imagine it could fulfil the related tasks without becoming involved in the application of all sorts of intrusive police powers and methods. And given this probability it would have perhaps been relevant to make a few distinctions in the matter at hand. For example, a distinction between the possession of executive powers and the participation in executive police work of national police forces. Another relevant distinction that could have been put forward is that between an EDIU/Europol that performs operational police tasks autonomously and an EDIU/Europol that takes part in Member State police operations only in a subordinate way. In any case it is a pity that the committee didn't take the opportunity to further the debate on this complicated issue.

The report on Europol

The report of the Committee on Civil Liberties and Internal Affairs contains numerous proposals with respect to international police cooperation. It would take us far too long to discuss the whole range of statements here, so we will limit ourselves to the issues raised in the previous reports.

It must first be underlined that this report defended the position that Europol be considered a completely Communitarian question, drawn up on the basis of Article 235 of the existing EEC Treaty. The main argument that was put forward to justify this option is based on the perceived disadvantages of an intergovernmental approach: the democratic deficit, the disturbance of the relationship between Community institutions, citizens and national authorities, and the lack of proper parliamentary and judicial control. It later stated that as Article 235 already forms the legal basis for other Communitarian regulations (especially in the matter of drugs), why not also for Europol? In the wake of this radically Communitarian perspective on Europol, Interpol was completely disconnected from this initiative.

As far as the question of executive powers is concerned, the report was really very unclear. On the one hand a lot of arguments were put forward saying that such powers cannot be allocated. On the other, it was proposed that Europol should be directed towards the fight against organised crime in general and particularly towards the fight against criminal offences which defraud the European Community. Europol should even have an exclusive competence in relation to the investigation of subsidy frauds. And of course this statement only makes sense if Europol achieves executive powers.

For several reasons this report is a curious document. First of all, it completely contradicted – without any comment – many of the conclusions of the other reports. In the second place, it ignored the policy that was laid down in the Maastricht Treaty; in this sense it leaves a quixotic impression. Third, it plainly denied the effectiveness of existing control mechanisms with respect to cross-border police operations, whereas no questions at all were raised as to the role of the European Parliament. Finally, it suggested that when Europol and Interpol become separate entities, their relationship within Western Europe will cease to be a problem. However, I am afraid that the issue is not that simple.

CONCLUSION

In the introduction the question was raised as to what extent Europol, as it has been conceived in the Maastricht Treaty, meets the expectations and proposals which in the last years have been put forward in the European Parliament with regard to the institutionalisation of international police cooperation, above all in conjunction with the containment of the illegal drugs trade. The answer to this question now is quite simple: the European Parliament incorporates divergent and completely contradictory perspectives on the way this form of cooperation should be institutionalised. Of course, this means that even with the Maastricht Treaty ratified, international police cooperation will remain a point of friction between the European Parliament and the European Council, the European Commission and the European Council of Ministers.

It can also be predicted that the European Parliament, superficially operating in this field, will soon become a sitting duck for the other institutions, as they are in a position to exploit its fundamental weaknesses and disagreements. Parliament can only overcome this unenviable position if its political parties develop a more balanced view on the complicated issue of international police cooperation. And it cannot be excluded from the realm of possibility that, in doing so, the European Parliament will legitimise its claim for a more privileged position in this matter than the Maastricht Treaty allows it.

NOTES

1. *Europa van Morgen*, June 1992, Doc. 52.
2. See page 2 of the 18 September 1992 press release.
3. *Europ a van Morgen*, December 1992, Doc. 73.
4. See European Parliament, 1986–7, Working Documents. PE 106.715/B/fin., respectively European Parliament, 1991–2, Session Documents, PE 152.380/fin.
5. See European Parliament, 1992–3, Session Documents, PE 202.364/def.

REFERENCES

Benyon, J., P. Davies and A. Willis (1990) *Police Cooperation in Europe; A Preliminary Investigation* (Leicester: University of Leicester).

Borricand, J. (1992) 'Crime organisé et coopération européenne', *Revue Internationale de Criminologie et de Police Technique*, vol. 45 (4), pp. 445–54.

Busch, H. (1988) 'Von Interpol zu TREVI; polizeiliche Susammenarbeit in Europa', *Bürgerrechte und Polizei*, vol. 2, pp. 38–55.

Fijnaut, C. (1987) 'The Internationalisation of Criminal Investigation in Western Europe', in C. Fijnaut and R. Hermans (eds), *Police Cooperation in Europe* (Lochem: J. B. van den Brink).

Fijnaut, C. (1992) 'Naar een 'Gemeenschap-pelijke' regeling van de politiële samenwerking en de justitiële rechtshulp', in C. Fijnaut, J. Stuyck and P. Wytinck (eds), *Schengen: proeftuin voor de Europese Gemeenschap?* (Antwerpen, Kluwer Rechtswetenschappen; Arnhem: Gouda Quint).

Fijnaut, C. (1993) 'The 'Communitisation' of Police Cooperation in Western Europe', in H. Scheormers *et al.* (eds), *Free Movement of Persons in Europe; Legal Problems and Experiences* (Dordrecht and Boston: Martinus Nijhoff).

Home Affairs Committee (1990) *Practical Police Cooperation in the European Community*, 2 vols (London: HMSO).

Jeschke, J. (1988) 'Organisierte Ausländerkriminalität und internationale Zusammenarbeit am Beispiel der Drogenkriminalität', *Der Kriminalist*, vol. 12, pp. 462–9.

Kendall, R. (1992) 'Drug Control: Policies and Practices of the International Criminal Police Organisation', *Bulletin on Narcotics*, vol. 44 (1), pp. 3–10.

Le Jeune, P. (1992) *La cooperation policière européenne contre le terrorisme* (Bruxelles: Bruylant).

Littas, R. (1979) 'The Sepat Plan and Its Development', *International Criminal Police Review*, vol. 34 (327), pp. 101–4.

Meyers, H. *et al.* (1991) *Schengen; Internationalisation of Central Chapters of the Law on Aliens, Refugees, Security and the Police* (Deventer: W.E.J. Tjeenk-Willink).

Mletsko, L. and M. Mletsko (1992) 'Europa ist mehr als die EG; ein Gespräch mit dem Generalsekretär der IKPO-Interpol', *Kriminalistik*, nrs 8–9, pp. 482–6.

Nadelmann, E. (1993) 'US Police Activities in Europe', in C. Fijnaut (ed.), *The Internationalisation of Police Cooperation in Western Europe* (Arnhem: Gouda Quint).

Pietsrsick, W. (1981) 'Der internationale organisierte Rauschgifthandel un die besonderen Problemen seiner Bekämpfung', *Poliseiliche Drogenbekämpfung, Wiesbaden, Bundeskriminalamt*, pp. 213–39.

Rachal, P. (1982) *Federal Narcotics Enforcement: Reorganisation and Reform* (Boston: Auburn House).

Rupprecht, R. (1991) 'Brauchen wir Europol? Zukunftsgedanken an der Schwelle Zum neuen Jahr', *Die Polizei*, vol. 82 (12), pp. 293–9.

Rupprecht, R. and M. Hellenthal (eds) (1992) *Innere Sicherheit im Europäischen Binnenmarkt* (Gütersloh: Bertelsmann Stiftung).

Summer, H. (1979) 'Bekämpfung des Heroinhandels; Moglichkeiten und Grensen internationaler Zusammenarbeit', *Kriminalistik*, vol. 7, pp. 314–20.

Tress, P. (1988) *Leitfaden für Instrukteure und Ermitlungsbeamte auf dem Gebiet der Rauschgiftbekämpfung* (Wiesbaden: Bundeskriminalamt).

Zimmermann, H. (1992) 'Europol; Anforderungen, Möglichkeiten und Fragen einer europäischer Zentralstelle Zur Verbrechensbekämpfung', *Schriftenreihe der Polizei Führungsakademie*, vol. 4, pp. 47–55.

Part IV
EU External Drug Policies, Enlargement and Drug Control

12 Money Laundering, the Developed Countries and Drug Control: the New Agenda

Ernesto Savona[1]

The 1988 Vienna Drug Convention was the turning point for international anti-money laundering policies. Before its adoption only Australia, the United States and a few other countries had adopted domestic anti-money laundering policies. Since the Vienna Convention, many countries have adopted either a partial or a complete set of criminal and regulatory policies against the laundering of the proceeds of crime. This process was strengthened in 1989 by the G7 Group of industrialised countries, which established the Task Force on Money Laundering. This provides the international community with a set of recommendations to address the problem.

In February 1990 the Financial Action Task Force (FATF) produced a report containing forty recommendations combatting money laundering. This was the first set of international 'soft laws' against the problem. The impetus behind this came from the Vienna Convention and the Basle Committee for banking regulations of 1988. In 1991 the European Community Directive on Money Laundering was enacted to harmonise the anti-money laundering policies of the twelve European countries. In 1991 the Council of Europe Convention took steps toward strengthening anti-laundering policies. This was accomplished by an international expansion of the area of criminalisation from drug trafficking crimes to all serious crimes and by instituting international police cooperation. In 1992 the Organisation of American States developed a set of recommendations for Latin American Countries which was strongly influenced by the FATF's forty recommendations.

In only five years, due to the initiative of all those mechanisms and through the leadership of G7's FATF, it has been possible to produce an international anti-laundering system, intended as a coordinated set of international, regional and domestic policies and mechanisms. These policies reflect two main strategies: attacking criminal organisations for the proceeds produced by their criminal activity, and defending the transparency of economic and financial systems from the infiltration of organised crime.

The policies originated from the concerns provoked by drug trafficking but are now being enlarged to encompass 'all serious crimes'. The main assumption behind this strategy is that by attacking the proceeds of crime it will become more risky for criminals to commit not only drug-related crime but all crime which produces high revenue. The perception of the increasing internationalisation of high-revenue crime makes the need for international cooperation in tracing, freezing and seizing criminal assets ever more apparent.

This will require substantial changes in the agencies charged with implementing the policies, not least the need for greater cooperation between them. New forms of analysis, investigation and organisation are required of law enforcement agencies to deal with financial criminal matters. The demand for financial intelligence is producing new and specialised agencies in the area of economic analysis and investigation such as FINCEN in the United States, TRACFIN in France, and AUSTRAC in Australia. Furthermore, banks may have to ease their secrecy, identifying customers and cooperating with enforcement agencies in reporting suspicious transactions.

As a reaction to the increased efficiency of anti-laundering strategies, criminal organisations are beginning to use more professionals in their money laundering activities and developing more complex strategies and schemes.

This chapter has several key objectives. It seeks to examine the dynamics of the money-laundering phenomenon, the measures which have been taken on the national and international levels to address it and the development of these diverse strategies. The problems of implementing anti-laundering policies will also be considered. A discussion of the ways in which it is possible to improve their effectiveness and efficiency will be discussed in the conclusion.

DRUG VERSUS NON-DRUG MONEY LAUNDERING: EMPHASIS IN THE FATF COUNTRIES

A 1990 study by the Financial Action Task Force[2] estimated that $85 billion a year is available for laundering and investment from the sale of cocaine, heroin and cannabis in the US and Europe alone. It is not possible to update this general estimate and at the same time it is impossible to say how much criminal money is circulating today in the world's economic and financial systems. Assessing it through the analysis of cash-flow between countries is extremely problematic, although that technique has been invaluable for identifying particularly suspicious situations.[3]

Pursuant to the recommendation n.30 of the Financial Action Task Force, tentative national estimates have been made and are being refined,[4] but they appear to be of limited utility. In the United States, analysts estimated that 'non-drug proceeds may account for a third or even as much as one-half of total illicit proceeds converted in or transmitting through US financial institutions'.[5] The crimes giving rise to this money include gambling, smuggling, pornography, loan-sharking, fraud, corruption and criminal tax evasion.

According to the US State Department's 1994 International Narcotics Control Strategy Report, approximately the same trend is found in Europe:

> Bankers, finance ministries and enforcement agencies report an apparent increase in non-drug money laundering and seem agreed that drug-related money laundering constitutes no more than three-fourths of illegal proceeds transferring through or being converted by West European financial institutions (exclusive of tax considerations), and may be at that level or slightly lower in Eastern Europe where large sums of crime syndicate funds are being invested.[6]

The perception of an expansion of non-drug-related laundering may be the result of many different factors. The first could be the new profile being given to criminal money that is not drug-related by international and regional bodies such as the FATF and the Council of Europe, coupled with bureaucratic fears that anti-drug programmes will no longer have the same budgetary appeal. The second could be a real expansion of criminal proceeds from sources other than drug-related crime, giving rise to the question whether drug-money accumulation is decreasing or other criminal money simply increasing. The third factor could be the process of professionalisation of money laundering activities, to be discussed below. This process allows criminals, especially organised groups, to exploit the same kinds of laundering schemes used by drug money launderers. This can be done directly by the organised criminals themselves or more likely by the same professional launderers who handle drug money. Capital being inherently mutable, once any readily identifiable bills (whether by serial number or drug traces) have been changed – which may be done by a separate exchange professional – the laundering investment professional has no reason not to mix funds derived from various criminal activities, further diluting the possibility of a direct association of those funds with a particular drug trafficking origin.

A recent analysis[7] shows that countries experience different problems with regard to criminal activity which creates a money laundering demand. Western Europe produces, exports and imports organised crime, but also a variety of economic crime not necessarily 'organised', such as fraud and corruption. Groups such as the Sicilian Mafia are spreading their activity into both Western and Eastern Europe, in addition to maintaining their traditional connections in the Americas. Organised crime from Africa (Nigerian gangs); from the East (mainly Chinese, Turkish and Russian organised crime gangs); and from the Western Hemisphere (Colombians) import drugs into Europe, and may receive payment through European banking channels. These are all opportunistic groups dealing with a variety of illicit goods and services. The prevalence of drug-trafficking crimes does not obscure the relevance of other crimes, such as arms trafficking or fraud. Central and Eastern European countries are potentially large exporters of organised crime, and seem to be areas of investment for money laundering. North America is a major producer of organised criminality and the largest import market for organised crime and its product lines of drugs, smuggled immigrants, etc. South America, Africa and Asia, with many local differences, are mainly producers and exporters of either organised crime products (cocaine, heroin, amphetamine), services (Nigerian courier networks), proceeds (Cali cartel bank accounts in Luxembourg), and organisations (Colombian cocaine cartel vertical distribution networks, Chinese Triads).

TWO GOALS, TWO STRATEGIES – FORTY POLICIES

The main goals governments want to pursue with their anti-laundering policies can be summarised as:

attacking criminal activities and disrupting criminal organisations;

defending the transparency of the economic/financial systems.

The first goal, an active one, seeks to discourage organisations from pursuing criminal activities by increasing the 'law enforcement risk' for criminals. This risk is a comprehensive term that encompasses both the risk of being identified, arrested and convicted and the risk that the proceeds of crime will be forfeited. Money and the other proceeds of crime have increasingly become the primary investigative trail used to trace criminal organisations. To this 'apprehension risk' it is necessary to add the 'confiscation risk', which is becoming more common with the wide use of seizure and confiscation.

By making it more difficult for criminals to keep the proceeds of their crimes, and by increasing the 'apprehension risk' there should be a great disincentive to incur the risk involved by generating these illicit proceeds. Indeed, for a criminal organisation, confiscation risk can be a more effective deterrent than apprehension risk. A criminal enterprise characterised by continuity and a hierarchical structure can control apprehension risk. Simple overstaffing or recruitment/replacement procedures, accompanied by layers of sufficient organisational insulation, financial rewards and a reputation for violence (to minimise the risk of an apprehended member jeopardising the 'safety' of the group or its core management), allow organisations like the Mafia, the Triads and the Boryokudan to survive the imprisonment of individual members without serious damage to organisational operations or profitability. None of those defence mechanisms, however, are effective at addressing a loss of confiscated funds, which tends to frustrate criminal organisational and individual goals and profitability. Forcing the organisation to work harder and take more risk for less return is, after all, a classic economic disincentive.

The second goal (protecting the transparency and integrity of domestic and international financial systems) is a defensive one.

Criminal money pollutes and infects these systems, altering competition in the market place. Legitimate money on which taxes are paid and whose cost for investment purposes is higher than criminal money cannot effectively compete with low-cost criminal proceeds. Criminal money also creates political advantages, making it easier for 'respectable strawmen' representing criminal organisations to infiltrate economic and political life. They are subsequently followed by members of gangs and the introduction of criminal practices and values.

Both goals of penal deterrence/control and protection of financial transparency/integrity are closely connected, even if the first is centred more on criminal legislation and the second on the exercise of regulatory powers. Frequently there is a cross-over, in which criminal penalties are applied to reinforce the transparency of the financial system, and regulatory policies are used to identify or deter criminal conduct.[8] Thus, financial institutions typically have regulatory obligations of customer identification, which impose both administrative and criminal penalties for deliberate non-compliance by an employee. They also apply criminal penalties to a customer intentionally violating those requirements, for example by furnishing false identity documents. These identification policies and reporting of large currency transactions, however, have historically emanated from law enforcement authorities seeking to enlist the assistance of banks and bank regulators in identifying and tracing the transfer of criminal proceeds through regulated financial institutions.

These two goals have received attention through the forty recommendations of the 1990 report of the FATF. This expresses three main objectives. The first is 'The Improvement of National Legal Systems to Combat Money Laundering', mainly measures making money laundering a criminal offence and empowering confiscation. They relate to the first goal of attacking criminal activities and disrupting criminal organisations. The second objective refers to the 'Enhancement of the Role of the Financial System', mainly policies directed at the second goal (making financial systems more transparent). The third refers to 'Strengthening of International Cooperation' as a way of achieving the two goals more effectively.

These forty recommendations have influenced the anti-laundering policies of many countries. Step by step, followed by regional instruments such as the European Directive, the Council of

Europe Convention and recommendations from the Organisation for American States, an international system of 'soft laws' and domestic 'hard laws' has been enacted. Beyond the difficulties of implementation at the different levels, the creation of this system has made it more difficult for criminals to launder their money. This system is totally new in the philosophy of crime prevention and control, and yet it could also initiate new organised crime activities.

THE GAME: HOW CRIMINALS AVOID CONTROLS AND HOW POLICY-MAKERS ESTABLISH NEW ONES

Looking at the main international criminal organisations, two trends seem to appear in their money laundering activities: trends toward professionalism and complexity. It is impossible to say how much these two complementary trends are influenced by the creation of the new anti-money laundering system or are the result of internal organisational developments.

The trend toward professionalism is demonstrated by:

the progressive separation of criminal activities and money laundering activities and in some cases the establishment of money laundering services offered to a wide range of criminals and to more than one criminal organisation.

the progressive involvement in money laundering schemes of professional launderers such as accountants, lawyers and private bankers.

This trend toward professionalism is due to the need to minimise law enforcement risk and maximise opportunities. There are three main ways in which criminal organisations try to do this: first, they have greater recourse to risk analysis and risk management; second, greater recourse to technology; and third, greater recourse to professionalism in the cycle of laundering and investment. This is a trend that can be found in all the main international criminal organisations.[9] The proverbial use of defence lawyers as house counsel ('consiglieri' in organised crime jargon, 'risk analysts' in management jargon) merits greater examination. In order to minimise risks, criminals (knowing the price of information) need to know the procedural requirements for law enforcement action. The flip-side to law enforcement wiretapping and electronic surveillance technology can be, for example, the hiring of American law firms by Colombian traffickers to 'obtain materials from the court, things that are in public record or things that are in criminal files released through the process of trials and courts . . . so they can study this material to see, for example, how long it takes the DEA or the FBI to get a wiretap application . . . Mainstream law firms and defense attorneys [are] doing risk analysis and risk management.'[10]

This reference to electronic surveillance emphasises that communications are the vulnerable point in criminal organisations. Criminals need to communicate and those communication networks can be penetrated and 'captured', yielding invaluable knowledge of the organisation's structure and activities as well as directly usable evidence. No single technical solution guarantees such penetration, but rather a series of continuous adjustments by law enforcement to the communication practices of the criminal groups. Cellular phones, especially used with stolen phone codes from operating phones, and anonymous pay telephones in hotels, restaurants and hospitals are most often used by criminals.[11] Crypt and digitalised communications are the evolving steps of this technology.

Criminal organisations frequently resort to expert advice for laundering and investing money. The notorious examples of the Italian bankers Sindona and Calvi acting with the Italian Mafia demonstrate the involvement of professional bankers of major institutions in the criminal process of laundering money. As the need for their advice grows, these professionals become more and more integral to criminal organisations. 'And you have got people who are involved in dealing with the financial side of the industry, dealing with the money, dealing with the controllers and accountants. I might add that these cartels rely very heavily on professional accountants. Many of these people are credentialed and decreed and licensed in several countries. They travel frequently to check on the investments in the investment centres of the financial world.'[12]

The metaphorical classification used for describing different levels of money laundering services, such as hand-wash, family washing machine, condominium washing machine and launderette[13] is intended to express the trend toward the professionalisation of money laundering activities. There are different kinds of 'launderette' operating in money laundering markets. Some of them are legitimate mechanisms such as banks and other financial institutions, sometimes with informal subsidiaries devoted to laundering, such as the black network of the Bank of Credit and Commerce International (BCCI). Other alternative systems operate in Asia as 'hawala' or 'hundi'. These are fully or quasi-legitimate alternative systems of informal banking widely used by traffickers. 'Casas de cambio' in Latin America and a wide range of import/export and commodity brokers are also frequently used by criminals. It is difficult to say if criminals are only the customers or also the owners of these services. In a continuous evolution of these private banking services, criminals as customers readily become the owners. The combination of law enforcement action, more effective regulation of banking systems, and demand for laundering services in corrupt business and official transactions seem to be stimulating international alternatives to traditional, well regulated, financial systems. The increasing number of off-shore banks, especially close to drug-producing countries, seems relevant in this regard.

Drawing on records seized through Colombian National Police raids and their own investigations, US government agents believe that the Cali cartel – which once handled all money operations internally – now employ financial controllers to seek bids from money brokers, who in turn may process money for more than one trafficking organisation. One side-effect of such massive document seizures has been that these controllers now minimise paper records, preferring to use computer discs and increasingly sophisticated communication devices, often linked to computers.

Money brokers are also buying cash in bulk, at a discount rate of around 20 per cent. The drug trader gets the proceeds back from the point-of-sale countries without having the burden of personal involvement.[14] This level of sophistication was not common several years ago and is still limited to the more developed money launderers, such as the Colombian cartels, who have historically been trend-setters in money laundering.

A trend towards more complex money laundering activities can be found by analysis of the schemes, methods and mechanisms involved and consideration of the strategies used. Some conceptual definitions are necessary to explain the money laundering system, which are best presented in a practical example.

Money laundering 'schemes' attempt to 'structure' (legitimise) a 'transaction' through the use of some 'mechanism'. For example, criminals may wish to 'smurf' (American slang for using anonymous helpers to divide a transaction into small parts that will not arouse suspicion) the proceeds of crime into many banks in order to avoid controls before bringing the funds together to buy stocks and shares through a brokerage account. Here, the scheme is the plan to launder the proceeds and structure the transaction, and the mechanisms are the banks and the brokerage house. A scheme could be as simple as the example or more complex, when more and different methods and mechanisms are involved – an overall conception or practice of combining or selecting schemes according to organisational goals could properly be called a money laundering strategy.

The phases of money laundering can go through bank and non-bank financial institutions (e.g. brokerage houses) and through non-financial institutions (export brokers), or all three in the same scheme. The main phases are commonly called 'placement', 'layering' and 'integration'. These can be seen in a continuum (from the placement to the integration) or alone – proceeds of crime may be laundered only through one of these phases. For this reason it is sometimes difficult for investigators to understand in which phase a single operation should be inserted.

The mechanisms are the main actors in the money laundering activity. Banks have traditionally had a prominent role but their reporting systems probably influenced the move away from the use of the banking system as a launderer: 'Knowledge by criminals of the BSA reporting requirements and the generally high compliance by the financial system with those requirements, often discourages the criminals' use of that system. And, even though some criminals still want their money in financial institutions because of the services only those institutions provide, the criminals are, as result of the BSA reporting requirements, compelled to be more creative and sophisticated in their efforts to insert their ill-gotten cash into the financial system. They are forced to engage in more complex or convoluted schemes which frequently require the employment of more individuals to make them work.'[15]

The two trends toward professionalism and complexity merge in the increase in money laundering activities on the part of non-bank financial institutions, as a recent US Senate investigation confirms.[16] The following are the non-bank financial institutions that have been involved in money laundering cases as reported by the police in Hong Kong, the United Kingdom and the USA: currency exchanges, money transmitters, parallel exchange markets, 'black' money markets, precious metal, stones and artwork dealers/brokers, auction houses, casinos and gambling businesses, automobile/airplane/boat/real-estate dealers and brokers and professionals such as attorneys, notaries, accountants, insurance companies and security brokers.[17]

Another trend emerging in the US is the utilisation of bearer bonds and bearer bond interest coupons to pay for narcotics. These bonds and coupons are being exchanged among some narcotics dealers just like cash. Again, much remains to be learned concerning the possible use of this type of scheme.

In conclusion, criminal organisations do not respect national borders and have exploited the globalisation of commerce. As international regulations and enforcement procedures are tightened to prevent money launderers using traditional or formal financial systems, launderers will turn increasingly to nontraditional financial systems, transfer mechanisms, and foreign financial systems where either few or no regulations exist, so as to disguise the source of their funds and to make them usable in legitimate economies.

The utility of the international payments system to money laundering networks has been successfully demonstrated by investigations into the operations of the Bank of Credit and Commerce International. These investigations have heightened global awareness of the money laundering threat and illustrated the necessity for foreign governments to modify bank secrecy laws and develop coordinated responses to combat the money laundering threat.

The mechanisms and methods described above do not necessarily demonstrate an evolutionary trend from simple money laundering methods toward more complex ones. Even today the simplest ways of laundering persist, such as physical smuggling across borders. There does, however, appear to be an evolution in the use of mechanisms, with more emphasis on non-bank financial institutions (where only banks are regulated) or on non-financial businesses and mechanisms (where both banks and non-bank financial institutions are regulated). All the recent regulation and forms of criminal control have shifted criminals to other less regulated activities, and the shift of laundering activity from traditional mechanisms to non-regulated or non-financial ones is highly characteristic of countries where anti-money laundering controls have been most effectively implemented.

It is also possible to detect an evolution towards greater complexity in the schemes utilised. A movement toward more internationalisation is obvious and may be the product of the new transnational dimensions of criminal organisations which do business on a global market – selling cocaine in Europe as well as in North America, buying heroin from Southeast Asia rather than Mexico if the price and quality promise better resale profits. Internationalisation in money laundering schemes may also be a conscious strategy to minimise law enforcement risk, taking advantage of imperfect investigative and prosecutive cooperation between countries, bank secrecy, corruption and absence of regulation in countries which may constitute weak links in the global anti-laundering chain. A sophisticated criminal organisation has the inherent capacity to use complex money laundering schemes to protect and utilise its assets, with its choice between traditional or innovative methods being a function of the environments in which it operates, derives its profits, and where it can find opportunities for placement, layering or integration of those assets.

The response to this increasing complexity of money laundering organisations which also use unregulated mechanisms has provoked a strong demand for regulation of non-bank financial institutions. FATF has written an interpretative note to Recommendations 10 and 11 regarding the application of appropriate anti-money laundering measures to the conduct of financial activities by non-financial businesses or professions,[18] and some FATF members are in the process of discussing and enacting new ways of effectively regulating such activities.[19]

THE WAY FORWARD

No more laws please: implementing the anti-money laundering system

The international anti-money laundering system is both large and complex. Mechanisms and 'soft laws' such as the FATF recommendations clearly address the domestic aspects of this system – the national legislators and national banking and financial systems, the law enforcement agencies and the criminal justice systems. In many countries these 'soft laws' have produced a homogeneous set of 'hard laws'.

The process of adapting legal norms and establishing new criminal legislation and financial regulations is occurring simultaneously in many regions and countries, North America and Western Europe leading the way. South America is following, although without uniformity; Asia is a big patchwork with some countries acting intensively against laundering while officials in others turn a blind eye. Eastern Europe has only recently begun to address the problem; and Africa has generally failed to develop anti-money laundering policies. There are therefore still many holes in the system despite the efforts of many in the international community to fill them.

After the problem of harmonising legislation, implementation may be the most important task. In those places where a domestic system has been created, there is ongoing discussion as to its effectiveness and efficiency, on its capacity to achieve the two above-mentioned goals at the least possible cost.

Despite the internationalisation of money laundering activities, the policy differences between countries reduce the effectiveness of the anti-laundering system. Criminals seek both to move money rapidly and to increase the return on their investments. They therefore seek out places where the risk of their money being traced and confiscated is low and returns on investments are high. The effectiveness of an anti-laundering strategy therefore depends upon the successful combination of domestic policies oriented to control the 'placement phase', and the international harmonisation of policies which equalises the risk for criminals. Domestic anti-money laundering systems and the international anti-money laundering system need to be strictly interdependent, the effectiveness of one depending on the effectiveness of the other.

Allied to effectiveness is the question of efficiency, namely what costs are incurred to produce the required effects? In addressing this question, one of the sensitive areas is the burden on the banks to comply with reporting procedures. Attaining the transparency of the financial system can reduce the traditional efficiency of that system. Criminal operators look for places where banking secrecy is highly enforced and where controls do not exist. In the international financial markets there are many available locations, such as some of the off-shore banks where secrecy and confidentiality are highly enforced and where it is possible to launder money easily. These are the preferred systems for criminals because they maximise their investments at almost no risk of confiscation. Until regulation reaches such banks – creating a 'level playing field' – these holes in the international financial system will foster unfair competition. Once again the problem is that transparency can be efficient only if its criteria are widely harmonised and equalised between countries.

Conditions for success

In summary, to have effective and efficient domestic and international anti-money laundering systems, two main conditions have to be met:

the establishment in each country of two sets of policies, one regulatory and the other crime control according to some minimum common criteria;[20]

the effective implementation of these policies.

The first condition (building a homogeneous legal framework) means that all countries should have regulatory and crime control policies containing at least some common criteria. For achieving this result an integrated system of international cooperation needs to be realised. International mechanisms and countries through multilateral and bilateral cooperation should solicit and help other countries participate in a common protective network, based on recognised criteria and worldwide regulation of non-bank financial institutions.

The second condition is more substantive. It requires that, in order to achieve the two previously discussed goals, law enforcement agencies and the financial system need the capacity and motivation to act. To achieve 'motivation for implementation', a system of incentives/disincentives for law enforcement agencies and financial institutions should be established. Even if the intensity of the problem varies between countries, past experience of implementing policies can be used to establish some general outlines for action.

Effective and efficient domestic and international anti-money laundering systems should have two aims. The first aim is cooperation between law enforcement agencies, banks and financial institutions. It is widely recognised that the greater this cooperation, the more effective the system. This cooperation cannot be achieved only on a voluntary basis and therefore should be regulated. But neither can it be pursued only through compulsion. It needs a degree of motivation that exceeds the resistance against it.

In order to achieve this, there is a need to establish new agencies where law enforcement expertise is combined with banking and financial expertise – such as Fincen in the USA, Tracfin in France, Austrac in Australia – and their development in other countries could be a viable solution to the problem. Alternative and additional solutions can be found which increase the level of cooperation, bearing in mind that the wheels of cooperation are oiled by incentives to control laundering and by disincentives against corrupt behaviour.

The identification of incentives and disincentives should be part of any analysis of the structure and organisation of law enforcement agencies and of the banking and the financial industry. Incentives for law enforcement agencies can be of an economic nature, such as sharing seized criminal assets, career rewards for participants, and training in the area of financial investigation. Disincentives could be related to the potential for corruption coming from money laundering activities.

Incentives for the banking and financial industry to report suspicious transactions and cooperate with law enforcement agencies, are directly connected to their reputation. Banks and financial institutions want to preserve and increase their standing because its value rests upon the market environment in which they operate. The greater the competition between banks, the more highly they value their reputations – after all, most customers are attracted to banks and financial institutions that are not involved in fraud or other economic crime. The willingness of banks to cooperate with anti-money laundering policies could be pursued through a system of incentives/disincentives directed at their reputations. Corporate sanctions against banks and financial institutions should be considered not only as an economic deterrent but also for their powerful labelling function.

A second objective of an effective and efficient anti-money laundering system is to maintain a high level of flexibility in the system. That means that the definition and implementation of regulations and criminal sanctions should be managed and monitored in order to optimise their effectiveness.

Criminals are very flexible at exploiting banking and financial systems for their money laundering activities. Once they realise that a control system is effective they try to avoid it. It is therefore possible that what has been for some time an effective system for controlling money laundering quickly becomes obsolete as it is circumnavigated by the launderers. If adjustments in the system are not promptly made, the controls will have no effects upon criminals and some negative effects in terms of efficiency. The ongoing discussion on the effectiveness of the present reporting system in the United States (which according to some analysts does not justify the burden upon the banks and financial institutions) is a warning light for the need to pay more attention to the efficiency issue.

International harmonisation

In order to develop effective domestic and international anti-money-laundering policies, there needs to be an international instrument to coordinate strategies formulated at the national and international levels. An anti-money laundering authority could be established in each country in order to monitor the development of the phenomenon, using information obtained from law enforcement and regulatory agencies. All these authorities could be drawn together at the international level in order to harmonise anti-money laundering policies worldwide. This agency could provide advice on potential new regulations and legislation, select priorities for action and evaluate the effects of legislative strategies and national and international policies.

In order for an effective international money-laundering policy to be developed in the future, it is imperative that it be placed on the international agenda today. Cooperation and coordination are sorely needed if the ever more powerful and complex phenomenon of money laundering is to be combatted successfully.

NOTES

1. This chapter is part of the research activity of the author supported under grant number 92–IJ–CX–0005 awarded by the National Institute of Justice, US Department of Justice, Washington, DC. Points of view in this document are those of the author and do not necessarily represent the official position of the US Department of Justice.

2. Financial Action Task Force on Money Laundering, Report, Paris, 7 February 1990.

3. President's Commission on Organized Crime, *The Cash Connection*, US Government Printing Office, 1986.

4. I have seen notes and tables by P. van Duyne on the cash flow sent back to the Netherlands. The cash flow repatriated in 1990 from foreign banks was Dfl3,691 million. This money includes criminal and legitimate sources such as savings from foreign workers, normal transfers of funds, and tax evasion/avoidance money. As Mr van Duyne says, 'anyhow the Dfl3,691 million seems the physical upper limit of the money-laundering cash flow following a cross-border circuit. The criminal money should be considerably lower.' FinCen (USA) is actually developing an analysis of the cash flow to the United States in order to quantify the criminal money. The research is still in progress.

5. US Department of State, *International Narcotics Strategy Report 1994*, p. 467.

6. *Ibid.*, p. 4.

7. E. U. Savona and M. DeFeo, *Money Trails: International Money Laundering Trends and Prevention/Control Policies*, report prepared for the International Conference on Preventing and Controlling Money Laundering and the Proceeds of Crime: A Global Approach, Courmayeur, Italy, June 1994.

8. For example, the requirement to report transactions over a determined amount of money is a regulatory measure to prevent criminals using banks for laundering purposes. This measure could also help law enforcement agencies trace a money laundering scheme.

9. E. U. Savona and M. DeFeo, *op. cit.*, Ch. 2.

10. Testimony from John Coleman, Assistant Administrator for Operations DEA at the US Senate, Subcommittee on Terrorism Narcotics and International Operations, Hearing on Recent Development on Transnational Crime . . . 20 April 1994 Stenographic Transcript p. 13.

11. Testimony of Mr Coleman, *op. cit.* p. 39.

12. *Ibid.*, p. 15.

13. See Savona, 1993, pp. 35–6.

14. INCSR, *op. cit.*, p. 479.

15. US Department of Treasury (1991) *The Reporting Requirements of the Bank Secrecy Act and Section 6050I of the Internal Revenue Code. Their Effectiveness and Utility*. Report to the Congress, December, pp. 3–4.

16. Staff Statement, US Senate Permanent Subcommittee on Investigations, Hearings on Current Trends in Money Laundering 27 February 1992, Appendix, p. 87.

17. US Dept. of Treasury and US Customs Service, *Typology of Money Laundering, Non-Traditional Financial Institutions*, document presented at the Financial Action Task Force II, 14–19 March 1991, Paris, pp. 14–25.
18. Financial Action Task Force on Money Laundering, *Annual Report 1993–1994*, 16 June 1994, annex 2, p. 33.
19. *Ibid.*, p. 23.
20. The recent report (June 1994) of the UN conference, 'Preventing and Controlling Money Laundering and the Use of Proceeds of Crime: A Global Approach', identifies seven minimum priorities which should be recognised worldwide: (1) Criminalisation of laundering of drug and non-drug criminal proceeds, (2) Limitation of bank secrecy, (3) Implementation of the 'Know your Customer' rule, (4) Identification and reporting of suspicious transactions, (5) Improved regulation of businesses/professionals conducting financial operations, (6) Asset forfeiture legislation; (7) Workable international cooperation mechanisms.

REFERENCES

Financial Action Task Force on Money Laundering (1990) *Report*, Paris, 7 February.

Financial Action Task Force on Money Laundering (1994) *Annual Report 1993–1994*, 16 June 1994.

President's Commission on Organized Crime (1986) *The Cash Connection* (Washington, DC: US Government Printing Office).

Savona, E. U. and M. DeFeo (1994) *Money Trails: International Money Laundering Trends and Prevention/Control Policies*, report prepared for the International Conference on Preventing and Controlling Money laundering and the proceeds of Crime: A Global Approach, Courmayeur, Italy, June 1994.

Savona, E. U. (1993) 'Mafia Money Laundering versus Italian Legislation', *European Journal on Criminal Policy and Research*, vol. 1 (3), pp. 35–6.

UN Conference on Preventing and Controlling Money Laundering and the Use of Proceeds of Crime: A Global Approach (1994), *Report*, June.

US Department of Treasury (1991) *The Reporting Requirements of the Bank Secrecy Act and Section 60501 of the Internal Revenue Code. Their Effectiveness and Utility. Report to the Congress*, December.

US Department of State (1994) *International Narcotics Strategy Report*, April, Washington, DC.

US Dept of Treasury and US Customs Service (1991) *Typology of Money Laundering, Non Traditional Financial Institutions*, document presented at the Financial Action Task Force II 14–19 March, Paris.

13 Drug Trafficking, Laundering and Neo-Liberal Economics: Perverse Effects for a Developing Country[1]

Humberto Campodónico

The distribution pattern of the proceeds of drug trafficking amongst the producing countries, between the cartels of traffickers and the producers themselves, has remain unchanged for some years. This means that approximately 90 per cent of profits continue to be made in industrialised, drug-consuming countries, whilst only 10 per cent return to the producing countries. Given the scale of the 'narco-dollar' problem, most governments are keen to show that they are doing something to combat money laundering and drug trafficking. Now and again operations are mounted, such as the famous 'Casquete Polar' at the end of the 1980s against the Medellin Cartel. Financial scandals are also made public, and those in power are imprisoned, as in the case of General Noriega of Panama. Curiously, accused and fugitives are always linked with the third world. Rare indeed are prosecutions against drug traffickers or financial institutions of the industrialised world, which is precisely where most of the proceeds of drug trafficking are kept.

What ensues is a 'double discourse' in the industrialised countries. On the one hand, it is suggested that money laundering must be policed through a series of specific measures and economic pressures have been brought to bear on countries such as Peru to toe the line. On the other hand, the multi-nationals also demand the unhindered free movement of capitals internationally. This makes it possible for the 'dirty money' of drug trafficking to be indistinguishable from legal capitals. As a result, international attempts to combat money laundering and to locate the profits of trafficking have had little success until now.

This chapter illustrates this double discourse, by examining how the neo-liberal economic policies foisted upon Peru by international financial institutions and the developed countries have acted as impediments to the fight against drug trafficking – and at the same time have brought about largely negative consequences for the Peruvian economy.

CONDITIONALITY IN ECONOMIC AND DRUG POLICIES OF THE NORTH

During 1990, at the same time that the newly installed Peruvian government was negotiating with international agencies and developed countries on economic questions, the government was also negotiating with the US government on the terms of a joint fight against drugs. The first priority of the US government was to sign an agreement with the new government of Fujimori similar to that signed with the Bolivian government in the first few months of 1990. The agreement was to be signed by September at the latest, so that the funds of the Andean Initiative could correspond with the fiscal year 1990 and be credited to that year. In other words, the Peruvian government had two negotiations of the utmost importance with the US: its reinsertion in the international financial system, and secondly the fight against drug trafficking and the signature of the anti-drugs agreement.

In the event, the Peruvian government rejected the signature of the anti-drugs agreement with the US in September 1990 because of the conditions included in it. It proposed new foci and scopes to deal with the drug-trafficking problem. As a result of long negotiations, the agreement was finally signed in May 1991. The postponement of the signature of the anti-drugs agreement by Fujimori led to a new and protracted period of negotiations concerning the reinsertion of Peru into the international financial system. The government of the US takes the view that it cannot endorse the support of multilateral organisations for governments not cooperating in the fight against drug trafficking. It is only since the signature of this agreement that the negotiations on reinsertion were set up, and signed with the IMF in Washington in September 1991.

To summarise, the reinsertion of Peru into the international financial system is subject to a new conditionality (the signing of the anti-drugs agreement) – in addition to the traditional economic conditionalities created by the IMF and the World Bank. At the same time, the anti-drugs agreement itself states clearly that neo-liberal programmes of reform (described by international institutions as 'coherent and viable economic policies') must be put in operation. What are the consequences of these interlocking conditions?

THE FUJIMORI GOVERNMENT AND ITS NEO-LIBERAL REFORMS

The Peruvian government's reforms, which started in August 1990 and gained force in March 1991, have had some negative consequences for the country. The reforms (for example, the programme of stabilization and the beginning of structural reforms) have been badly designed and poorly implemented (in terms of their sequence and the speed of execution). The economic consequences have been largely negative as well. Here we restrict ourselves to the aspects of the reforms which have implications for drug trafficking.

Liberalisation of currency exchange

Before the coming to power of the Fujimori government, all movements of currencies coming into or going out of Peru had to be registered with the Peruvian Central Bank (Banco Central de Reserva or BCR). Currencies obtained for exports or imports fall within this category. However, already in 1988 the government of Alan Garcia had relaxed the means of control of currency exchange, which increased the flow of currency inside Peru. In 1990 the Prime Minister Hurtado Miller decided that traders could dispose fully of the currencies derived from exports, and that importers would be free to buy dollars on the market, without registration with the Central Bank.

This meant not only that the Central bank no longer had it in its power to register the movements of capitals coming from international trade (this information can now only be obtained from customs) but also that importers could avail themselves of dollars from the parallel economy in order to buy imports. In reality this means that drug trafficking money can be bought by any agency, and used to do business abroad.

Liberalisation of the banking system

In addition, the government of Fujimori has proceeded to liberalise the banking system. This means that there is now free movement of currencies between Peru and the rest of the world. This has contributed to the legalisation of money laundering in the Peruvian financial system since it is possible to deposit dollars in Peru without any restrictions and without having to provide information about their origin.

Consequently, hundreds of millions of dollars have come into Peru, in order to benefit from the high rates of interest available on the national market. This highly mobile capital is called 'capital golondrino': golondrino means 'rolling stone', so 'foot-loose capital' would convey a similar meaning. Included in this flow of capitals, are of course the 'narco- dollars' as we shall see.

Over-valuation of foreign currency

At the heart of this new economic model is an orientation towards external trade, which has been called 'the export-led model'. As a result of this orientation, the influx of drug trafficking money has contributed to the increase in the supply of foreign currency into the Peruvian economy. However, this has led to an over-valuation of foreign money which has made exports more costly and imports cheaper.

Up to the time of writing (June 1993) this over-valuation continues, in the same way as all purchases of dollars in the parallel economy continue to be made with the help of our financial institutions. It was hoped that the World Bank would put in place policies capable of reversing the tendency to over-value, and allow the intervention of the Peruvian Central bank in order to stem the 'legalised' flow of drug trafficking money. However, the World Bank has not adopted this policy.

Narco-dollars

Owing to the over-valuation of foreign currency and to the diminution of tariffs, imports have increased enormously these last few years, reaching a record 4 billion dollars in 1992. This generates a deficit in the balance of payments of the order of 567 million dollars. Furthermore, financial services have increased steeply, due in part to the external debt, generating a deficit of 910 million dollars in 1992.

This deficit in the current account of the balance of payments is paid for mostly by the *capitales golondrinos* (mobile or footloose capital), remittances from abroad and the dollars of drug trafficking. The unpredictability of these incomes render the situation of the balance of payment most vulnerable and very dependent on narco-dollars. It also makes the task of balancing the books dependent on factors external to the Peruvian economy. It is doubtful that these flows of capital are stable. (For further information, see: GRADE Anàlysis Trimestral de Coyuntura Ecómica, May 1993, p. 34).

RUINING OF SMALL FARMERS

Undermining alternatives to coca cultivation

The neo-liberal economic policies of the government have the effect of removing the means of business from small farmers. At the same time, the protectionist policies of the governments of the north towards their own agricultural sectors make small farmers uncompetitive. There are consequences not only for trade in legal goods, but also for coca (see Painter, 1994; and Chapter 14) – since only a reasonable price for agricultural produce can offer an alternative to coca cultivation.

One of the explicit objectives of the neo-liberal reforms is to roll back the state. In the case which concerns us, the present government has eliminated the Agricultural Bank (Banco Agrario) which was the main source of credit for farmers in mountainous regions, where most of the coca is cultivated. The withdrawal of the Banco de Fomento, including the Agricultural Bank, the near complete disappearance of the system of *mutuales* and *cooperativas*, as well as the high cost of borrowing national currency – all these have virtually eliminated the traditional sources of access to borrowing for small farmers. This is particularly noticeable in the north-eastern high regions, the main area for coca cultivation.

If we add to this factor the low prices paid for alternative crops (such as coffee, for example) as well as the increase in imported food products, which is now unhindered, we find a situation where there are, for land owners, strong incentives to introduce the cultivation of coca. One of the main problems encountered by the growers of north-eastern regions is related to the subsidies that the OECD countries grant towards certain agricultural products. In 1992 these subsidies reached over 300 billion dollars (Agricultural Policies, Markets and Trade, Paris 1992).

The subsidies have the result of lowering the price of agricultural products on international markets. What I wish to say is that the OECD subject the growers and cattle breeders of third world countries to unfair competition. In the Peruvian case, in order to attempt to remedy this unfair competition a system of surcharges has been put in operation. This increase of the tariff on imports of agricultural products has the effect of approximating prices to what they should be without subsidies. This way Peruvian growers and cattle breeders are protected. This policy, which is one followed in many countries, is one which has been adopted by the Ministry of Agriculture and also by the Constitutional Assembly (Congreso Constituente). However, the Inter-American Development Bank, Washington DC, with the agreement of the Ministry of Finance, has asked the government to withdraw the surcharges in order to follow a 'policy of free trade without any distortions' [sic] – i.e. without surcharges. If those are not eliminated, the IDB has threatened not to grant the credits which have been promised to the government. This would undeniably lead to an increase in the cultivation of the coca leaf in the north-eastern region of the country.

Cultivation trends

Indeed, according to both foreign and national data, the cultivation of the coca leaf for trafficking has been expanding northwards and now reaches the middle regions of the Huallaga. This accords with findings of the United States State Department. Senior officials of the Peruvian government responsible for the 'emergency zones' in Upper Huallaga Valley have reportedly made estimates of the extent of this cultivation:

> The Commandant General of Frente Huallaga, General EP Eduardo Bellido Mora, pointed out that at the end of 1992 . . . it was estimated that some 180,000 hectares of land was cultivated with coca. According to the Department of Agriculture, the cultivated area has increased by 210 thousand hectares.
>
> (*El Comercio*, 20 March 1993, p. A12).

The General in Command of the Armed Forces, General Nicolas De Bari Hermoza Rios, stressed that the commercialization of cocaine carried out by the traffickers themselves was increasing:

> The production of coca is increasing,as well as the commercialization of the drug, and the drug traffickers are using some of the aerodromes in the area in order to transport cocaine in its unprocessed, washed form. The Chief in Command of the Armed Forces, General Nicolas De Bari Hermoza Rios said that the traffickers land and load the drug into the planes at the aerodromes of Saposoa, Bellavista, Sion and Puerto Pizana. The landing strip at Saposoa is watched by the air force, but unfortunately because of logistical problems, this surveillance is only possible for a few hours a day. The rest of the time the force is at the base of Santa Lucia, and the aerodrome is left at the mercy of the traffickers.
>
> (*Ibid.*)

As General Hermoza Rios has indicated, there were attempts to improve the situation but the traffickers had the upper hand because of the logistical problems encountered by the army: indeed, he said the traffickers held the army 'by the short and curlies'. From the height of the Loma where the anti-subversive base of Saposoa is located, 'at night, all that could be seen was the two lights (of the small planes) when they arrive at the aerodrome. After about three minutes they are ready to go again' (*El Comercio*, 20 March 1993, p. A12).

General Eduardo Bellido Mora, the Commandant General of Frente Huallaga, estimated the value of the production in the area to be of 4,200,000 kg of basic coca paste (in Spanish, PBC) and 2,940,000 kg of grey coca paste (Pasta Basica Lavada or PBL) per year (*El Comercio*, 20 March 1993). If we consider that the price of basic paste is 200 dollars per kilo (taking the lowest prices of these last few years), its total value would be 840 million yearly. If we take as reference the price of basic paste (also taking the lowest price these last few years, 400 dollars a kilo), we end up with a figure of 1.2 billion dollars annually. If we suppose that 50 per cent of this money stays in Peru, either in national or foreign currency, this means an estimated 500 million dollars annually. This sum represents a significant inflow of currency from drug trafficking into the country.

CONSEQUENCES IN TERMS OF MONEY LAUNDERING

Drug trafficking money in the Peruvian economy

It is difficult to know with any certainty what quantity of dollars enters Peru for the purpose of drug trafficking. Estimates vary, for example from 100 million dollars, according to Hernando de Soto (a figure he mentioned at the end of 1990, whilst negotiating an anti-drug agreement with the US), to 200–300 million dollars given by Luis Novoa Soto (*Expreso*, February 1993). Others mention figures varying from 500 million to 1 billion dollars.

The author's own estimate is that the influx of foreign currency for the purpose of drug trafficking corresponds to at least 15 per cent of exports, that is to say approximately 500 million dollars. We are therefore confronted with a phenomenon which impacts deeply on the national economy and is of the utmost importance. It must be noted, however, that none of the estimates available are derived from a systematic and direct methodology that would permit an evaluation of the flow of narco-dollars. In fact, all estimates are indirect, general and come from various sources. The majority of estimates are derived from the study of supply carried out in the Upper Huallaga Valley and consist in estimating the value of production. The value is calculated by aggregating factors such as the activity there (calculated from official and non-official statistics), the surface cultivated, the average production per acreage, national and international prices and indices based on the processes of transformation of the coca leaf into cocaine.

Other estimates are based on economic modelling of under-ground economies, their manpower requirement and include aerial photography as a complementary methodology. The majority of estimates of supply do not come from observation on site but from references to fieldwork studies which do not necessarily represent an accurate picture at the national level. Furthermore they are only reliable within strict parameters which themselves change according to a number of national variables. The methodological problem has its roots in the variable and dynamic nature of coca cultivation. Cultivated areas respond to internal and external economic and non-economic variables and the result is often unpredictable. Economic models are over-simplistic, since they do not allow for the disaggregation of regular monetary flows from contraband money. There is, however, ample theoretical discussion assessing the consistency and the ability of such indirect estimates versus the information collected thorough micro-economic fieldwork. Finally, it is difficult to rely on estimates obtained through an aggregation of indirect methods (of economic methods, that is) because of the lack of knowledge about the economic and financial consequences of the cycle of production and about the number and speed of transactions.

The international picture

The following discussion sets the Peruvian situation in its international context, as far as money laundering is concerned. There is no dearth of studies or of politicians' pronouncements on the impact of drug trafficking on international finance. Estimates again vary between yearly figures of 900 billion dollars (Institut St Gall, Switzerland) to figures under 50 billion dollars. An estimate of 500 billion dollars has been made by the ex-General Secretary of the United Nations, Javier Pérez de Cuéllar. GAFI, the International Finance Task Force created by the Group of Seven and which has experts from the OECD, IMF and the International Bank, has presented official estimates relating to drug trafficking and money laundering. In 1990 GAFI estimated that the total income derived from the sale of drugs at world level reached 120 billion dollars, of which 85 billion were laundered through financial institutions. Official publications of the government of the US state that 80 per cent of such income is obtained illegally. This means, if we accept the figure of 120 billion dollars, a sum of up to 97 billion dollars annually – a figure very close to that for total Latin American exports in 1992. As these figures indicate, the variation between estimates is quite considerable. However, none of the estimates can be treated as 'entirely reliable', because of the illegal nature of drug trafficking.

Assuming that the level of profits has remained stable these last ten years (and this is a conservative estimate), we reach a figure of over 1.2 trillion dollars (without taking into account accrued interest). However, all the indications are that profits are increasing. In January 1993 a North American study stated that the 1990s could be identified as a boom period in drug trafficking, partly because of organisational changes in industry (Centre for Strategic and International Studies, 1993, p. 3). We can also deduce that the demand for drugs in the industrialised countries, coupled with the illegal character of their consumption, has led to huge profits for drug traffickers of the very same industrialised countries.

CONCLUSION

It is clear that the approach adopted by the international financial institutions and the developed countries to combat money laundering and drug trafficking has had little success so far. In particular, the 'double discourse' in the external policies of industrialised countries has had a negative impact on the economies of drug producing countries. Economic life for Peru is made conditional upon neo-liberal economic policies – which in turn require cooperation on drug control on terms set by the industrialised countries! Ironically, the neo-liberal economic reforms have contributed to the increase of narco-dollars in the national economy and to the cultivation of coca. This conditionality lays upon Peru the responsibility to stop coca cultivation, whilst at the same time denying her the possibility of doing so.

NOTE

1. This chapter is an editorially re-ordered, shortened and re-presented version of the original published Spanish text. Changes have been introduced that are the responsibility of the editors, bearing in mind a

European readership and the aims of the book. Some sections, references and other details have been omitted. Please see original: Campodónico, 1994. The original was translated for the editors by Simone White, Research Associate, ISDD. The editors are grateful to the author, the translator, and the Andean Commission of Jurists for permission to use the material in this way.

REFERENCES

Campodónico, H. (1994) 'Importancia economica del narcotrafico y su relacion con las reformas neoliberales del Gobierno de Fujimory', in Comision Andina de Juristas, *Drogas y control penal en los Andes* (Lima: Comision Andina de Juristas) pp. 149–68.

Centre for Strategic and International Studies (1993) *The Transnational Drug Challenge and the New World Order* (Washington DC: Centre for Strategic and International Studies).

Painter, J. (1994) *Bolivia and Coca: A Study in Dependency* (Boulder: Lynne Rienner; Harlow Longman).

14 Borderline Criminology: External Drug Policies of the EU

Nicholas Dorn

The external policies of the EU shape its drug policies *vis-à-vis* other trading blocks and countries. These external policies may be broken down into two broad categories:

1. Global external policies. The EU has ratified a number of international conventions bearing on drug control, where the Treaty of Rome, Single European Act, or Treaty of Union give it the competence to do so. The Treaty of Rome covers matters of trade, so the EU has an interest in the control of precursors – chemicals that may have widespread uses in industry, but also may be used to manufacture illegal drugs such as amphetamines, or to convert plant drugs products such as opium or coca leaves into heroin and cocaine respectively. The Single European Act (the basis of the Single Market in goods, labour, services and capital) requires the good running of banks and other financial services, leading the EU to adopt regulations designed to combat money laundering.

In these areas, the EU simply reflects the international consensus (or balance of power, as it may be); and it attempts to apply the policies globally, that is to say, to *all* regions and countries of the world.

In the following pages, global aspects of external policy of the EU and its member states will be represented by a few words on money laundering, followed by a short but critical commentary on precursor control. Questions will be raised about the effectiveness of precursor measures, and about possible geographical displacement and other negative side-effects. It is suggested that the EU should take a more active stance in relation to the formulation and reform of international policy in these matters – good intentions may not be good enough.

2. Sectorial external policies In addition to its global external policies, the EU has distinct sectorial policies, in the fields of enlargement of the Union, security policy, development policy and external trade.

These aspects of external policy are not global in their reach, but bear in different ways upon different regions and countries of the world – providing quite a *variety* of contexts for the articulation of the Union's external policies on drug-related matters. For example:

Enlargement, security *and* development concerns apply to many of the countries of Eastern Europe, and hence frame EU drug policies there.

Security concerns of the EU, but not enlargement prospects, apply to Russia (apparently not a candidate for membership of the EU) and to countries to the south of the Mediterranean, so security concerns frame EU drug polices in those contexts.

Development and trade policies (but not security concerns) underpin the political rationale and practical application of the EU's drug policies vis-à-vis the Latin America countries.

It is from this perspective that the EU's external drugs policies are discussed in the latter part of this chapter: trying to understand the diversity of interventions in terms of the broader sectorial policies that it 'makes sense' for the EU to apply in different parts of the world.

Understanding that drug policies are embedded in broader and more powerful policies does not mean we have to think of them as unchangeable, the author believes. Quite the contrary: understanding the context should help to illuminate the levers of change. In each of the spheres of EU external policy discussed – especially in those described as sectorial, where the democratic institutions of the Union may be consulted or have some decision-making power – there may be room for manoeuvre. Wherever possible in this chapter, problems inherent in existing external drug policies are highlighted and directions for potential improvement are signposted.

GLOBAL POLICIES OF THE EU ON DRUGS

These policies include international action against money laundering and control of precursor chemicals. The EU participates in the development and implementation of controls in both these areas, but with results that, from the perspective of developing countries, are at best mixed.

Laundering

Whereas ensuring that credit and financial institutions examine with special attention any transaction which they regard as particularly likely, by its nature, to be related to money laundering is necessary to preserve the soundness and integrity of the financial system as well as to contribute to combatting this phenomenon; whereas to this end they should pay special attention to transactions with third countries which do not apply comparable standards against money laundering. . .
(European Council, 1991, preamble)

Money laundering and the prospects for anti-laundering measures to reduce drug problems have been discussed, albeit from quite different perspectives, by Savona (Chapter 12) and by Campodónico (Chapter 13). For this reason, this section will be very brief. Following the 1988 International Convention (Vienna Convention, 1988), the Council of Europe Convention and the 1988 Statement of Principles of the Basel Committee on Banking Regulations and Supervisory Practices, the developed countries meeting at the 1989 Paris Summit convened a Financial Action Task Force on Money Laundering. The FATF published a string of recommendations, aimed initially at the G28 – OECD countries, plus Hong Kong, Singapore, the EC, Gulf Cooperation Council and the EC Commission. Implementing legislation in the countries concerned either obliges banks and other financial institutions to report movements of money that exceed a certain quantitative threshold (the US approach) or those that may be suspicious for other reasons (the EU approach). It is notable that these controls were conceived by the developed countries. Problems might therefore be expected in their application to developing countries, and this has been the case:

The geographical extension of the FATF programme is still limited as few developing countries have participated . . . [discussion of possible sanctions against non-compliance by developing countries]. Most Latin American countries do not accept the G28 guidelines. Some perceive that they benefit from the import of laundered money; others believe uniform monitoring standards are difficult to achieve because their banking and legal systems are not sophisticated enough. . .

(Hopkinson, 1991, p. 36)

Another view, represented by Campodónico in the preceding chapter, is that it is the more general economic policies that the G28 and international financial institutions urge upon the developing countries which are the dynamo behind money laundering. This seems to be an area worth including in evaluation of EU policies on aid and the development of financial and market infrastructures in the South.

Perverse precursors

Precursor chemicals are those required to manufacture drugs in refined forms. Measures against precursors are by no means new. Since the early 1980s domestic policing in developed countries has employed precursor monitoring and reporting systems in undercover policing, in relation to drugs such as amphetamines. Precursor control 'went international' in a big way in the 1990s due to the a combination of factors – including pressure from the Andean countries, who called for greater action from the EU, US and other parts of the developed world, where most precursor chemicals are produced. Without such action, it was argued, it would be hypocritical for the developed countries to press the developing countries to take action against plant drugs; after all, the plant drugs were relatively harmless as such.

So, in contrast to anti-laundering measures, international precursor control arose at least partly from the initiative of the South. Such action was by no means resisted by developed countries, whose domestic policing agencies had gained experience of precursor monitoring, and they generally supported more of the same. Add to this the fact of competence in this area by the

European Community (since precursors are matters of trade and also of interest from the point of view of customs), and the stage was set for European action. In 1988 the Community ratified the UN Convention Against Illicit Traffic in Narcotic Drugs and Psychotropic Substances and it subsequently legislated on precursors (European Commission, 1993).

In spite of the fact that pressure from the developing countries was a factor in the internationalisation of precursor control, the latter may turn out to out to be something of a 'Catch 22', for many reasons. Of course, we will have to await evaluations of the effectiveness of the EU's 1992 Regulation, which requires licences for the export of such chemicals from Europe, provides for penalties for corporations that do not comply, and requires exporters to obtain import certificates from importing countries where the latter request this (European Commission, 1993). Meanwhile, there are doubts over the effectiveness of controls, even in the European context (European Parliament, 1991). Moreover, their efficacy in the context of trade with developing countries seems particularly doubtful, for a number of reasons.

1. It seems likely that the effectiveness of such controls decreases the further we get from the original place of manufacture and the main export/import routes. After all, chemicals such as acetone, hydrochloric acid and sulphuric acid have widespread legitimate uses in industry. It seems unlikely that such chemicals can be monitored effectively and their distribution restricted in developing countries, especially in contexts where there is a continuity between legitimate agro-industrial elites, the informal or shadow economy, and drug trafficking (Dunkerley, 1984). Elite group access to precursor chemicals becomes even easier when there is national government and international encouragement for development through industrial expansion and liberalisation of the economy (see Chapter 13). Precursor monitoring therefore seems likely to be somewhat ineffective in such settings. Moreover, informal reports (personal communication, Atkins/CIIR) suggest that some groups have developed ways of 'recycling' some of the chemicals involved (which at least would be good for the environment).

2. There seems to be a 'slope' in the impact of precursor controls:

greatest impact in developed countries;

some degree of impact in those developing countries and regions thereof which are most accessible to control by the authorities;

little or no impact in areas which are geographically and politically remote from control agencies.

Thus, one consequence of precursor controls is to shift the various processes of drug production 'downwards', away from the countries of the North, away even from transit zones such as Colombia, and closer to the cultivators. Falls in price for drugs have a similar effect, since those low down in the supply chain may attempt to compensate by producing the 'next step up' in the drug production process. Both these processes, falling prices and action against precursors, occurred in the 1980s. Following action against large cocaine laboratories in Colombia, much of the production process was broken down into smaller operations, and shifted to many places in Peru and Bolivia. The result was higher availability of more refined coca products throughout the Andean region. Inevitably, some of these highly refined (and hence dangerous) drugs end up on the street of Lima, La Paz and the other cities and towns of Latin America. This is not what was anticipated when these countries lent their voices to calls for the EU and others to clamp down on precursors. But it inevitably follows from the fact that such controls *cannot* deny common industrial chemicals to those trafficking groups within developing countries who have sufficient organisational capacity and the material resources to circumvent controls at their weakest point.

3. Where precursors *can* more readily be controlled is where the persons who would use them are relatively powerless and have fewer opportunities to circumvent the controls. This takes us back to the peasant farmers themselves. It is ironic that, in areas of acid soil which would normally be improved through the use of lime, this chemical is controlled because it can be used as a precursor at the level of the cultivators, in converting the coca leaves into coca paste. As Painter puts it:

Although the Chapare [in Bolivia] has a number of diverse microregions, the region as a whole is not particularly suitable for growing other crops due to heavy erosion, the excessively high rainfall, and the high level of acidity and aluminium toxicity. Lime could help to neutralise the acidity and toxicity of the soil to allow plants to absorb nutrients more readily, but lime is one of the controlled substances in the Chapare because it is used in the manufacture of coca paste, the first stage in the manufacture of cocaine.

(Painter, 1994, p. 9)

It is not only standard agricultural inputs such as lime that can get caught up in precursor control, and hence denied to farmers, but also other basics, such as kerosene, an essential lighting and heating requirement in remote areas (Elizabeth Joyce, personal communication). It is deeply unfortunate that Andean countries' enthusiasm for international control of 'western' precursors should, when implemented within these counties, result in restrictions on such basic items, needed for subsistence, let alone development. Such deprivations of course would not be tolerated in developed counties, nor in the towns and cities of developing counties; clearly, it is a measure of the powerlessness of the low social strata of which the farmers are a part. Needless to say, the restrictions on lime and kerosene which keep these items from the farmers do not stop middle-men getting hold of them – so the coca is refined, just the same. The upshot is that precursor controls hit the farmers specifically rather than the drug trade generally.

So far we have been speaking of the impact of precursor controls specifically in the Andean context (no doubt the impact of controls in other regions of the world will differ), and it would be wrong to generalise from the above to, say, Asian cultivation of opium poppy and production of opiates. Nevertheless, it is possible to mount a broader and more general critique of precursor controls – based on the experience of drug enforcement agencies through the world.

4. For synthetically produced drugs, the production cycle of drug trafficking becomes geographically displaced. For example, amphetamines, illicitly manufactured in developed countries such as Britain and the Netherlands until precursor monitoring was introduced by the police and proved somewhat effective (Dorn *et al.*, 1992), thereafter became partially displaced to other sites where such monitoring was either absent or less effectively carried out (in the 1980s, Poland).

5. Within developed countries, traffickers' increasing awareness of the possibility of precursor monitoring leads them to abandon the most common 'routes' for synthesising drugs, and to develop

new routes using precursors that are as yet not listed as such or alternatively are so common that effective surveillance is extremely difficult. The end result is that the same drugs are produced as before, but with a different set of contaminants, corresponding to the new routes of production, whose effects are unknown to the producers, consumers and authorities. To the extent that in future precursors control could be made more effective within the developing countries, similar effects could be expected there.

6. Finally, counter-measures against precursor monitoring leads illicit producers to favour new drugs, where precursors are not yet under surveillance. Thus for example, it took some time for the precursors of Ecstasy (MDMA) to become monitored, and a shift 'sideways' to another product starts the game again. The result: new drugs, more of them, and new impurities, more of them, with a wider range of unknown effects.

In the context of policing in developed countries, it seems fair to say that there is an inverted U-curve of effectiveness of precursor control as measured against time. First, effectiveness increases rapidly as new surveillance methods take effect. Effectiveness may remain high for many years, depending on how successful the authorities are in disguising their methods (the least professional traffickers may never learn). Then, as most traffickers adapt to the situation and adopt counter-strategies, we are over the top of the curve and plunging downwards – perhaps crossing the horizontal axis and producing negative side-effects of enforcement, as noted above. At least there is the initial phase of enhanced effectiveness. But this may not be the case in developing countries, where the consequences for drug control and for country development may on balance be negative from the start.

The lesson seems to be that even though something (e.g. international precursor control) looks good politically, in terms of fairness and reciprocity (the developed world trying to do something about *its* contribution to production of dangerous drugs), even so, problems may occur. Control models created in developed countries may suffer from problems of transferability, and turn out to be 'inappropriate technology' in a development perspective. The EU has competency in this area and its European Monitoring Centre for Drugs and Drug Addiction has been authorised by its founding regulation to provide information on such topics (EMCDDA Priority Areas 2 and 4:

see European Council, 1993). The EU and EMCDDA should be pressed to initiate studies on precursor control in the context of trade and development. The challenge for the EU must be to involve its development partners in dialogue about possibilities of fine-tuning enforcement measures, so as to more constructively engage the circumstances on the ground – and to help all parties to think through, at a conceptual level, the potential consequences of new measures.

EU SECTORAL EXTERNAL POLICIES

We turn now to those areas of external policies which the EU applies differentially to different regions and countries of the world, depending on historical links and contemporary conditions.

Common foreign and security policy and drugs

The Maastricht Treaty designates the Western European Union (WEU) as the defence arm of EU Common Foreign and Security Policy (CFSP). It was anticipated that, by 1998, there might be sufficient progress in the development of the WEU and of CFSP for the security responsibilities of the USA to be reduced – as far as the regions immediately surrounding the EU are concerned (Treaty on Union, Title V, Article J.4.(6)). CFSP also provides the political context within which the EU articulates concerns with democratisation and human rights, and:

> An initial example of joint CFSP action would be systematically to include the 'drugs' questions in the political dialogue conducted by the Union with third countries, based on the experience already acquired in the fields of democratisation and human rights, with a view to enhancing awareness of the drugs phenomenon at the highest political levels. And if the dialogue partner were to maintain a resolutely negative attitude the Union might choose to review or even suspend the envisaged or existing cooperation.
>
> (European Commission, 1994a, pp. 22–3, para. 51)

The ways in which such a general inclination might be put into effect vary with the external policies of the EU in relation to the different geographical regions of concern, and the political situations that arise within those regions. The CFSP/drugs linkage has arisen especially in relation to those regions bordering the EU, to the east and to the south.

EU ENLARGEMENT TO THE EAST

The popular press and some serious commentators present a gory picture of the dangers posed by drug traffickers from the CCEE (Russian 'Mafia', and so on, on the doorstep of the EU). Indeed, there is a tradition in Europe of describing drug traffickers in terms of foreign nationalities and, in particular, to equate *organised* trafficking and other criminality with nationalities outside the present EU. This tendency is rife in the internal ministries and policing agencies of the EU member states, who effectively formulate pan-European anti-trafficking policy. For example, in 1994, drugs intelligence units of the member states were asked to carry out national studies of drug trafficking and organised crime, in which foreign nationality appeared to be accepted as a criterion for what counted as 'organised'. In the view of the author, without wishing to set aside the dangers of drug trafficking, it seems fair to recognise the extent to which (a) xenophobia and, (b) internal EU political conflicts and stalemates play their part in generating counter-productive levels of anxiety amongst European policy-makers and drug enforcement practitioners. These anxieties may prevent the thorough-going review of the basic assumptions of EU drug control that is so badly needed.

Challenges of EU enlargement

CFSP concerns of the EU sit alongside its plans for enlargement to some, but not all, of the countries of central and eastern Europe (CCEE). At the time of writing, Hungary, Poland, Rumania, Bulgaria and the Czech and Slovak Republics have associate status, through 'Europe Agreements', and all or most of these are expected to join the EU soon after the latter's 1996 Intergovernmental Conference. Next, the Baltic States and Slovenia are expected to become associated. It is in this context of enlargement of the EU that its policies in relation to drug control and the

CCEE are formulated. It is anticipated that transition to EU membership will underpin some degree of economic development and political stability in these CCEE (in contrast to greater economic difficulties and possible political crisis for those others likely to remain outside the Union – see below). Serious candidates for membership of the EU are obliged by the terms of prefatory agreements to construct western-style market mechanisms, democratic political systems, legal systems and policing agencies.

Functioning legal systems and policing agencies are essential for control of drug trafficking and money laundering. A large number of western agencies are assisting in this, including the PHARE programme of the EU, the Council of Europe, and many ministries and enforcement agencies of the member states. In practice, the work is disjointed and observers have called for tighter coordination (personal communication, Europol source, 1994). Better coordination does seem difficult to achieve, given the fact that both the internal and foreign ministries of most or all of the fifteen EU countries seem likely to run their projects in the CCEE.

More fundamentally, the building of judicial systems and cooperation in the east throws up a question that EU member states find so controversial and difficult to address within the present boundaries of the Union: should there be separate, sovereign, criminal justice systems and policing agencies in each member state, cooperating with each other at arms' length – or should there be the creation of a common European criminal justice space and enforcement institutions? Until some degree of consensus can be reached on this question, possibly in the years following the EU's 1996 Intergovernmental Conference (though that seems optimistic), then member states and their agencies inevitably will be playing a double game in the CCEE. This game may be called, as Frank Sinatra sang it, 'I did it *my way*'. For example, the British teach the CCEE enforcement agencies to do it the British way (cooperation between policing agencies, but no integration), whilst the Germans do it their way (integration of policing agencies on the German model, c.f. former east Germany). When these sorts of conflicts are mapped onto the rather disrupted circumstances in the CCEE – and also considering the intrinsic difficulties of drug enforcement – there seems little reason to expect rapid progress.

Moreover, the enlargement of the EU to the east throws into doubt some of the fundamental principles of police cooperation against drug trafficking within the EU. These assumptions may be summarised in the following terms:

1. That plant drug products such as heroin are imported from outside the EU and not cultivated or refined within it. But with the expansion of the Union to poppy-growing areas of the east (starting with Poland, possibly later encompassing the Ukraine), this assumption becomes negated.

2. That the external frontiers of the Union can in principle be secured ('fortress Europe'), thus permitting lowering of internal borders. This seems increasingly doubtful (unless enlargement is quite slow), suggesting that another vision of control may arise.

3. That exchange of drugs intelligence and forms of criminal intelligence is feasible within the EU, given necessary safeguards (about which the member states were in dispute at the time of writing). Enlargement adds further questions: in Poland, for example, the overthrow of the communist state entailed legal reforms of a type that make exchange of intelligence illegal (source: drugs intelligence officer).

Clearly, the present situation in Europe generally, and particularly the challenges of enlargement of the Union, raise quite new issues of crime control and drug control. New ways have to be found to talk about the evolving situation. One can hope that the closed sessions of Councils of Ministers and those functioning to advise them have devised a framework to facilitate this new thinking.

Exclusion, insecurity and drugs

Strikingly absent form the list of candidates for membership of the EU in the foreseeable future is Russia. As far as Russia itself and other constituent parts of the former Union of Soviet Socialist Republics are concerned, it is a truism to say that the late 1980s saw the partial disintegration, not only of its social and economic order, but also of the political institutions holding the federation together. By 1995, with fighting within the ex-USSR itself adding to the long-running armed conflicts within ex-Yugoslavia, the difficulties of the UN, NATO and the EU over defining their respective roles and responsibilities in relation to 'regional policing' came to the fore once again. It seems likely that, from the point of view of the EU, the Russian Federation is too close for comfort. It will continue to be defined as both 'foreign' and potentially dangerous. The dangerousness follows in part from the lack of prospect of accession to the EU (or any other stabilising and supportive union). In these circumstances, the EU's drug polices in respect of Russia may be difficult to conceptualise except in terms of military security. Some commentators envisage a stepping up of involvement of member states' military intelligence services and/or of NATO in this area (Clutterbuck, 1990). This would have the 'knock on' effect of strengthening the position of the internal security services in relation to drug enforcement, both in the CCEE and in the present members of the EU.

There has indeed been a debate about the desirability, or otherwise, of internal security forces and external security services taking a lead at EU and member state levels within the Union. The practical consequences of that are hard to anticipate, but would probably include greater reliance on long-term surveillance, infiltration of trafficking organisations, disruption of them through false information, generation of uncertainty, rip-offs under the guise of competing criminal groups, and other *agent provocateur* actions. Disruption of trafficking and money-laundering organisations by such means is already occasionally practised by ordinary policing organisations – but generally only if circumstances are such that arrests cannot be made or evidence cannot be brought to court (e.g. without endangering informants, or imperilling a more important operation). Such measures are more the stock-in-trade of the security services, as indicated in the case of the BCCI case, known to have been used by Britain's (internal) Security Service (Bingham, 1992, Appendix F) in order to gather information and conduct operations, rather than to initiate prosecutions. According to the investigation of the US government (Kerry and Brown, 1992), when finally the US authorities forced the hand of the Bank of England and BCCI was closed down, the Security Service was first into the building – seizing files of concern to them, whilst files valuable for prosecution were allowed to go to Abu Duabi. The security services, unlike the police, have no particular investment in bringing offenders to court, and so little interest in making arrests or generating evidence that would stand up in court.

The prospect is that non-judicial measures could become more common, as non-police agencies expand their involvement in anti-trafficking work. Whether these methods would be more effective than present methods in combatting drug trafficking and laundering at upper levels is arguable. But legality and accountability would suffer, no doubt. Furthermore, security agencies would become more influential in policy-making, since they will be in a position to claim that they understand the situation best, through their monopoly on high-level drugs intelligence. No civil agencies would be in a position to check this. Thus, what is at stake in the CCEE as far as drug enforcement is concerned is rather like what is at stake within the present EU member states: political values of transparency of operation, judicial oversight/supervision of the agencies of drug control and, ultimately, truth.

THE SOUTHERN FLANK

As far as the southern flank of the EU is concerned, CFSP and drug control have become increasingly intertwined in the thinking of the European Council and the Commission:

Common Foreign and Security Policy offers a new dimension allowing the full weight of the Union's political and diplomatic relations to be added to the commercial and development cooperation mechanisms already in place. The European Council has identified the fight against trafficking in illegal drugs as an area suitable for common action under CFSP and has identified the MAGHREB and the Middle East as priority regions in that context.

(European Commission, 1994a, p. v in Summary)

At first sight, the assessment of these as 'priority regions' in the fight against trafficking in illegal drugs is perplexing. After all, the plant drug most often cultivated in the MAGHREB and the Middle East is cannabis. So, as far as the middle 1990s are concerned, it might appear that the nearby production areas for cannabis have been assessed as presenting more of a security threat than the more distant sources of heroin (further to the east) or cocaine (Latin America). Presumably this cannot be because of the relative dangers of cannabis and other drugs: opinion may differ about the harmfulness of cannabis, but it is generally accepted to be less harmful than the highly refined products, such as cocaine or heroin. However, public policy about drugs and the priorities for control are never simply about the drugs themselves. Drug policies are always about other matters as well. In relation to drug users, for example, public debates and control policies are related to concerns about the social regulation of pleasure, or youth and the family, or ethnic groups facing social discrimination, or the need for social discipline and respect for law, or the proper sphere of operation of the market economy, or fear of crime and public disorder, or human rights. . . and so on. In relation to drug traffickers, debates and policies are not simply about the drugs they supply – the 'threat assessment' may often be much coloured by perceptions of the traffickers and the threat to public order and public security that they are felt to pose. In other words, it is not so much what you do as a trafficker, but rather who you are, and where you do it, that makes you a target for active control.

In this context, defining the MAGHREB and Middle East as areas for CFSP may be understood. Since the early 1970s the EC has recognised these areas as important for economic reasons, in its competition with US and Japanese capital; and also as a supply of external labour, with the political difficulties that implies. The Global Mediterranean Policy agreed in 1972 has, however, faced difficulties, particularly since new entrants to the EU, such as Spain, Portugal and Greece, have no interest in admitting cheap manufactured goods or agricultural produce from the non-EU Mediterranean countries on favourable terms (Yesilada, 1991, pp. 359–72). In spite of the strategic importance of the Mediterranean region in terms of trade, oil and labour, economic ties between the EU and this region have, if anything, deteriorated in recent decades.

This economic deterioration coincides with a political development – the rise of what is sometimes called Islamic 'fundamentalism' on the EU's Mediterranean flank, running from the Middle East across Africa (and notable in the French ex-colony of Algeria). This is certainly considered a security issue. The combination of economic and political uncertainties has led the EU to re-emphasise security matters in its planning vis-à-vis the Mediterranean (Yesilada, 1991, p. 370), and this is the context in which CFSP action on cannabis now falls. The prospect of a Euro-

Mediterranean Economic Area, not covering free movement of persons, seems unlikely to shift the underlying political realities, as perceived by the EU: 'sources of instability leading to mass migration, fundamental extremism, terrorism, drugs and organised crime' (European Commission, 1994b).

The rise of drug policy in CFSP context may have implications for the police and for domestic drug policies in EU member states. It seems unlikely that the member states could easily project a strong external stance against cannabis trafficking (through CFSP), and at the same time move in the direction of liberalisation of supply of cannabis at home (through domestic ministries of health and the interior). So, on the face of it, the CFSP/drugs interaction may add political weight to the arguments against experiments such as the coffeeshop system of the Netherlands (Chapter 5). Perhaps also there might be pressure against toleration of personal possession and use of cannabis.

The broad point is that there may be interactions between foreign policies and domestic drug controls. A rounded understanding of the relationship between external and internal drug policies of the EU would need to cover the implications for specific substances, control systems and enforcement agencies.

TRADE, AID, DRUGS AND ANDEAN COUNTRIES

If during the 1980s and early 1990s the EU/Mediterranean situation turned somewhat from economic cooperation to security policy, then the EU/Latin America relationship is weak on both these dimensions. On economic matters, for example, the EU does not have a very well developed economic policy vis-à-vis Latin America. Historically, EU 'concessions' on terms of trade have been directed towards the ex-colonies of France and Britain, through the Lomé Convention. As commentators have noted:

Despite their close ties with Spain and Portugal, Latin American states are not covered by the Lomé Convention, and their relations with the Community are confined to commercial and cooperative agreements.

(Llaesch-Mougin *et al.*, 1991, pp. 343–57)

It is equally true that the EU has few vital security interests in South America generally (leaving aside the Falklands/Malvinas issue). It is the US which still takes a security interest in this continent.

How, in such a weakly defined field from the EU point of view, does the EU formulate the drug policy element of its foreign policy? There seem to be two broad possibilities. The first possibility would be that EU drug policies towards Latin America reflect US drug policy in this region. In this case, EU member states and the Union acting as such would support and, possibly, participate in US-led crop eradication programmes, and militarisation of the war against trafficking. The second possibility would be that the policy of the EU regarding drugs and development has its own characteristics.

US/Latin America drug policy: cocaine and conditionality

In the first half of the 1990s the US Drug Control Strategy, overseen by William Bennett, allocated half of its budget for Andean anti-drug measures to law enforcement. This split echoed the compromise arrived at between the US and Andean countries at the Cartegena Summit in 1990, between President Bush and the presidents of Bolivia, Peru and Colombia. There, the US recognised that economic issues underlay the cultivation of coca in Latin America – whilst the Andean governments acknowledged a role for the military (as distinct from police) in drug control.

In practice, a combination of factors has meant that the military side has been more to the fore than economic aid. The reasons include: the historical shakiness of democracy and rule of law within Andean countries (Andean Commission of Jurists, 1991); linked to that, the tendency for military rule, which in some cases subordinates the police to army command, even though the army may be implicated both in human rights violations and drug trafficking (Washington Office on Latin America, 1992); and the tendency for US economic aid and cooperation from international financial institutions to be made *conditional* on short-term targets for eradication of coca that are hard to achieve (c.f. Chapter 13). In a study of Bolivia, for example, James Painter (1994) reports that the greater proportion of US financial support for anti-drug activities in Bolivia goes to the military, with a lesser amount being given in the form of balance-of-payment payments relief to the government to make up for loss of coca-dollars, and a relatively small amount spent in support for replacement crops in the coca-growing areas. On the basis of available figures, Painter (1994, p. 142) writes:

Bolivian armed forces were rewarded with more US aid in one year than coca growers received for eight years (1983 to 1990). This imbalance between money for interdiction and money for alternative development (actually disbursed) will come as no surprise to many observers despairing of US policies for [drug] 'producer countries'. It is worth reiterating, however, that such an emphasis fails to address the essential manner in which the coca–cocaine trade manifests itself in Bolivia – as a development problem that affects thousands of poor farmers and needs development-orientated solution.

Generally speaking, there is strong linkage between US economic aid and the extent to which Latin American countries can show that they are meeting targets towards eradication of coca cultivation and cocaine supply. This conditionality of development aid is an instance of what may be described as a process of 'coca-isation' of discourse on Latin American countries. US perceptions of the cocaine threat become the lens through which all other issues in Latin America, such as country development, are viewed. From such a perspective, Latin America countries (and particularly Colombia) and their peoples become synonymous with cocaine and violence and the proper response is very 'resolute', indeed somewhat coercive. In Europe, however, even if these perceptions carry over to some extent in media representations, they do not provide the mainstay of policy towards the Andean countries.

EU/Andean drug policy: trade and development?

It is true that some EU member states, including Britain, have given training and other forms of aid to the security forces in some Latin American countries, notably Colombia. In this respect – security policy – some EU member states assist the US in its drug policies in these countries. But this cooperation is relatively low key; and there seems to be little political support within the EU for a general militarisation of drug control in south America (Instituto de Relaciones Europeo-Latinoamericas, 1988). Unlike the US, the EU has few strategic security concerns in South America generally or in the Andes specifically. Other dimensions of policy – trade and development – provide the context for the EU's distinct line on drugs in this region.

From 1991 onwards and again in 1994, the EU implemented special trade preferences with the Andean countries Bolivia, Peru, Colombia and Ecuador, and with Central American countries, within the framework of the Generalised System of Preferences (GSP). These have the effect of reducing the application of EU tariffs considerably: for Colombia, from over nine-tenths of its primary exports, to under one-tenth. Unusually, the preferences were given for four years rather than the usual one year, making it easier for exporters to plan ahead. The aim of these tariff reductions is to support the construction of economic alternatives to coca; but they are not conditional on progress towards crop substitution. Nevertheless it was hoped that: 'The wider opening of the Community market to these countries via the GSP can help transfer production from illegal to legal activities, the product of which will enter the normal economic circuit' (European Commission, 1990, p. 15).

Perhaps these EU initiatives are more acceptable to Andean countries than most past US initiatives – but can they really work in terms of development of the peasant farming regions, and hence in drug control? There seem to be four reasons to doubt this can be so, each of which would sound familiar to students of development:

First, the cultivators are peasants [most of whom] farmed for the domestic market and or family consumption, growing crops such as rice, beans, maize, sugar and bananas. The international market for these is already glutted. Such crops, grown under peasant farming conditions, cannot hope to compete with large-scale agribusiness in the export market. Lowering trade barriers is likely to benefit mainly large-scale agricultural producers, who are not those directly involved in drug-linked cultivation. Second, zones of drug-linked cultivation are usually isolated, lacking the transport facilities and communications to market their produce successfully at the national level, let alone on international markets. Thirdly, perhaps three-quarters of the coca trade from the Andean regions comes from Bolivia and Peru, and only a quarter from Colombia. Yet Bolivia and Peru have been the least able to take advantage of the [European] Community's trade concessions. . . Finally, while trade concessions have been in place, other processes have continued to undermine the viability of legal rural enterprise in the Andean regions. . . [with] falling commodity prices, with their terms of trade turning against the rural populations as they received less and less for the same produce. This situation remains and has been exacerbated by trade liberalisation measures which have exposed farmers to competition from cheap imported foods (whose production is often subsidised by the EC or the US).

(Atkins, 1993, pp. 22–3)

Summarising, the benefits of trade concessions may be insufficiently focused upon peasant coca growers to enable them to cease that cultivation. When it comes to export markets, peasants are uncompetitive with larger production units, so the advantages of general tariff reductions go primarily to the latter. Falling commodity prices further disadvantages small peasant production, which is only viable in export markets under favourable conditions. Since re-distributive policies and 'trickle down' processes are modest, EU tariff reductions concerning Latin American produce are welcomed by those countries but their impact on cultivation of the coca bush may be modest.

What might this mean, for Latin America and the EU? On the face of it, economic incentives point in the direction of continuing cultivation of coca for those least well placed in terms of domestic or export markets. Indeed, a combination of reduction in price of export commodities and reduction in the international price of coca products (a coincidence prevailing since the mid-1980s) faces small farmers with a simple choice: intensification of poverty, or a search for economically viable alternatives. Since the international price for heroin has been relatively stable, that avenue is open.

Surely the implication is that further fine-tuning of EU development policy is urgent, and that it should address the infrastructural and economic realities of life for the peasant classes. One possibility would be to target resources more closely upon coca-producing regions and the farmers there. Several member states and the EU collectively have supported development programmes of the UNDCP (United National Drug Control Programme); some observers suggest that these programmes are more realistic in their demands upon subsistence farmers than are the USAID programmes (Painter, 1994). There are doubts that crop substitution can come up with crops that are viable for the peasant farmer, as long as export is the aim. But crops for sale in local markets, for local or regional consumption, may have a better chance of financial viability. The political problem likely to remain is that the political classes are unlikely to be much in favour of development programmes that reduce coca and poppy cultivation through helping the peasant farmers to develop economically and socially, but do not help the elites themselves to expand their agribusinesses or to export.

On balance, the European response to drugs in the Andean region may be seen as development first and security second, with the US response being the other way around – reflecting differences in EU and US perceptions of their interests in this region during the 1980s (America's 'backyard', and the EU's distant cousins). The 'Cocaine Threat' functioned as a powerful metaphor for US speakers, linking coca and violence in Latin America, and linking 'crack' and violence in western inner cities. In Europe, however, many observers recoiled from both the international and domestic implications of this vision. Local drugs markets throughout Europe were indeed troublesome, but not to the extent represented in the US. Even where crack became more significant (which it did relatively slowly and to varying extents), ways of handling the situation were evolved. Indeed, if in Europe there was the appearance of loss of control by the authorities of some aspect of drug problems, the new 'dance' drugs seemed to be implicated rather than coca products (see Part 1 of this volume; also ISDD, 1995). The lessening of the rhetorical pressure on the Latin American countries opens up for the EU the opportunity to deepen its understanding of development needs and drug problems.

Moving now to the boundaries of the EU: those countries who are candidates for membership (i.e. most of central and eastern

Europe, given time, and possibly even the Ukraine) have an incentive to adopt western-style legal systems and police cooperation, on drug enforcement as on other matters. In this context, demands made by the EU upon the CCEE that they must join in the common task of fighting drug trafficking may be seen in a politically progressive light – since the passage of anti-trafficking laws and reorganisation and retraining of policing agencies are part of the modernisation of these countries. But those countries further to the east, or to the south of the Mediterranean, where EU membership is not on the agenda (leaving aside any surprises), will continue to be regarded by the EU in a external policy framework. EU drug policies articulated in such a framework may be quite volatile – tending towards the security solution and military intervention in some circumstances, or towards the trade and development approach in other circumstances, or balanced between the two. Just as US drug policy manifests itself in Lain American countries, in fact. For good or ill, the future seems set to give the EU an opportunity to explore this balance around its external frontiers.

The links between the external and domestic drug policies of the EU are not easy to trace, since both the external drugs trafficking situations and drug policies, and the internal (national and local) trafficking situations and drug policies, are quite diverse. No general model has been advanced here, other than the principle that drug policies have to be understood as arising within and between these wider EU policy contexts. Just as political realities in Europe have broken through the borders between member states, so our thinking about the construction of policies in this complex geopolitical space needs to be developed. So much needs to be done.

REFERENCES

Andean Commission of Jurists (1991) *Drug Trafficking: A Year after Cartagena* (Lima: Commission Andeinadejurists).

Atkins, A. (1993) *European Drug-control Policy and the Andean Region, Narcotics and Development Discussion Paper 6* (London: Catholic Institute of International Relations).

Barber, L. (1994) 'Europe Recovers its Sense of Direction', *Financial Times*, 12 December, p. 2.

Bingham, Lord Justice (1992) *Inquiry into the Supervision of the Bank of Credit and Commerce International* (London: HMSO).

Clutterbuck (1990) *Terrorism, Drugs and Crime in Europe after 1992* (London: Routledge).

Dorn, N., K. Murji and N. South (1992) *Traffickers: Drug Markets and Law Enforcement* (London: Routledge).

Dunkerley, J. (1984) *Rebellion in the Veins* (London: Verso).

European Commission (1990) *Commission communication on the response to the Cooperation Plan presented by Colombia*, Com(90)254 Final.

European Commission (1992) *Progress Report: Programme of North–South Cooperation*, reports for May and June.

European Commission (1993) *Community regulations in Precursor Matters (External Trade): Integrated version of legislation applicable from 1.1.93* (Brussels: DG XXI).

European Commission (1994a) *Communication from the Commission to the Council and the European Parliament on a European Union Action Plan to Combat Drugs (1995–9)*, COM(94)234 Final (Brussels).

European Commission (1994b) *Strengthening the Mediterranean Policy of the EU*: Establishing a Euro-Mediterranean Partnership, COM(94)427 Final (Brussels).

European Council (1991) *Council Directive of 10 June 1991 on Prevention of the Use of the Financial System for the Purpose of Money Laundering* (Brussels).

European Council (1993) Council Regulation (EEC) No 302/93 of 8 February 1993 on the Establishment of a European Monitoring centre for Drugs and Drug Addiction, *Official Journal of the European Communities*, No L 36/1, 12 February.

European Parliament (1991) *Report by the Committee of Enquiry into the Spread of Organised Crime Linked to Drug Trafficking in the Member States of the European Community*, Session document number A3-0357/91, April.

Hopkinson, N. (1991) *Fighting Drugs Trafficking in the Americas and Europe*, Wilton Park Papers 43 (London: HMSO).

ISDD (1995) *Drug Misuse in Britain 1994* (London: Institute for the Study of Drug Dependence).

Instituto de Relaciones Europeo-Latinoamericas (1988) *Dangers to Democracy in Latin America: Development, Debt and International Conflict*, IRELA Conference Report number 1/88 (Madrid: IRELA).

Kerry, J. and H. Brown (1992) *The BCCI Affair: A Report to the Senate Committee on Foreign Relations* (Washington, DC: US Government).

Llaesch-Mougin, C. and J. Raux (1991) 'From Lomé III to Lomé IV: EC-APC relations', in Hurwitz and C. Lesquesne (eds), *The State of the European Community* (Boulder: Lynne Rienner; Harlow: Longman) pp. 343–57.

Painter, J. (1994) *Bolivia and Coca: A Study in Dependency* (Boulder: Lynne Rienner; Harlow: Longman).

Vienna Convention (1988) *Convention against Illicit Traffic in Narcotic Drugs and Psychoactive Substances* (reprint) (London: HMSO).

Washington Office on Latin America (1992) *Peru under Scrutiny: Human Rights and US Drug Policy*, issue brief number 5, 13 January (Washington: WOLA).

Yesilada, B. (1991) 'The EC's Mediterranean Policy', in L. Hurwitz and C. Lesquesne (eds), *The State of the European Community* (Boulder: Lynne Rienner; Harlow: Longman), pp. 359–72.

Index

267